PENGUIN BOOKS

DANIEL JOHNNES'S TOP 200 WINES

Daniel Johnnes, one of the most respected wine personalities in the country, is the Wine Director and sommelier for Montrachet, which is among New York's finest three-star restaurants. He is also a partner in Drew Nieporent's Myriad Restaurant Group, which owns and operates The Tribeca Grill, Nobu, TriBaKery, Layla, Zeppole, and Rubicon.

In May 1995, Johnnes was named the nation's top sommelier and given the Outstanding Wine Service Award by the James Beard Foundation. In July 1993, he was named Wine Master of the Year by the Fine Wine and Food Federation. And in 1991, he was chosen as one of the top ten sommeliers in America in a competition sponsored by Food and Wines from France.

In 1993, Johnnes founded Jeroboam Wines, a wholesale company that imports French wines. All imports bear "A Daniel Johnnes Selection" label. In 1995, he founded Deux Chapeaux, a negotiant business, with his colleague, Master Sommelier Larry Stone. Together they select top examples of wine, blend them, and bottle them under their own label.

Johnnes lived in France from 1974 to 1978. He worked in the kitchens of Guy Savoy in Paris in 1982, and speaks fluent French. He now lives in Brooklyn, New York, with his wife, Sally, and his two boys, Lionel and Barnaby.

Michael Stephenson first fell in love with wine when, as a young man, he spent a long, hot summer picking grapes in the Rhône. Though that year turned up a lousy vintage, the love of wine stayed. In 1990, he produced, with Robert Joseph, *The Essential Guide to Wine,* which won the prestigious Wine Writers' Guild award.

DANIEL JOHNNES'S TOP 200 WINES

An Expert's Guide to Maximum Enjoyment for Your Dollar

DANIEL JOHNNES

WITH MICHAEL STEPHENSON

FOREWORD BY ROBERT M. PARKER, Jr.

PENGUIN BOOKS

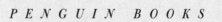

PENGUIN BOOKS

Published by the Penguin Group

Penguin Books USA Inc., 375 Hudson Street, New York, New York 10014, U.S.A.

Penguin Books Ltd, 27 Wrights Lane, London W8 5TZ, England

Penguin Books Australia Ltd, Ringwood,Victoria, Australia

Penguin Books Canada Ltd, 10 Alcorn Avenue,Toronto, Ontario, Canada M4V 3B2

Penguin Books (N.Z.) Ltd, 182-190 Wairau Road, Auckland 10, New Zealand

Penguin Books Ltd, Registered Offices:Harmondsworth, Middlesex, England

First published in Penguin Books 1996

1 3 5 7 9 10 8 6 4 2

LIBRARY OF CONGRESS CATALOGING IN PUBLICATION DATA

Johnnes, Daniel.

[Top 200 wines]

Daniel Johnnes's top 200 wines : an expert's guide to maximum
enjoyment for your dollar / Daniel Johnnes with Michael Stephenson.

p.   cm.

ISBN 0 14 05.1316 7

1. Wine and wine making.   I. Stephenson, Michael.   II. Title.

TP548.J58   1996

641.2′2—dc20   95-25387

Printed in the United States of America
Set in Bulmer
Designed by Jessica Shatan
Illustrations by Sally Johnnes

*This book is lovingly dedicated
to Sally, my companion for life,*

to my two beautiful boys, Lionel and Barnaby,

*and to my mother, Abby Johnnes,
who took me to France in 1973.*

FOREWORD

I first encountered Daniel Johnnes at New York City's superb Montrachet restaurant, where he was introduced to me as "the sommelier." In a lifetime spent enjoying wine, I have had too many confrontations with pretentious, insufferably arrogant sommeliers, who took themselves far too seriously. A sommelier is a critical position, a vital link between the restaurant's wine cellar, patron, and the chef's cuisine. It did not take long for me to realize that Daniel Johnnes was the antithesis of the outdated old snooty school of sommeliers that I had so frequently encountered. He was engagingly candid, exceptionally knowledgeable, and brilliantly skilled in making the customer feel comfortable and relaxed. Those first impressions were reinforced at later meetings. It seems to me that if our country's restaurants employed more like-minded professionals, such as Daniel Johnnes, the enjoyment of wine and food would no longer be such an intimidating proposition for so many Americans.

Since that first memorable encounter (and a delicious meal as well) with Daniel Johnnes, I have followed his career as not only the wine sommelier at Montrachet but at several other exceptional New York restaurants. In addition, I have applauded the plunge he took to become a small specialty importer dedicated to finding handcrafted, artisanal wines for his customers. It seems only logical that his passion and contagious enthusiasm for fine wine, whether it be a rare hundred-dollar-a-bottle Burgundy, or a small fifteen-dollar treasure from France's Midi, would eventually compel him to author a book.

It is a privilege to write this book's foreword, and I hope this work will be the first of many gems from Daniel Johnnes. He has plenty to say about wine, and he does it in plain English, in an authoritative, caring manner. Whether someone is just beginning to enjoy and learn about wine, or is a seasoned veteran, this book will benefit everyone. What comes across so poignantly is that, above all, he is a wine consumer as well as an enthusiastic communicator and educator. No doubt as a sommelier he long ago recognized that the dialogue between the customer and wine steward had to be a two-way street. This refreshing, knowledgeable, exceptionally informative book showcases Daniel Johnnes's pro-consumer, educationally oriented, no-nonsense approach.

And as a result, the entire school of precious silly wine rhetoric that has served only to make this fascinating beverage more mysterious and elitist has been further pushed to the back of the theater. Daniel Johnnes is the right person, at the right time, with the right ideas, and his book effectively celebrates the pleasures of wine in its many diverse forms. I say bravo!

—Robert M. Parker, Jr.

CONTENTS

PART THREE:
THE DANIEL JOHNNES TOP 200 • 171

APPENDICES

INDEXES

ACKNOWLEDGMENTS

I have two very special acknowledgments to make. First to Drew Nieporent, proprietor of Montrachet, founder of the Myriad Restaurant Group, and my partner in several other ventures.

I first met Drew Nieporent in 1984 at Le Régence restaurant in the Plaza-Athénée Hotel in New York City. I was a waiter; he was a captain. I quickly recognized that he had the vision and the determination to be one of the country's great restaurateurs. When he left to open Montrachet in 1985, I persuaded him to hire me as a waiter. I had had little experience with wine at the time, but it was enough to let him allow me to take over the daily duties in the wine cellar. As I became more experienced and knowledgeable, the wine program expanded, and Drew allowed this to happen. I brought it up one level at a time—first by improving our selections of white Burgundies (one of which is, after all, what the restaurant is named after) and then by expanding our selections of wine from other regions of France and the United States. As I and the wine program evolved, Drew watched and continued to give me the support and opportunity to pursue my passion. It is for this confidence in me that I will forever be indebted to him. Without opportunities we cannot grow.

My second special acknowledgment is to Al Silverman, who first approached me with the idea to write a book in the spring of 1993. I was thrilled and flattered. But I was naive to think I could do it overnight. I had no idea what I was getting into. I would write and give Al pages to read. He was polite and supportive in his criticism, and he provided the gentle encouragement I needed in order to struggle on. Many a time I nearly tore up the manuscript and hoped he would just come to me and say, "Well, we tried. Maybe sometime when you have more time, we'll try again." But I found the time, and he never gave up on me. And I'll never forget his trust, loyalty, patience, and guidance for helping me get through it.

This book would not have been possible to write without the invaluable assistance and encouragement from many friends and colleagues.

I raise my glass to:

My childhood friend, Mark Goldberg, who is always there for me and whose advice I cherish.

My brother, Abba, and sister, Sarah, who drove me to drink at a very early age.

My dear friend Larry Stone, M.S., arguably the most wine knowledgeable person in the world, whose confidence, support, and friendship are of immeasurable value to me.

Dawn Drzal, my wine-loving editor who reassured me that everything would be all right, and made sure it was.

Beena Kamlani, my wine-loving line editor who wouldn't let me rest until this book was in shape. She's the best!

The following people who gave me support, advice, and assistance in completing this book: Broadus Anderson, Philip di Belardino, Hal and Arlene Bergwall, Paul Bocuse, Michael Bonadies, Ed Bradley, Joel Butler, M.W., Scott Carney, M.S., Kimberly Charles, Clive Coates, M.W., Tim and Ellen Cochrane, Michael Connolly, Roger Dagorn, M.S., Fred Dame, M.S., Jean Pierre De Smet, David Gordon, Josh Green, Robert Lescher, Tom Matthews, Katrin Naelappa, Robin Kelly O'Connor, John Osborne, Peggy O'Shea, Robert M. Parker, Jr., Shelly Pressman, Frank Prial, Alan Richman, Jancis Robinson, M.W., Marcy Rosenblum, John Rossant, George Sape, Lorenzo Semple, Marvin Shanken, Martin Shapiro, Kip and Faiga Shaw, Peter Sichel, Nikki Singer, Phil Stafford, Carol Sullivan, Serena Sutcliffe, M.S., Stephen Tanzer, Madelaine Triffon, M.S., Patricia Wells, Kevin Zraly.

My publicist Barbara Edelman, whose thoroughness and professionalism are unsurpassed.

All my friends at Sugarloaf who helped me understand the true meaning of value.

All the importers and distributors who sent me well over a thousand bottles of wine to sample in search of the best values in their portfolio. A special toast to Lauber Imports, Seagram Chateau and Estate Wines, Winebow, Martin-Scott Wines, Jorge Ordonez from Fine Estates from Spain, Peerless Importers, Steve Metzler from Classical Wines from Spain, Pat Iocca from the Portuguese trade commission, Michael Skurnik Wines, Kobrand Corp., Neal Rosenthal, Vin Divino, Peter Weygant, Robert Kacher, Terry Theise, Rudy Weist, Priscilla Fetton, President, Australian Wine Importers Association, House of Burgundy.

Drew's partner Tony Zazula for allowing me to spend more than a million dollars of his money on wine over the years.

All the good customers at Montrachet, without whose confidence I wouldn't have a job.

The great chef at Montrachet, Chris Gesualdi.

Don Pintabona, chef at Tribeca Grill, and Nobu Matsuhisa, chef/owner of Nobu, Traci des Jardins, chef at Rubicon in San Francisco, Jim Mullen, Fred Wambolt, and the rest of the award-winning staff at Montrachet, whose great interest and knowledge of wine make me look good on a daily basis.

Michael Stephenson, my co-author, without whose vision, organization, persistence, love of wine, and friendship this book would probably still be spread out all over my desk and I would be desperately trying to figure out how it should all go together.

On nights I took off from the restaurant to write, I never felt the customers were being deprived of sound advice by my absence. This is largely due to the presence of Tim Kopec, my assistant and certainly one of the best sommeliers in the country.

And finally to all the great winemakers of the world.

PART ONE

THE
ESSENTIALS

INTRODUCTION

> In Europe we thought of wine as something healthy and normal as food and also a great giver of happiness and well-being and delight. Drinking wine was not a snobbism nor a sign of sophistication nor a cult; it was as natural as eating and to me as necessary.
>
> —Ernest Hemingway, *A Moveable Feast*

Wine is my *métier,* my profession. As the wine director of Montrachet, Tribeca Grill, Nobu, and Layla—four of New York's premier restaurants and nationally famous for their wine lists—as well as owner of Jeroboam wines, the importer of the Daniel Johnnes Selection of fine wines, and co-owner of the wine label Deux Chapeaux, I spend a good part of my life immersed in the business, technicalities, and economics of wine. Most of the time I deal with wines of the highest quality and matching price levels, but that is not always the most satisfying challenge for a wine dealer, whether you're selling in a store or in a restaurant. I dislike the hype and pretension that often surround the whole subject of wine. To me, the thrill is to find the unpretentious, honest wine of quality that delivers mouth-filling satisfaction. That relationship between quality and price, what I call "flavor per dollar," represents good value—and that is the guiding star of this book. These ideas were rooted in my earliest experiences as a young man working in French vineyards and restaurants.

My education in wine began early. In 1973 I had just graduated from high school, and, like most suburban kids my age in the

United States, my life revolved around my friends, playing baseball, and earning a little pocket money doing small jobs around
the neighborhood. My father had died not long before, and my
mother made the fateful and, as it turned out, fruitful decision to
move us all to France; she to write fiction, us kids to follow our
serendipitous paths.

I can't pretend that I was completely thrilled at the prospect.
In fact I can remember being downright scared at the thought of
leaving my friends, my dog, my neighborhood. As a pretty green
eighteen-year-old, I had "traveled" only from Westchester, N.Y.,
to Yankee Stadium in the Bronx. Now we were headed for the
tiny village of Le Barroux in the depths of Provence.

Le Barroux is about twenty miles north of Avignon, in the
heart of the Côtes-du-Rhône-Villages wine area and just another
fifteen minutes from the town of Châteauneuf-du-Pape. It sits in
one of the wildest and most dramatic—as well as one of the gas-
tronomically best-endowed—regions of France. The markets are
a cornucopia of local produce: vegetables, fruits, olives, cheeses,
breads, and herbs. The wines of the region are mostly red, rich in
color and flavor, full-bodied, and chewy. Like the people they are
outgoing and direct. And what they may lack in finesse they more
than make up for in generosity, power, and opulence—definitely
wines for indulgence rather than reflection.

In a village that thought a "foreigner" was someone from Avignon, we must have struck the residents as being as exotic as
Martians, but they were fascinated by *"les Américains,"* offered
their help, and threw open their prodigal kitchens. Even though
my mother and father had brought me up to appreciate food, I
can remember being stunned by my first meal as a guest in a simple family home. I walked into the house and tasted the air. I was
engulfed by the rich fragrance of garlic, vegetables, thyme, rosemary, bay, lavender, *sarriette* (wild savory), beef, red wine, olive
oil. The dish, a classic *daube provençal,* had been slowly cooking
en casserole for several hours while the aromas and flavors deep-
ened and intensified. Remember, this was at a time before *coulis*

and *concassé* had become as commonplace as catsup, and before all things Provençal could be Mayle-ordered. For me it was an epiphany.

The lustiness and earthiness of that *daube,* well supported by a bottle of local wine, changed forever my understanding of what having dinner meant. It was a *celebration* of flavors, friends, and life. When I was eighteen, wine had been mostly a vehicle for having a little fun. Now it was much more—an integral part of the meal, as necessary as bread or salt. There is an ancient sacramental echo when we take wine with food, and for the first time I had heard it.

One of the guests that evening was a local farmer, Maurice, who cultivated apricot, cherry, peach, and olive orchards, as well as vineyards (the wine that accompanied the *daube* had been his). His first language was Provençal, a dialect descended from the medieval troubadours and full of antique expressions, poetic imagery, and melodic cadences. It has almost disappeared now, but then could still be heard spoken by country folk.

Before long I was helping Maurice with the winter pruning of his vines. The word for the famous Provençal wind, *mistral,* has an appealing, romantic softness to it, but when you are perched on the back of a tractor at 6:00 A.M. on a freezing January morning with that relentless wind gnawing at your bones, you realize that work in a vineyard—even a Provençal vineyard—can be hard and raw. At about 8:00 A.M. we would stop and rest behind a line of trees that, leaned on by the *mistral* throughout their lives, had taken on a permanent, slightly tipsy, thirty-degree lurch. A robust garlic sausage, bread, and Maurice's good red wine made a fine breakfast, after which I would fall asleep while Maurice got into another session at the vines.

A lot of time has passed since I worked and slept in Maurice's vineyard. My education in wine and cooking started during those three years in France (including a memorable stint as a waiter and sous-chef in a nudist colony; luckily the chefs were allowed to wear aprons), and I have always loved the unpretentious strength of the wines from that region of France.

After returning to the United States and finishing my college education, I went back into the restaurant business (this time fully clothed), starting as a waiter at the Landmark Tavern in Manhattan. After a year learning the basics from the chef and pastry chef at the Landmark, I went off to apprentice with Guy Savoy in Paris. The thrill of learning classic haute cuisine from a master was matched only by the thrill of returning to France for the first time in four years.

Following a four-month spell at Poujauran, one of Paris's finest boulangeries/pâtisseries, I moved to the southwest of France, to Les Landes, the heartland of foie gras, cèpes, duck confit, Armagnac, and hearty red wines. Bordeaux was not far away, and on my days off I would visit the small châteaux and domaines, as well as making longer forays into Italy and Spain. By now I was truly caught up in the spirit of traditional winemaking and decided to give up my career as a chef and devote myself to wine.

Today I am responsible for purchasing a million dollars' worth of wine a year. Since each of the restaurants for which I buy has a different style and clientele, and needs a wine program that reflects those distinct personalities, I taste between one hundred and two hundred wines a week. The wines range in price between twenty and five hundred dollars a bottle, and believe it or not the five-hundred-dollar bottles do not always taste the best—although admittedly they often do!

As a professional I have to take many factors into consideration when I taste wine. I ask myself how the wine will evolve over time: Will it be more pleasurable in a year, or five, or ten, or is it at its peak now? I also look at the wine's personality: Is it representative of its region, grape variety, and vintage? Are there any flaws? Is it too alcoholic, too tannic, too acidic? These are just a few of the considerations that preoccupy me as a wine professional, but they are not important to the average customer who is simply looking for a good bottle to accompany a meal. What he or she wants is something that tastes delicious and represents "flavor per dollar"—not necessarily bargain-basement wine, but value for money. And that is what this book is about.

Price alone is not what makes a wine a good value. The deciding factor is the relationship between price and quality. If I taste a bottle of Beaujolais-Villages and it's delicious and falls within the price boundaries for wine of that type, then it's a candidate for great value. An inexpensive bottle of Chardonnay that tastes awful is a lousy value at any price. Likewise, a forty-dollar red Burgundy could be so seductive that even with that relatively high price tag, it is still a great value compared to similar wines.

You will stand a much better chance of finding good values in wine when you stop being impressed by familiar brand names and fancy châteaux that command high prices because of their reputation. This "designer label" method of buying wine is relatively low risk because the brands have been tested over time, but you pay a premium for the reputation, and there cannot be an absolute guarantee of quality. My aim is to point you toward the less obvious, the little-known winery, the up-and-coming producer, allowing you really to score on value for money.

Today, perhaps more than at any time before, there are hundreds of relatively inexpensive wines that really deliver flavor per dollar. They are not necessarily grand (although wines for special occasions are also included here) but they are the mainstay of uncomplicated, convivial drinking—the sort of wine to share around a dinner table when the most likely topic of conversation will be the day's events, or politics, or the movies, rather than how long the prefermentation maceration took, or whether the wine was aged in French or American oak.

As a wine professional I am constantly aware of people's inhibitions and insecurities about wine. They will often tell me that they have had a bottle and enjoyed it, but because it wasn't a famous name and because they are not experts, it can't have been that good. Wrong. Reactions to wine are always subjective. Some prefer sweet, others bone dry; some prefer red, others white. It's a matter of taste. Wouldn't it be a tragedy if you didn't go to a gallery because you didn't know enough about art, or to a concert because you couldn't read music? It is also true, though, that once you have dipped your toe in the water it's much more rewarding to learn how to swim. So, although this book does not attempt to be an encyclopedia of wine, it does give background information that helps explain some of the factors that make for good-value wines.

Above all, this is a book about enjoying wine, and about drinking it now rather than collecting it or speculating in it as though it were a commodity on the futures market.

As the owner of Jeroboam Wines, specializing in French wines, I was tempted to include some of the wines I import in this book. I bring those wines to this country because I believe that they are great examples of their appellations and because they represent terrific value. However, in the interest of avoiding any accusations of conflict of interest as the author of this book, I have omitted all mention of them. If a reader should wish to know more about the wines I import, I can be contacted at Jeroboam Wines, 90 West Street, New York, NY 10006. A quick way to learn about my selections would be to visit my site on the Internet. The name is Interactive Gourmet at http://www.cuisine.com.

GRAPE
VARIETIES

Given the number of grape varieties there are in the world, it's amazing how few have the potential to make quality wine. There are about twenty different species of grapes but only one of them—*Vitis vinifera*—produces all the grapes used in wine (some wine is made from the wild grape *Vitis labrusca,* whose "foxy" off-flavor rules it out as a serious wine producer). However, within the *vinifera* species there are estimated to be as many as ten thousand strains, clones, and hybrids. Most of them do not have a recognizable taste, which means that most of the world's wines depend on perhaps thirty to forty grapes, of which an even smaller number are what might be called "classics."

A winemaker's main concern with the *vinifera* is to strike the right balance between sugar and acid. There has to be sufficient sugar in the juice of a wine grape for yeasts to feed on and turn into alcohol (it's strange to think that a great aristocratic wine such as Château Pétrus is, like all wine, based on yeast excreta!). Too much sugar and the wine becomes cloyingly sweet or boringly flabby; too little and it will be thin and unsatisfying.

Sugar develops in the grape as it grows, so that in cool climates such as Burgundy, winemakers may have to resort to adding sugar (a process called "chaptalization," see page 67). Hot climates like parts of California and Australia have the opposite problem: The grapes ripen quickly and produce an abundance of sugar. The winemaker's job in such areas is to time the harvesting so that there is still enough acid in the juice to balance the sugar content. Of course, different grapes have different characteristics and various growing and ripening speeds that depend not only on the type of grape but also on such factors as climate, soil conditions, and rainfall—just some of the variables the winemaker must juggle. Some grape varieties, such as Cabernet Sauvignon, have relatively small berries with a larger proportion of skin and seeds to pulp than do others. The thicker skin not only cuts down the evaporation of water from inside the grape during hot weather but also gives the wine its characteristically deep color. The seeds and skin together (along with the stems, if they are included in the mash) contribute tannins that act as a natural preservative but also add a bitter astringency. Again, the winemaker will have to make decisions about how much pigment and tannin he or she wants to extract.

Other grapes, such as Pinot Noir for example, have thin skins and tend to produce lighter-colored wine. The thin skin also allows for more evaporation from within the grape and so makes Pinot Noir less easy than Cabernet Sauvignon to grow successfully in hot climates. Wines made from thin-skinned grapes also tend to be less structured compared to those made from thicker-skinned varieties.

RED WINE GRAPES

Cabernet Sauvignon

It has been described as the world's most successful grape, although even in the Bordeaux region, where it is associated with some of the world's greatest red wines, it is not as widely planted as Cabernet Franc. Cabernet Sauvignon, however, retains its special status. It is easy to grow and harvest, has a relatively low yield—lower-yielding vines generally produce an intense, concentrated juice that translates into a more resonant, complex wine—and is tolerant of cold and wet but also does well in warmer climates.

Cabernet Sauvignon is often referred to in Bordeaux as *Vidure,* a name that gives us a clue to one of this grape's most important characteristics. *Vidure* means "from hard wood," which describes not only its hardiness but also the "hard" taste that comes from the extraction of abundant tannins from the skin and seeds. (Cabernet Sauvignon has about twice as much skin and seed in proportion to pulp as Sémillon, for example.) The skin and seeds release bitter tannins that are essential as preservatives and give Cabernet Sauvignon its great aging potential. By Bordeaux standards, the wine should remain in the bottle at least ten years before it is ready for drinking, although this varies depending on the producer and the vintage.

Cabernet Sauvignon has a great affinity with oak, and when the wine is aged in oak barrels it develops complex aromas and flavors. In great Cabernet Sauvignon, spicy oak, tobacco, and cedar combine with intense black-currant/plum flavors, resulting in tightly structured wines that need time to develop. No 100 percent Cabernet Sauvignon is made in Bordeaux because the relatively cool climate means that the grapes often do not ripen fully, and their hardness needs to be softened and rounded out by blending with other, less tannic grapes such as Cabernet Franc and Merlot.

In the United States and Australia, where the climate ripens the fruit completely, 100 percent Cabernets are more the rule. They may lack some of the nuances associated with great Bordeaux, but they have a big, forward, fruity presence, and the best are magnificent by any standard. (There is a growing movement in California to use the same kinds of blends as Bordeaux.)

Merlot

In the Bordeaux region there is twice as much Merlot as there is Cabernet Sauvignon (it is *the* grape variety of Saint-Émilion and Pomerol, as well as being very popular in Bourg, Blaye, and Fronsac), but somehow it does not seem to have the muscle or toughness and longevity of its more aristocratic neighbor. In the Médoc and Graves it is used as a blend (along with other varieties, such as Cabernet Franc, Malbec, and Petit Verdot, for example) to round off some of Cabernet Sauvignon's sharp corners.

Merlot is fruity and comparatively high yielding, as well as being lower in tannin and higher in sugar than Cabernet Sauvignon. It ages quickly, and wines made from it can be drunk young. *Cru classé* Saint-Émilion (see page 85) may not have the legs to go the three decades of a *cru classé* Médoc, but at least most of it can be drunk after only four or five years.

In recent years it has enjoyed success as a 100 percent varietal (especially from California, Washington State, Australia, and New Zealand) and at its best is fleshy, plummy, with a chocolaty aroma, but because it doesn't have the tannin and acid to give it structure (especially when grown in warm climates), it can collapse into jammy dullness.

Pinot Noir

Pinot Noir is the sulky prima donna of grapedom. Difficult to grow, quick to mutate into offshoot clones, low in tannin, prone to frost *and* rot (what a double whammy that is!), it is nevertheless capable of making the most seductive wines in the world, be they *grand cru* Burgundy or *grande marque* Champagne. Where great Cabernet Sauvignon has a certain toughness, Pinot Noir is all supple lusciousness, with complex undertones of smoky, aromatic black cherry, anise, cinnamon, and cloves. In older Burgundies, violets, truffles, and even game crop up in tasting notes.

It is *the* grape of Burgundy and thrives in cooler climates (even though it needs added sugar to bring up the alcohol level).

In the heartland of France it is fermented in large open vats at quite high fermentation temperatures, creating a friendly environment for wild yeasts. In the cooler regions of California, particularly Carneros and Central Coast, and Oregon (Willamette Valley), interesting Pinots are being produced, but their winemaking techniques (smaller vats, cultivated yeasts, lower fermentation temperatures) tend to be more conservative than the wild Burgundians, and the wines less complex. Pinot Noir is a grape that yields uncertain results.

Gamay

Gamay has a lilting, fruity note: fresh raspberry when young (famously in Beaujolais Nouveau), and hints of chocolate in older Beaujolais *crus* (it represents 98 percent of the crop in the Beaujolais). It is high in acid (which accounts for the vibrancy of its fruity and floral cherry flavor) and low in tannin (which accounts for its early drinkability), with a blue pigment in the skin that gives the wine its characteristic violet hue. Gamay can age, though, as witnessed by the ten *crus* of Beaujolais (see page 78).

Syrah

A big ox of a grape producing dense, dark, tannic, alcoholic wines that are prone to oxidation and flabbiness. It has been described as a "black" wine tasting of smoke and creosote, but inside the forbidding frame lurks a deep, sweet raspberry richness that needs age to show itself. It can smell of violets, black pepper, and wild herbs. Hermitage and Côte-Rôtie in the northern Rhône are eloquent reminders that even oxen can sometimes be noble beasts indeed (in fact, in the nineteenth century Château Lafite was cut with Hermitage to give it more body and richness). Mature Côte-Rôtie can be quite elegant and refined.

In Australia it is known as Shiraz and represents about 40 percent of all the red wine produced. As a result most of it is taken for granted (in fact it can taste like twice-boiled jam)—except for Penfold's Grange Hermitage from the Barossa Valley, the mother of all Aussie Shirazes and a truly monumental wine.

Syrah or Shiraz should not be confused with California's Petite Sirah, which is known as Durif in the south of France.

Cabernet Franc

No grape that is primarily responsible for Château Cheval Blanc, one of the *premiers crus* of Saint-Émilion, can be dismissed easily. It is a greener, "grassier" version of Cabernet Sauvignon and is usually blended with the softer Merlot (in Saint-Émilion and Pomerol) to rub down some of its sharp angles, resulting in a wine described as having "raspberry," "violet," or "pencil shaving" and "cedary" nuances.

It is the most popular variety in Chinon, Bourgueil, and Saint-Nicolas-de-Bourgueil, as well as being the primary grape used in the luscious rosé of Cabernet d'Anjou and the strawberry-flavored sparkling rosé of Saumur. It is grown extensively in northern Italy, most notably in Grave del Friuli, where it produces a light but ripe red.

Grenache

A big, alcoholic, blowsy variety low in acidity and prone to oxidation. It is found mainly in the Languedoc-Roussillon, Provence, Côtes-du-Rhône, and Côtes-du-Ventoux, and is used as part of the blend for Châteauneuf-du-Pape. The rosés of Tavel, Lirac, and Provence owe their peppery tang to Grenache. As with syrah—an equally full and potentially flabby grape—carbonic maceration (see page 23) can help to keep it lively.

It is the most widely planted red variety in Spain, where it is called Garnacha or Garnacha Tinta. It is found mostly in the north in Navarra, Rioja Baja, and Aragón.

Nebbiolo

Not very fruity, and so high in acidity and tannin that its longevity has been pronounced "awesome." When it is well made it can produce enormous, deep-colored, and complex wines with hints of leather, chocolate, and prunes. Try Barolo for a long-lived big mouthful, and Barbaresco for a slightly gentler version. Nebbiolo d'Alba is perhaps even more approachable, while in the Valtellina region the grape manifests itself in dark, alcoholic wines such as Sassella, Grumello, Spanna, and the forbiddingly named Inferno.

Carignan

Responsible for producing more red wine throughout the world than any other variety. Lacking any precise flavor, Carignan does have the virtue (at least from a business point of view) of being high yielding. It is deep colored, alcoholic, and has strong tannin extract. It turns up in a lot of Rhône blends, and in Provençal rosés. It is at its finest in Fitou (part of the Languedoc) and in the strong, full-bodied reds of the Minervois and Corbières. Best from old vines and low yields.

Mourvèdre

Known as Monastrell in Spain, where it is the second most planted red variety after Garnacha, and as Mataro in the United States, it is the predominant grape in Bandol. It is quite popular throughout Provence and now in the Languedoc-Roussillon. As a late ripener it needs a warm climate to achieve the best results. It shows more class than Carignan but less than Syrah. It is sometimes described as earthy, gamy, leathery, and at its best shows depth of flavor and complexity.

Barbera

If Nebbiolo produces the monumental wines of Italy, Barbera provides friendly everyday drinking. At its best it is chewy and fruity with firm acidity. It is altogether a very amenable grape, lending itself to light or full, dry or sweet, rosé, and even sparkling versions.

Zinfandel

Its origins are vague, but it really is considered a true American grape variety. And because of the spectacular success of white Zinfandel, or blush, wine in the 1970s, many venerable old Zinfandel vineyards were spared the plow of those that wanted to rip out these vines in favor of the more glamorous Cabernet Sauvignon. These old vineyards are producing some of the most beguiling, heady red wines in California today. Because it is a grape variety that ripens unevenly, it can make a wine that is a bit tart and green tasting or one that resembles port. Although it has these many faces, the best Zins have a spicy, brambly, mulberry / blackberry, peppery aroma, rich flavors, and good acidity.

Sangiovese

Italy's most widely planted red grape, Sangiovese at its best can produce the most exciting, herby/spicy wine in Italy; at its worst it is "cheap mouthwash." Its quality and complexity vary among its main sites in Tuscany (Chianti, Brunello di Montalcino, and Montepulciano) because of cloning. The very best wine is made from isolated, jealously husbanded varieties. Top Chianti will contain as much as 90 percent Sangiovese.

Low in tannin, light colored, with moderate alcohol and good acidity, the wine is often described as having rustic "farmyard" tones.

Because of the increased popularity of Italy's super-Tuscan

reds, it has newfound interest among California wine producers and consumers.

Tempranillo

The grape that gives Rioja (where it is the dominant partner in a blend that includes Garnacha [Grenache] and Graciano) its dry, scented flavor. In the hands of a great winemaker such as Miguel Torres, it is used as a foil for Cabernet Sauvignon, much as Merlot is in Bordeaux.

WHITE WINE GRAPES

Chardonnay

Easy to grow, hardy, early budding, naturally vigorous, a consistent cropper with naturally high potential alcohol, Chardonnay is a heaven-sent blessing to winemakers. And it is precisely because it is so reliable, even predictable, that it sometimes comes over like the Big Mac of the wine world. And just as fast-food manufacturers have moved away from over-the-top grease-outs, so too have New World producers of Chardonnay toned down and refined the big alcoholic oaky sledgehammers of the 1970s— wines so exotically fruity that they tasted as though they had been made out of Carmen Miranda's more heavily laden hats. Today, however, it is quite easy to mistake top-quality Californian Chardonnay for first-rank Burgundy. In the cooler areas of Australia (Yarra, Padthaway, Mornington Peninsula, Adelaide Hills, and Tasmania, for example), the style is definitely more refined and French, less blatantly overoaked than in warmer areas.

In Burgundy, Chardonnay can produce the greatest white wine in the world, and some of the worst. The flavors and aromas vary from region to region: "butter and hazelnut" (Meursault), "gun flint, steel, and lemon" (Chablis), "fresh apple and melons"

(Mâconnais) are just some of the descriptions wine writers have used. Its natural affinity for oak gives it a delicious toasty complexity.

Chardonnay is used as part of the classic Champagne blend (with Pinot Noir) to give a yeasty, nutty, buttery flavor. When used as a 100 percent varietal it is called Blanc de Blancs and is usually more delicate and refreshing.

Chenin Blanc

Some have called it one of the wine world's most undervalued treasures while others denounce it as being merely "blandly fruity." Vouvray in the Loire Valley represents the grape at its best. There the tart acidity of the wine softens with age (sometimes a great deal of age: twenty years is not unusual) to reach its peak—*moelleux*, "full of marrow." Then the wine opens like a flower, with flavors of apples, quince, honey, apricots, and even a "damp straw" *goût de terroir*.

Chenins from the United States, Australia, New Zealand, Chile, and Argentina are all too often predictable but can retain a nice acid zing.

Sauvignon Blanc

Produces wine for early, and refreshing, drinking. The grape can make aromatic wine that can have a "grassy" undertone to it. It has bracing acidity. In Bordeaux it is blended with Sémillon and the wines can soar into another dimension: Château Haut-Brion is one example, while the sweet wines of Sauternes with Château d'Yquem at the top end are another.

In recent years there has been an upsurge of interest in the flinty wines of Sancerre and the Loire (Quincy, Reuilly, and Touraine), and the smokier wines of Pouilly Fumé. In the Napa Valley, Robert Mondavi created Fumé Blanc, a wine that sounds generic but is in fact Sauvignon Blanc that is aged in oak barrels to soften its grassy edge.

New Zealand with its cool climate is producing stunning Sauvignon Blanc, equal to the best of Sancerre and Pouilly Fumé.

Sémillon

Being thin skinned can be an advantage. For grapes it means susceptibility to rot. Not any old rot, but *pourriture noble,* the elegantly Gallic way of describing an attack by the bacterium *Botrytis cinerea.* The result? The greatest sweet wine in the world, Château d'Yquem of Sauternes.

Although it can produce flabby table wine, Sémillon is also capable of making the golden whites of Bordeaux, which are represented at their peak by Château Haut-Brion. In fact, Sémillon represents the major white wine grape in the Gironde, and in Chile, it is responsible for 75 percent of all white wine (after France, Chile is the largest grower of Sémillon).

Riesling

Some have called it the greatest white wine grape of all, and certainly it is the only one that can give Chardonnay a run for its money. In fact it has a couple of advantages over Chardonnay. It can make equally good sweet and dry wines, and its potential for aging is much greater than that of Chardonnay. Its great versatility comes from the fact that its acid content does not diminish as the grape builds up honey ripeness.

The problem is that the very name has been devalued by misuse and misappropriation. For example, jug wine from eastern Europe is made from an inferior grape, the Welschriesling, sold as "Riesling," while in Australia almost any white wine is called "Riesling." It is ironic, then, that some of the best Riesling around comes from Australia, a lean, flinty wine that takes on an attractive smoky undertone with age. The cooler areas of the New World are the best bet for this cold-climate variety: Chile and New York State's Finger Lakes and Niagara Peninsula, as well as Michigan, are worth exploring. But for the very top examples, look at Alsace, Austria, and German Rieslings.

Gewürztraminer

"Roses," "lychees," and "exotic fruit" are among the more commonly used descriptions (*Gewürz* means perfume). Low in acid but very high in potential alcohol (up to 14 percent), Gewürztraminer needs the restraining hand of a cool climate. If grown in too hot temperatures, that exotic fruitiness can turn into a sticky sweetness. Alsace, where the juice is fermented out to dryness but still retains a fabulously rich, "sweet" bouquet, is the prime producer of top-grade Gewürztraminer. The exceptions are the *vendange tardive* and *sélection de grains nobles* dessert wines, in which late-picked grapes have been affected by botrytis.

Pinot Gris

It is hard to imagine that the generally lightweight if not downright wimpy Italian Pinot Grigios have much in common with the full-bodied, pistol-packing Alsatian Tokays (a completely different animal from Hungarian Tokay, which is a blend of Furmint, Hárslevelü, and Yellow Muscat) and German Ruländers. In Alsace the grape produces a full golden wine, dry or slightly sweet, that is wonderful with food. When it is late-picked *(vendange tardive)* it can produce "monumental" dessert wine.

Pinot Blanc

Not considered as good as its cousins Pinot Noir and Pinot Gris, because it is higher yielding and does not have the concentration or aging potential. In Alsace it can be rich and nutty; in Germany either dry or, more traditionally, off-dry *(halbtrocken)*. In Italy's Alto Adige region it can produce good, fragrant, dry white wine.

Trebbiano (Ugni Blanc)

The world's most prolific wine grape and the mainstay of Orvieto and Frascati—which is not much to boast about when you think how degraded much of the wine from these areas of central Italy has become. In fact good wine from these regions owes very little to Trebbiano and much more to the skill of the winemaker who has blended it with other varieties. In France it is called Ugni Blanc, which is used as base wine for Armagnac and Cognac.

HOW WINE
IS MADE

RED WINE

1. Crushing. Freshly picked bunches of grapes are put into a mechanical crushing and destemming machine. Occasionally the stems are left in to increase the amount of tannin in the wine. The crushing at this stage is light—just enough to break the skins.

2. First fermentation and maceration. The grapes and their juice (called "must") now go into a vat. In the past the vats were made of oak (some still are) but nowadays they are more likely to be stainless steel or even concrete. Wild yeasts that occur naturally on the grapes or are present in the winery start to feed on the sugar in the juice (increasingly now, though, cultivated yeasts are introduced that enable the winemaker to control the fermentation process more carefully). Yeasts break down the sugar into carbon dioxide and alcohol. Heat is also produced by this organic chemical reaction, and the winemaker must watch the fermentation temperature carefully. Too high a temperature will burn out any fruit flavors and result in a characterless, unstructured wine; too low a temperature will prevent enough alcohol from being created or affect the color and tannin extracted, resulting in a thin, unsatisfying wine.

The length of time the juice is left in contact with skin and seeds determines the depth of color and tannin extract. The carbon dioxide pushes the solids up to the surface (unless they are restrained by a mesh), and the juice will have to be pumped over this "cap" of skins in order to extract color. For most fuller-bodied red wines this process takes about four weeks. For lighter reds a slightly different technique, known as carbonic maceration, is often used.

Carbonic maceration: Whole clusters of grapes are covered with a blanket of carbon dioxide. The sugar in the grapes feeds off the carbon dioxide and begins an intracellular fermentation. After a couple of days the alcohol accumulated within the skin causes the grape to split open and the must completes its fermentation by feeding off the yeasts contained on the skin's surface or by the addition of yeast strains. This process usually takes only about one week, and the wines need to be drunk young because they lack the tannin necessary for aging. Beaujolais Nouveau is probably the most famous example of this process.

3. Pressing. The juice that has come from the grapes before they are pressed mechanically is called "free run" and is considered the best quality. It is drawn off the fermentation vat and put into tanks. The remaining grape solids are then mechanically pressed to extract a highly tannic, dark wine ("press wine") that is sometimes added to the lighter free-run juice to give it more structure.

4. Second (malolactic) fermentation. A natural conversion of the astringent malic acid into a softer lactic acid, the second fermentation adds depth and complexity to the wine.

5. Maturing. The wine is now stored in barrels, usually oak, where the tannins can soften and the wood introduce its own subtle hints of vanilla. Quality red wine will spend at least a year in oak barrels; it is periodically racked off into clean barrels, leaving behind a yeasty sludge called lees. The wine will also usually be clarified, or "fined," with egg white or bentonite clay sprinkled on the top and allowed to drift down, picking up impurities as it goes. This process also softens astringent tannins.

6. Bottling. Before bottling, the winemaker may decide to pass the wine through fine-mesh filters or, more radically, put it in a centrifuge that will spin out impurities at very high speed. If this is done too violently the wine will be stripped of flavors and character. A quality red wine will almost certainly be aged in the bottle before being released for sale.

WHITE WINE

1. Crushing. The grapes are transported as quickly as possible back to the winery to cut to a minimum the amount of oxidation. The grapes are destemmed and crushed, and for heavier-bodied wines, the juice is allowed to macerate with the skins for about twenty-four hours. For lighter wines the juice will be quickly separated from the solids and run into a stainless-steel fermentation vat.

2. Pressing. The grapes are pressed (the gentler the pressing, the better the result). The pressed juice is put into settling tanks to allow any solids to fall to the bottom (in modern wineries it may be spun in centrifuges to separate the debris of stems, seeds,

TANNIN

Tannin is a natural chemical that, like the anthocyanins that make up a grape's pigment, or color, is a phenol. It's a powerful astringent that is found in many plants (dill and tea have particularly high amounts) and acts as a preservative. Its ability to toughen and coagulate protein has made it indispensable in the leather business, where it plays a part in curing hides. The grape has high concentrations in its stalk, pips, and skin, and so the longer they are in contact with the juice the "harder," more astringent, the juice will be. In grape must (the destemmed crush of skin and juice) the composition is about 70 to 85 percent water; 12 to 27 percent sugar; 1 percent acids; 0.1 percent tannin; 0.5 percent minerals; and 0.01 percent amino acids. The longer the juice is left in contact with the skin, the deeper the pigmentation (yellow for white grapes, red for black) and the higher the concentration of tannin. Oak barrels, particularly new ones, also leach tannin into the wine. American oak barrels contain a higher percentage of tannin than do French. Some grapes, such as the Cabernet Sauvignon, are higher in tannin because they are small and there's a higher proportion of skin to pulp. Black grapes have much more tannin, and anthocyanins, than do white.

What do tannins do? They help preserve the wine and give it the capacity to age. Bordeaux Cabernet Sauvignons, for example, are often highly tannic and mouth-puckeringly astringent in their youth, but they will last twenty to forty years and more, and in fact shouldn't be drunk within their first ten years. The Gamay that goes into Beaujolais, on the other hand, is a less tannic, "softer" grape and is better if drunk younger. Tannins also stabilize the wine's pigment, but with age the tannin molecules bond with the anthocyanin pigment molecules and precipitate, which is why red wine fades to a brickish color in time (and if left long enough will turn an unattractive brown). Tannin also contributes body to wine and helps in clarification by linking with protein molecules that have been released by dead yeast cells. When these linked tannin/protein molecules get large enough, they also precipitate, and the wine will become softer and less astringent.

and skin from the juice). Once cleaned, the juice is added to the free run in the fermentation tank, along with sulfur dioxide for chemical stabilization.

3. First fermentation. Usually in temperature-controlled stainless-steel tanks or in oak vats. If the fermentation temperature is cool (eight to eighteen degrees Celsius) the resulting wine will be fresh, aromatic, and fruity. At higher temperatures (eighteen to twenty-five degrees Celsius) it will be fuller and more complex. Barrel fermentation, especially in small oak casks, will add an oaky vanilla character and increase its aging potential due to the tannin extracted from the wood. Extra yeasts may be added to speed the fermentation, and sugar or acid (tartaric or citric) may be added to correct any imbalances.

4. Second (malolactic) fermentation. The softening conversion of harsh malic to gentler lactic acid will take place naturally unless the winemaker wants to keep more malic acid to counterbalance the high sugar content of very ripe grapes, in which case the process can be stopped by removing the yeasts through filtration or centrifugal extraction.

5. Maturing. The wine will be cleaned by "fining" with egg white or bentonite clay before it is racked off to another vat prior to bottling. Some wines, notably Muscadet, are left on their yeast lees (the label will say *"sur lie"*) in order to pick up some of their characteristic flavors. Apart from fining, the wines may also be cleaned by filtration or centrifugal extraction at this stage. Some wines may be "cold stabilized," that is, chilled to turn any tartaric acid into crystals that can be easily removed. (If you find crystals in white wine, they are quite tasteless and harmless and don't indicate an "off" wine.) Sulfur dioxide is added to protect the wine. The winemaker must judge the dose carefully to guard against a bad-egg stink.

6. Finishing. Most quality wine is aged in oak casks; lesser wines are bottled immediately after processing. The newer the oak, the more aggressive the vanilla/oak flavor.

ROSÉ

The simplest way to make rosé is to blend white and red wine, and a lot of cheap stuff is made this way. In France, though, it is banned (except in making rosé Champagne). Most decent rosé is made by allowing crushed or merely broken black grapes to macerate with their juice (all grape juice is clear, whether it comes from black or white grapes) for twelve to forty-eight hours until the skins have colored the juice a little (the French call it the *saignée* method, meaning to let a little wine "bleed" out of the fermentation tank). The free-run juice is then drained off—never crushed out—and fermented.

SPARKLING WINE

Champagne Method

1. Pressing. Pinot Noir, Chardonnay, and sometimes Pinot Meunier grapes are crushed in shallow presses to prevent too much juice running over the crushed grape skins and becoming colored by them. The best-quality wine is made from the first free-run juice, lesser qualities from the result of heavier and heavier pressing. The juice is now pumped into chilled vats, where sediment is allowed to settle or is fined out with bentonite clay. It is then pumped into stainless-steel fermentation vats.

2. Fermentation. Careful watch is kept on the fermentation temperature, and sugar and cultivated yeasts are usually added to promote the fermentation. The fermented wine is now racked off its lees, filtered, and fined again for clarity. Often, the malolactic fermentation is allowed to take place.

3. Blending. Tasting after tasting is carried out to come up with the "house blend." The mix is again clarified by chilling, fining, and filtering. Just before bottling, a solution of sugar and yeast *(liqueur de tirage)* is added to kick-start a secondary fermentation.

4. Second fermentation. The second fermentation takes place in the bottle, and as the sugar undergoes its transformation into alcohol, carbon dioxide gas is given off that is trapped and absorbed into the wine (cold temperatures help keep the process under control).

5. *Remuage* and disgorging. After the second fermentation is over, the bottles will contain yeast sediment (lees) that has to be removed. A skilled worker called a *remuer* gradually tilts and riddles the bottles so that over several months they are gradually moved from a horizontal position to a vertical (neck-end down) position and the sediment has collected at the cork (modern wineries now use a machine called a *gyropalette* for *remuage*). Next the bottle neck is dipped into freezing brine, the cork is removed, and a plug of frozen wine and lees is shot out by the gas pressure within the bottle. The lost wine is replaced with a sugared wine solution *(dosage)* and the bottle is immediately recorked. The wine is labeled and released for sale.

Cuvé Close, Charmat, or Tank Method

Used as an alternative to the time-consuming and expensive process of fermenting in the bottle, this method is used for basic sparklers. The second fermentation takes place in steel tanks rather than in the bottle.

THE TALE OF
TWO CHÂTEAUX

What makes a good wine? Although there's a gray area of personal taste, there are nevertheless some objective benchmarks of quality. Let me illustrate these by following the life of a grape through two very different wineries. One poor grape is subjected to villainous, abusive treatment at Monsieur X's Château Beaucoup, where the only concern is to squeeze the maximum amount of juice out of the crop and to make as much, albeit indifferent, wine as possible. On the other hand the same grape variety will be nurtured through its life cycle by Monsieur Y at Château Exubérant. His overriding concern is to help the grape grow as healthily as possible and produce the finest wine of which it is capable. Although I've given this little illustration a French slant, it's true for every wine-producing region of the world. Let's assume that both châteaux are located in the same region, sharing the same soil, climate, and grape varieties.

CHÂTEAU BEAUCOUP

With one thing in mind—money—Monsieur X wants to make as much wine as he can and sell it for the highest price the market will bear. First he decided on grape varieties that are high yielding. High yields have a direct correlation to low quality. By allowing a great many bunches of grapes per vine, the nutrition provided by the sap has to be spread among many grapes, resulting in a low sugar content per grape. Since it is sugar that will be converted into alcohol, the natural potential alcohol level for these grapes will be low and may need to be boosted by adding sugar (chaptalization) to raise the alcohol level enough to meet the requirements of the appellation.

Because Monsieur X wants an abundant crop he will spray chemicals to protect it from pests and rot. Chemicals can play a useful role in the prevention and cure of a range of serious problems, but if they are used indiscriminately, they will eventually deplete the soil, with devastating long-term consequences.

Although the local appellation sets limits on how much a vineyard can produce, there are ways of reaching and even surpassing those limits by declassifying excess juice. So, for example, if Monsieur X has produced eighty hectoliters per hectare when the appellation rules stipulate only sixty, he can sell it off as industrial alcohol. The problem is that the remaining sixty hectoliters were still the result of diluted overproduction. Never mind. It's legal.

At the harvest the tractors are sent in the moment he deems the grapes, or enough of them, are ripe. If he waits for full ripeness he risks the vagaries of the weather. There may be early frosts or rain that could affect his production. It's true that by waiting he might get a higher natural sugar content, but he would rather do the doctoring later on. The mechanical harvesters cut the bunches indiscriminately and save on the expense of handpicking. The ripe and the unripe go into the hoppers, even though the green and unripe grapes will taint the wine with an unpleasant bitterness. The harvesters will also certainly break stems, which will release their concentrated tannins and add harshness to the wine. This winemaker's main concern is to maximize the use of the machines, so grapes are left on trailers, where they grow warm, split, and start to oxidize until there's a large enough bulk to transport to the winery.

Once the grapes are in, the winemaking begins. And of course the choice of equipment is crucial. The first major piece is the press. White wines are pressed before fermentation; red after. Monsieur X uses the same press—an old, traditional, vertical model—for both. When the grapes are loaded in, a plate descends and juice flows out through vertical slats. The greater the pressure, the more juice, but also the more high-tannin extract from seeds and skin. Monsieur X presses on.

We have now reached the critical stage of the vinification, at which the yeast cells that live on the grape skins and in the air of the winery must become active and start feeding off the sugar in the juice (their by-products are carbon dioxide and alcohol). At this point the winemaker must decide to wait for the natural yeasts to start their work or add a cultivated yeast that will be much more predictable. The natural yeasts will add much more character, but they're not as efficient as the cultivated strains. Monsieur X, of course, opts for the cultivated yeast. There's nothing complex about Château Beaucoup.

Once the wine has completed its fermentation it is filtered to get rid of unwanted yeasts and impurities. It's a defensive step to insure against any bacterial problems. At this point the wine can be aged in tank or barrel until bottling. Monsieur X likes to add a good dose of sulfur at this point to be absolutely certain the wine is inert. The wine is now subjected to sterile filtration that will leave it sparkling, consistent, and stable but stripped of flavor and

aroma. Now it is pumped under tremendous pressure to the bottling line and *voilà!* one immaculate and characterless bottle of
wine.

CHÂTEAU EXUBÉRANT

Just as the grapes at Château Beaucoup led a tortured life, those
at Monsieur Y's *domaine* lead a charmed one. He knows that
people are drinking less but better quality. When it came to planting his vineyard he chose low-yielding clones. As the vines grow,
Monsieur Y respects the cycles and caprices of nature. If the
vines escape the attention of pests and diseases, he lets them be.
He will treat the soil with organic fertilizer, and if a wet summer
causes mildew and rot, he will treat them with a narrow-band
spray rather than the broad-band scatter-gun approach of his
neighbor. The less he interferes the better he likes it. As do his
grapes.

During the growing season he will monitor his vines to estimate how much fruit is going to be produced and will crop thin
or green harvest to contain the yield for maximum fruit concentration. As the grapes reach maturity and the harvest approaches,
he will check for an optimum combination of ripe tannins, high
sugar levels, and balanced acid, and at this point will send out his
handpickers to gather the ripest parts of the vineyard first. The
human eye and hand are much more discriminating than the
machine, and so only the best is selected and carefully picked,
leaving those bunches that are still unripe, or perhaps have been
damaged by hail or disease and could impart off-flavors to the
wine. The grapes may well be harvested at night, when temperatures are cool, and are quickly brought to the temperature-
controlled winery.

Once in the winery the green grapes are put into the press for
white wine, while black grapes go into fermenting tanks and, after
fermentation, into a press. Monsieur Y uses a pneumatic press in
which a balloon inflates, gently pressing the grapes against the

wall of the press. This free-run juice is the best, and it is Monsieur Y's choice for his wine. If he increases the pressure he will get much darker juice containing a lot of tannins and pigments from the seeds and skin. This he will keep separately, perhaps using a little to add some structure to the free run; the rest will be sold off as bulk—perhaps to Château Beaucoup.

Now, if white, the juice is allowed to flow into a vinification tank or barrel. The fermented red wine is brought to a tank or barrel for its secondary or malolactic fermentation (see pages 24, 26) and aging. A small amount of sulfur has been added to prevent oxidation and provide just enough protection from bacteria that could turn the juice into vinegar. Monsieur Y nurses his wine through the aging process, tasting and testing it for off-flavors.

When the white wine is ready to bottle it is transferred by gravity, not pump, to the filtration and bottling line. The filtration will be very light and intended only to remove any large particles and sediment. The red wine is also gravity-fed into the bottling plant, but it isn't filtered. Since it has spent a lengthy time in barrel, all the sediment has settled on the bottom, leaving the wine naturally clear. This gentle treatment has allowed it to retain all its aroma, flavor, and personality. It's exuberant!

EVERYTHING YOU WANTED TO KNOW ABOUT THE WINE TRADE . . . BUT DIDN'T KNOW WHO TO ASK

Since value implies a relationship between the quality of a wine and its selling price, it's interesting to look at some of the factors that influence price.

How does a winery establish a price for its wine?
One way a winery owner can establish a price for his or her wine is simply to check out what his or her competitors are charging. The market plays a large role in establishing price. For example, consumers may willingly pay $12 for a bottle of Chardonnay but balk at $35. So a winery owner must ask herself where she wants to position her product and then work her costs so that she can make her price with enough left over to still afford to go to the movies once a week. Or an owner may start at the other end of the equation and determine all his fixed (land, equipment, buildings) and variable costs (the fluctuating cost of grapes, if they are bought in) and see what options they allow in terms of positioning his wine at the low or luxury ends of the market.

Some wines are more expensive than others because of supply and demand (the high price of French Viogniers such as Condrieu, for example, is partly a reflection of small supply and high demand), land costs, the price of grapes, as well as production cost variables. Chardonnay is popular and fetches relatively high prices at retail. The grapes are more expensive because of this demand, and so the spiral of higher costs continues. Colombard grapes, by comparison, are cheap because there's no great demand for them. Some grapes, such as Pinot Noir and Viognier, are just difficult to grow and produce small crops that sell at premium prices.

Land costs are an important factor. For example, an acre of land classified for a relatively basic Bordeaux Supérieur appellation sells for $5,400 to $13,000, whereas an acre of classy Pomerol will go for from $100,000 to $300,000. An acre of Côte de Beaune Chardonnay will sell for from $300,000 to $500,000, while an acre of land in the same region used for Pinot Noir cannot command such a high price ($70,000 to $80,000). In theory the best land for any particular wine will cost the most and the wines will therefore sell for more. But sometimes the value of the land, and the subsequent price of the wine from it, have been established as much by tradition as by intrinsic worth. For example, Cabernet Sauvignon vineyards in California's premier wine region, the Napa Valley, average $30,000 to $50,000 an acre, several times the cost of an acre of Cabernet Sauvignon in Washington State. There's no doubt in my mind that Washington's Cabernet can not only compete with anything from the Napa but pretty much with anything from the rest of the world, including Bordeaux. But the wine industry in Washington is new and has yet to build the same kind of "brand loyalty" enjoyed by Napa wines. And that's why Washington's wines are such terrific value (see page 136 for more on Washington).

The price of a wine is obviously affected by marketing and packaging costs. But the decisions the winemaker takes concerning production costs have an enormous impact. First, if yields are limited to increase the quality of the juice, there's a cost involved. Second, the choice of expensive equipment such as crusher-

destemmers, presses, fermentation tanks, cooling equipment, and aging barrels, as well as the type of wood and percentage of new barrels in each vintage, will have to be taken into consideration. So at every turn, quality production, whether in the vineyard or the winery, involves added costs.

How does a wine store establish its price?
The general rule of thumb is to add a 50 percent markup to the wholesale price. However, there is tremendous competition among retailers because wine consumption is dropping but there's an enormous choice of decent wines out there from which the consumer can pick and choose. Discounters may slash prices by as much as 20 to 30 percent off the suggested retail price. But be careful—these stores are working at bare-bones profit. They probably can't afford very knowledgeable staff or, more important, proper storage facilities. Poor storage is the single biggest problem in the trade today, and a baked bottle of wine is a bad bottle of wine at any price. Be sure to buy at a discounter's as soon as possible after a shipment has arrived. Don't wait for the wine to cook.

How do restaurants establish a price for their wines?
There's no hard-and-fast rule here. The most common formula is for the restaurant to double or triple its wholesale cost. Sounds

high, doesn't it? I'm quite familiar with press criticisms about restaurant wine pricing, but I'm convinced that the press doesn't understand the costs of running a restaurant and how these costs dictate the pricing of food and wine (or they choose to ignore the context because controversy sells more magazines and newspapers). Prices vary to reflect the fixed and variable costs of the restaurant, which are much higher than those of a retail wine store. For example, a ninety-seat restaurant will have about four thousand square feet of prime real estate and about twenty to twenty-five full-time staff. The wine has to be properly stored; inventory has to be maintained and spoilage taken into account; appropriate stemware has to be bought and serviced. Wine is a valuable source of income for a restaurant, and alcohol is one of the highest-profit items (although not as high as coffee!), but it has to be seen in the context of the running costs of the restaurant as a whole. Besides, who complains when a $2 chicken sells at a nine-times markup for $18?

If a bottle of Beaujolais costs $10 in the store, what does it cost at the winery?
The importer will pay about $3 a bottle at the winery in Beaujolais. Then there are costs for labeling and label registration, shipping, insurance, warehousing, and fixed overhead that will add another $2 to 2.50 per bottle. The bottle is then sold by the importer to a distributor for $5.50, giving the importer a 50-cent profit. The distributor now sells the wine to a retailer for $6.65, giving the distributor a profit of $1.15, out of which he has to cover warehousing and shipping, as well as overhead. The retailer sells the Beaujolais for $10, giving him a $3.35 profit. Although the retailer is making the greater profit margin per bottle, the importer relies on volume to make up for a slimmer margin per bottle.

SERVING WINE

GLASSES

Just as we tend to serve reds too warm and whites too cold, we also tend to serve them in too small a glass. If the volatization of esters is key to the enjoyment of wine, then we should have glasses with big enough bowls to allow the wine to be swirled and release its bouquet. The top should be slightly tapered in order to funnel and concentrate the aromas.

Certain glass shapes have, through the accretion of tradition, become associated with certain types of wine. But we do not have to genuflect before every tradition. In fact some are plain wrong. For example, the Champagne "saucer" allowed bubbles to escape rapidly. Even the Champagne flute that succeeded it does not allow for the collection and concentration of bouquet and is usually overfilled anyway. (In fact no wine glass should be filled to more than about one-third capacity.)

Although Keats's "beaker full of the warm south" would do very nicely for a *vin ordinaire* from the Midi, there is no doubt that fine glass enhances wine. The Austrian glass manufacturer Riedel carried out blind tastings in which wine was consistently upgraded depending on the quality of the glass from which it was drunk. They found that wine in thin, generous-size glasses scored about 15 percent higher than exactly the same wine in inferior, thicker ones.

If you have to choose just one shape for both white and red still wines, choose the one favored by most professional wine tasters: an eleven- to thirteen-ounce tulip-shaped bowl, slightly tapering toward the top; the Riedel "Overture" glass is the most preferred. And remember to keep them clean! Too many glasses do a disservice to the wine because they have not been properly rinsed after being washed and still have detergent odors; others have picked up dust by being stored rim down on dirty shelves. Wash and rinse in very hot water. Let the glasses drain dry. Polish with a clean, lint-free linen cloth.

TASTING

The tasting ritual in a restaurant is often no more than that, a hasty, slightly embarrassed formality. Whether you are tasting the first pouring of a bottle at home or in a restaurant, it is worth taking a little time and doing it properly. It is not just a question of checking out if the wine is corked or dirty or served at the right temperature or is actually the wine you ordered (all of which *are* important), but it is also a pleasure, a sensual appreciation, and an anticipation that should not be rushed.

Color

Hold the glass by its foot or stem, but not by the bowl because the heat from your hand will quickly raise the temperature of the wine, especially the relatively small quantity you will have for tasting. Hold it up and look at the color. Since white wines tend to darken as they age, paleness will indicate youthfulness. Grapes grown in hot climates, such as Australia or California, have more robust pigmentation and tend to be a deeper hue. Whites with a good deal of barrel age will also have a deeper tinge.

THE GENTLE ART OF OPENING BOTTLES

I've had many a laugh watching the contortions people go through to open a bottle of wine. First there's the problem of the implement itself. There are hundreds of types of corkscrews, and people can get quite hot under the collar about which one is best: "butterflies," double-action doodads, zigzags, two-pronged extractors, simple pulls designed to give you a hernia, tricky little pumps, Victorian contraptions that look as though they had been designed for the Spanish Inquisition, and so on. And there's always a strange choreography involved in figuring out how to hold the bottle to get maximum leverage. Under the arm? Between the legs? On a table? The floor? I suppose whatever works is all right, but for me this simple act should be a kind of graceful ceremony. After all, it is the prelude to one of life's more civilized pleasures and deserves to be done with a simple elegance. It should be an act of kindness to the wine and a gesture of hospitality to your guests.

I find that the best tool is the unfancy and inexpensive waiter's corkscrew. It looks like a penknife, with a short blade at one end, a lever at the other, and a worm screw in the middle. Using the blade, cut the capsule (the foil or plastic cover) just under the lip of the bottle's neck. Wipe the top of the cork and rim with a clean napkin. Screw down through the center of the cork and fix the notch of the lever to the top of the bottle's neck. Pull up on the handle and take out the cork. Wipe the top and inside of the bottle's neck to remove any cork debris or mold that may have been left. Pour yourself a small taste before serving your guests. Champagne should also be tasted. A lot of people think that if there are bubbles the wine must be fine. Not true. Champagne has a cork, and it too can be corked (for more on corked wine, see page 42, and for serving, see pages 38, 45).

With reds, the color can depend on where the grapes came from. Look at the surface of the wine where it meets the glass. A vibrant purple is indicative of a young, full-bodied wine, perhaps from the Rhône. A ruby tinge might well suggest a Beaujolais, while a chestnut tone can indicate a more mature wine. Now swirl the glass.

Smell

By swirling the wine we release some of the volatile esters that produce aroma or bouquet. Take a good deep sniff—it will tell you more about the wine than your tongue ever can. Our sense of smell is more primal, more evocative than any of our other senses, and many professional wine tasters trust their noses much more than their palates. First of all, there should be a smell of fruit, but it is incredible how diverse the various aromas of wine can be. There's a whole vocabulary given over to them: fruits, flowers, woods, spices, and even the less likely analogies of "wet wool," "sweaty saddles," and "cat's pee." (See page 330 for "A Tasting Vocabulary.")

Taste

Take a generous sip and roll it around your mouth ("chewing"). The heat of your mouth volatizes the esters, which will pass up into the nasal cavity. But what your palate registers has more to do with balance and texture: "mouth-feel." In fact, the tongue can register only four tastes: sweet (on the tip); sour (on the sides); salty (on the upper surface); and bitter (at the base). Does the wine have a light or full body; is there a balance between its sweet and acid elements? In professional tasting the wine is spat out, but in a restaurant or at home this is usually discouraged—as it should be, for one of the most telling things about a wine is the sensation in the nose immediately after the wine is swallowed. Breathe out through the nose in short bursts, trying not to sound like a hog in hot pursuit of a truffle, and you will get a wonderful sense of the wine's character and its satisfying length and weight (assuming it has any).

ON CORKS AND CORKED WINE

The sheets of cork from which corks are cut are sterilized in vats of chlorine, a process that very occasionally can result in the growth of a penicillin-induced mold called 2-4-6 trichloroanisol. Wine tainted by a cork with 2-4-6 trichloroanisol has the smell of "damp cardboard," "beets," or "garden soil." It can be differentiated from dirty or otherwise faulty wine because the off-flavor and aroma will get worse the longer the wine is in the glass ("bottle stink," for example, is a temporary smell that disappears as the wine airs).

There's no consensus as to how many bottles become corked. The wine industry tends to play down the problem, suggesting that it is much rarer now than it used to be and perhaps affects one bottle in fifty—about 2 percent. Some Californian wineries reckon on 5 percent spoilage due to cork infection, an estimate that was confirmed by a 1990 Wine Spectator *survey.*

Our ability to detect corked wine is amazing. With five million olfactory cells, we can smell trichloroanisol in concentrations as low as four parts per trillion. And what can we do about it? Nothing, except open another bottle and hope for better luck.

Should the wine waiter always offer me the cork to smell before he pours the wine?

This is a pretty redundant ritual. A "corked" wine cork will smell musty, but the real test is tasting the wine. Regular corks smell just like cork. A dry, crumbling, or shriveled cork may indicate bad storage, but the main reason for checking the cork is to reassure yourself that it is the right cork for the wine—that is, that the legend printed on the cork corresponds with what the wine purports to be. As for such expressions as *mis en bouteille au château,* they are almost meaningless: Lousy wine can be bottled at the château (and traveling bottling services make it possible for even the most run-down operation to claim the *cachet* of on-site bottling). It is true, though, that fine wines tend to use longer (up to 57 mm) and superior corks, while lesser wines will often make do with short corks made up of cork-dust agglomerate.

What if my cork crumbles into the wine?
Line a plastic funnel with several layers of clean cheesecloth and decant. If the whole cork has fallen into the wine, you can keep the cork out of the way with a clean skewer until the first glass has been poured. After that the wine can be poured without using the skewer, and won't be any the worse for it. If you are serving a wine whose cork has developed a crust on top, wipe it clean before using your corkscrew. That way if the cork falls into the wine you won't get dusty sediment in the wine.

How do I extract a cork that has broken halfway down?
Put your corkscrew in at an angle to get a grip on the cork, and then pull it manually. Alternatively, if the stub of cork seems pretty good and tight, just start over as you would for a full cork but take it easy as you screw in. You can buy fancy prongs that slip down each side of the cork rather than screwing through the middle, but they're a bit tricky to use and quite expensive considering the few times (you hope!) you will get to use them. If you are storing wine for any length of time, store the bottle horizontally so that the wine covers the bottom of the cork and keeps it moist.

COMMON MYTHS
ABOUT WINE

Wine contains more sulfites than other food and beverage products.
Every bottle of wine, in the United States anyway, carries the slightly
scary warning "Contains Sulfites," even though the levels of sulfur in
wine are minuscule. It is there as a warning to asthmatics, who may
have an allergic reaction to sulfur. Sulfur gets into wine in two ways.
First, sulfur compounds in soil and rain find their way into grape
juice. Second, sulfur has been used for centuries as a preservative
and cleansing agent. Barrels are sometimes disinfected by burning
sulfur, and sulfur is added to wine to stabilize it and kill unwanted
bacteria. Dry red wine has less sulfur (160 milligrams per liter [mg/l]
according to European Community rules) than white [260 mg/l]. It
is impossible to produce an entirely sulfur-free wine since sulfur
dioxide is a natural by-product of fermentation. Some sweet white
wines have 400 mg/l but many fruits and vegetables are treated with
greater levels of sulfur than we find in wine. When will we see a government warning on a head of lettuce?

It is essential to smell the wine cork before sampling the wine.
Corks smell like corks. If you taste it, it will probably taste like

one, too. In itself, it tells you very little about the wine. However, I like inspecting the length, texture, and overall quality of the cork. It is an indication of how much attention the winemaker paid to detail. Some corks indicate the name of the winery and the vintage, which makes it useful as protection against foul play. If it's dried and shriveled, it might indicate poor storage. If it has little holes in the top, it may have been attacked by tiny worms that are sometimes present in cellars and can cause great damage after many years—a rare occurrence yet worth noting. A "corked" wine is a wine that has been tainted by a faulty cork (see "On Corks and Corked Wine," page 42). When the cork is bad it can be identified simply by smelling it. Yet the most accurate way to tell if a wine is corked is to smell and taste it. This is why wine should always be tasted before it is served. This is true for all wine—even Champagne.

White wines should be served thoroughly chilled and red wines at room temperature.
Generally we drink red wine too warm and white wine too cold. The red-wine problem has something to do with the misuse of the term *chambré,* which means to serve the wine at room temperature. This was probably fine during the nineteenth century, when the custom started. Rooms then would have been about sixty degrees Fahrenheit, not the little ovens of seventy to seventy-five degrees Fahrenheit central heating has since made them. Fine red wine should not be drunk at more than sixty-five degrees, while fruity young red wine, such as Beaujolais or Loire reds like Bourgueil or Chinon, should be served at about fifty-five to fifty-eight degrees Fahrenheit—in other words, lightly chilled. At too high a temperature alcohol evaporates, rises into the sensitive nasal cavities, and obliterates the other volatile esters that go to make up the complex thing we call bouquet.

Most of the "taste" of wine (or food, for that matter) has more to do with our noses than with our mouths. The odiferous (smelly) part of wine is very volatile and therefore very

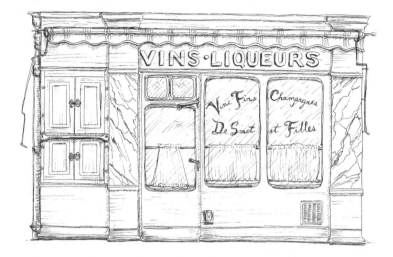

temperature-sensitive. Almost no single factor affects our appreciation of wine as much as the temperature at which it is served. I am
more particular about this aspect of wine service than any other. It
can either enhance our enjoyment of it or kill it off altogether.

Our obsession with refrigeration does a disservice to the better
wines. If we chill them back to the Ice Age, we also suppress their
aromas and flavors, leaving only the acids and alcohol. What
should be characterful has now become bland. Of course, for very
basic jug white wine, a subsubzero temperature is probably the
best thing, but for a decent white, especially a good white Burgundy that has some subtlety and character, a serving temperature of about fifty to fifty-five degrees Fahrenheit will allow it to
perform. Lighter whites and dry rosés, along with dry Champagne, should be served at a lower temperature, around forty-five
degrees Fahrenheit.

It is worth remembering that it is not only the temperature of
the wine that affects our appreciation. Experiments have shown
that humidity has an impact on our sense of smell. The danker
the atmosphere, the more heightened our sensitivity, which
explains why cows lie down before an impending storm—they
can smell it coming!

It is a sad and ironic fact that by age sixty, we have lost about 50 percent of our taste buds and 40 percent of our olfactory capacity, just at a time when most of us have painstakingly gathered the wherewithal to be able to afford the odd bottle that is capable of putting an *olé* into olfactory!

CORRECT WINE TEMPERATURES

Champagne and sparkling	Very cold	42–45 degrees F
(Warmer for mature and full-bodied Champagnes)		
Sauternes and sweet wine	Very cold	42–45 degrees F
(Warmer for mature wines)		
Light whites	Well chilled	45–48 degrees F
Medium/full whites	Very cool	48–50 degrees F
Rich and great whites	Cool	52–55 degrees F
Light reds	Slightly chilled	56–58 degrees F
Medium reds	Cool	60–62 degrees F
Full reds	Room temperature	65 degrees F

All wines should be decanted and left to breathe before they are poured.

There is probably more debate about airing wine before pouring than about almost any other aspect of wine service. Some authorities denounce the whole business of airing. The great French enologist Professor Peynaud, for example, contends that wine should hardly ever be aired, and if it has to be, then only a minute or two before serving. The principal reason for decanting is to remove sediment from red wines and port, but many people feel that wines with a lot of tannin (Bordeaux and Portuguese reds, for example) are softened by oxidation.

The general consensus among those who favor airing is that young reds should get one to two hours' airing; a mature wine and an old wine do not need any airing at all. But there are always exceptions. Hugh Johnson, author of *World Atlas of Wine,* notes:

> The only general rule I have found is that the better the wine, taking both origin and vintage into account, the more it benefits from prolonged contact with the air. Sometimes a wine that is a distinct disappointment on opening changes its nature entirely. A bottle of Château Pontet-Canet 1961 (in 1982) had a poor, hard, loose-fitting cork and, on first tasting, a miserable timid smell and very little flavor at all (although the color was good). Twenty-four hours later it seemed to have recharged its batteries; it opened up into the full-blooded, high-flavored wine I had expected. The moral must be to experiment and keep an open mind.

Though Hugh Johnson's Pontet-Canet 1961 benefited considerably from extended airing, this is not always the case with older wines that have already aged in the bottle. In my experience, young wine does need to breathe. It's part of the aging process of wine. It is a gradual oxidative process that allows a wine to develop its bouquet (that is also why many wine drinkers swirl the wine in their glass when drinking), to shed its hard, astringent tannins (in the case of a red wine), and to evolve from a youthful brilliant color to a maturer one. Wine breathes in the barrel before it is bottled and again in the bottle with the help of a porous cork.

If a young tannic red needs air to soften its tannins, the wine must be poured into a decanter or glasses, where a relatively large surface of wine is exposed to the air, and left for a half hour to an hour. If the wine is left in the uncorked bottle, so little of it is exposed to the air in the bottle's thin neck that there will be an extremely slow evolution before it is finally ready for drinking. Burgundy is rarely decanted and needs little airing because the Pinot Noir produces a much more fragile and volatile wine than, say, the relatively "closed" tannic wines of Bordeaux.

The price of a wine is a reflection of its quality.

At Restaurant Montrachet we have some bottles that sell for three thousand dollars each. Some of the great white Burgundies will sell for one thousand dollars a bottle. The question I'm most often asked is, "Is it really worth it?" or, "Is it really so much better than a wine selling for a hundred dollars or even fifteen dollars?" It's a difficult question to answer. Is a Picasso worth millions? Is a BMW worth more than a basic Honda? After all, they both get you from A to B. To some extent the price is established by what the market will pay. People have different values, preferring to spend their money on vacations rather than wine, antiques rather than BMWs. Having said that, there are identifiable and demonstrable differences of quality between wines just as there are between a BMW and a Honda. A great Bordeaux château such as Lafite or the Burgundy Montrachet has consistently proved over the years how a commitment to high quality control can pay off. Only a very small amount of wine is available from these vineyards, so its scarcity automatically pushes up its price. Some people value the rare, exquisitely crafted over the cheap and mass-produced. Obviously rarity alone can become something of a snobbish obsession—a vulgar way of impressing— and there's no doubt that this impacts on price. Then there's the collecting market, in which wine is all too often reduced to a commodity. It always amazes me that some of the most passionate collectors regale you with tales of their fantastic cellars while popping a well-chilled soda at dinner. This is the wrong way to experience wine. It's meant to be enjoyed for itself rather than as a maneuver in the snob game.

Most fruity wines are very sweet.

When I use the word "fruity" to describe a wine, I can see people roll their eyes. They jump to the conclusion that it means cheap and syrupy, the sort of stuff you were forced to drink at your aunt's Passover Seder. Over the years, I've avoided using it, but now I've decided to come out of the fruit closet. Fruity is fine.

After all, wine is made from fruit—grapes—which have to be ripe and sweet in order to make good wine. If you can't taste the fruit in the wine, there is something wrong. It will taste hard, dry, and coarse, and it will not have a very long life. Good wine carefully balances sugar, acid, alcohol, and tannin. Without ripe fruit, there will be insufficient sugar, and the wine will be imbalanced. At the other extreme, a wine with too much fruit and too little acid, alcohol, and tannin will not have enough structure and will be characterless. It's all in the balance.

WINE AND FOOD MYTHS

White wine should be drunk with fish and red wine with meat.
This is the most common myth. Though taken as gospel, it just isn't true. The colors don't always match.

Think about intensity of flavors and richness: light vs. heavy. Think about preparations: poaching, grilling, steaming, sautéing, etc. Generally, light wines go better with lighter foods and fuller, richer wines work with heavier food preparations. Many fish with stronger flavors, like tuna and salmon, work very well with light red wines, especially Pinot Noirs. Often a white wine is just too light. It doesn't have the body to complement the dish. Grilled fish is best with red wines, even fuller-bodied reds, because of the grill and smoke flavors it absorbs in the cooking process. This type of preparation completely overwhelms most white wines.

You can't drink wine with salad.
Wrong. The salad dressing is usually very high in acidity. Choose a wine that is also highly acid, such as a Riesling. It can compete.

You can't drink wine with chocolate.
Wrong. The best wines with chocolate are Ports and Madeiras. Also worth trying is Banyuls, a Port-like wine made in the Roussillon area of the south of France.

Red wine should be drunk with cheese.

It ain't necessarily so. I have seen more great red wine ruined by the wrong kind of cheese than I care to think about. There's an old wine merchant's dictum in France that, translated, means, "Sell with cheese, buy with fruit." Cheese will often soften harsh tannins, while fruit highlights them. Young, vigorous reds are good with soft, ripened, strong-tasting cheese, but older reds that have already shed some of their tannins and softened can be over-whelmed by strong cheese. Older reds can work wonderfully with hard, aged cheese, such as sheep's-milk Pyrénées, or a semi-soft, mild cheese, such as Chaumes or Saint-Nectaire.

However, the most exciting combination is cheese and white wine. Chilled white wine, higher in acids than red, offers a refreshing foil to the richness of cheeses such as Camembert or to the tartness of goat's cheese. Try a Pinot Blanc or a Chardonnay with a ripe Brie, or a spicy Gewürztraminer with a strong farm-house Munster, or a crisp Sancerre or Sauvignon Blanc with a young goat's cheese. But perhaps the most magical combination is a sweet Sauternes with a creamy Roquefort.

Experiment and see for yourself, but please don't serve those venerable old reds with a strong, creamy cheese.

Wine and spicy foods don't mix.

Wrong. Wine can work very well as long as you choose the right wine. The heat in spicy food is exacerbated by alcohol, so you need to choose something light, such as a Riesling, Muscadet, Entre-Deux-Mers, Soave, or Vinho Verde, because it will cool and refresh the palate. Perhaps the best choice, though, is something with a touch of sweetness, such as a German Riesling Kabi-nett. The truth is that if your palate has really been set on fire by highly spiced food, neither wine, beer, nor water is the best extin-guisher. Eat bread or yogurt.

PART TWO

HOT SPOTS

INTRODUCTION

People are constantly asking me, "How can I find good value wines in my local store?" "What do I look for?" "I don't know if I can trust my wine merchants. Aren't they just trying to push their highest-profit items?" Well, I can't wave a magic wand, and there's no simple formula. The great thing about wine is that you get to learn about it by drinking it. Don't be hidebound by the wine scores found in guidebooks and magazines. High scores are usually awarded to wines with the most potential. They may be great for the collector but tannic monsters if you want to open a bottle now.

Nevertheless a few pointers can be helpful, and here I've chosen those wines and regions of the world—my hot spots—that I think offer some of the best values in the market today. Often they are well-established wine regions that have been overlooked. The wine business is as subject to the cycles of fashion as the food and clothes businesses. Perhaps a wine style (Riesling, see page 101, is a good example) gets neglected because it's simply not the *vin du jour*. Cabernet Sauvignon has ruled the red-wine roost for many years, but now we're seeing a serious shift to Merlot and Pinot

Noir. Italy, once in disgrace, is now chic, especially Sangiovese-based wines.

A region becomes hot for a number of reasons. It may be by association with a neighboring and much more famous one whose topflight wines fetch topflight prices. The lesser neighbor will work hard to improve the quality of its wine but still offer real values by comparison. That's certainly the case with Burgundy's Côte Chalonnaise, just south of the great Côte d'Or, from which come Burgundy's Rolls-Royce wines; it's also true of Fronsac (next door to Pomerol), and of the Côte de Castillon next to Saint-Émilion.

A wine may become hot because of its parent's fame. (This might be called the "second-label syndrome.") Rosso di Montalcino is not exactly a second label, but its relationship to Big Daddy Brunello di Montalcino is similar. The Brunello—pretty tannic in its youth, especially in a strong vintage—is a sturdy and quite expensive red from Tuscany, made from the Sangiovese Grosso grape. The Rosso is made from the second-choice grapes from the same vineyard as the Brunello but can be sold after one year, rather than four for the Brunello. It's much more approachable, and much cheaper!

In France and California, for example, second-choice grapes are used to make very-good-value "second-label" wines (see page 87 for more details). For example, the very grand Grand Vin Château Margaux has Pavillon Rouge as its second label. Laurel Glen, a Cabernet Sauvignon producer, has a secondary wine called Terra Rosa, which is just about the best-value Cabernet anywhere (see page 235). Second labels are something like the ready-to-wear lines of haute-couture houses—brilliantly made but not quite so handcrafted.

Public taste can heat up a hot spot. The word gets around that great values are coming from X winery and soon the whole region has caught fire. Take Bodega Pesquera in Spain's Ribera del Duero region, for example. Until 1982 there was one world-class bodega in the area, Vega Sicilia. But since its emergence and enormous success other bodegas have overhauled themselves, and suddenly the whole Ribera region is on the rise, and for prices that make them great value.

The wines of Australia, Chile, and Italy are popular now, and I expect them to be joined soon by South Africa, Spain, Portugal, Austria, and Argentina. I just wish Germany's wines were better understood (and better labeled), because they represent some of the best values and most delicious white wines available in the world.

BURGUNDY
VALUES

"Burgundy is too expensive!" My back stiffens and my blood pressure rises when I hear that. It's not true because it is too generalized. The great Côte d'Or Burgundies, such as Chambertin and Montrachet, are very expensive indeed, but they represent only a tiny proportion of all the wine produced in Burgundy (made up of the two parts of the Côte d'Or—Côte de Nuits and Côte de Beaune—and the Côte Chalonnaise, Côte Mâconnais, Beaujolais, and Chablis).

I firmly believe that Burgundy is a great region for the novice wine drinker. For one thing there are only a few grape varieties to remember: Chardonnay and to a lesser extent Aligoté for the whites, Pinot Noir and Gamay for the reds. Although Chardonnay and Pinot Noir express themselves differently depending on soil and climate, they both have a gentle and appealing style. The reds are soft and fruity with low tannins and moderate alcohol, which makes them very flexible with food.

Even when we talk about the expensive and famous vineyards of the Côte d'Or, values can be found. When buying a simple

Bourgogne Rouge from a great estate like Michel Lafarge in Volnay, for example, we are buying wine made with the same care and expertise as Lafarge's more expensive wines. The winemaker will often go through his or her cellars and sample from the barrels. Some lots may not be up to the standard for the *village, premier cru,* or *grand cru* wines and so go into a lower appellation. Perhaps the vineyard has vines of varying ages. For example, Jean-Pierre de Smet at Domaine de l'Arlot in Nuits-Saint-Georges will bottle wine from the youngest vines in his *premier cru* vineyards as simple Nuits-Saint-Georges rather than Nuits-Saint-Georges *premier cru* because he feels that the younger vines do not produce a wine of enough depth to go into the more prestigious appellation. The simpler Nuits-Saint-Georges will have the breeding of the *premier cru* but will be less intense, rich, or complex. And, of course, it's much cheaper.

The key to finding good value in Burgundy is the grower's reputation (see "Hot Shots," page 62). Don't buy on the basis of the appellation or vintage but on the standing of the winemaker. A good winemaker will make good wines year after year. And this rule of thumb will serve you well for every wine you buy.

GETTING A HANDLE ON BURGUNDY

Burgundy is about detail—the subtle distinctions between microclimates and soil (grapes grown only a few yards apart can produce totally different wines) and the way the ownership of the land has been fragmented over the last two hundred years.

Burgundy produces only about half as much wine as Bordeaux. Where Bordeaux has the relatively easily comprehended "château" as its basic "unit" of wine production, usually owned by one family or company, the equivalent in Burgundy, the village, has long since been broken up into multiownership. A cru classé *Bordeaux has much more consistency than its equivalent in Burgundy. Gevrey-Chambertin on the Côte d'Or, for example, is* owned by several hundred individual wine growers, all with their own tiny slices of land. Sometimes they bottle their own wine, and sometimes they sell it to a négociant, a merchant who blends and matures wine from different growers in the village.

Burgundy is much more of a vinous crapshoot than is Bordeaux. The stakes are high and the rewards can be celestial, but so can the disappointments. Arguably Burgundy produces the most sublime wine in France, but it also produces some of the most hyped and overpriced. It has a wayward genius that can be much more exciting than Bordeaux, but it doesn't have the solid dependability of its cousin to the west.

The weather in Burgundy is much more variable than that in Bordeaux (which is tempered by its closeness to the ocean), and this, together with the topography and geology of the region, make for small climats, or parcels of land, each distinctive in subtle ways.

The history of the region has reinforced the patchwork created by nature. Before the French Revolution the major landowner and wine producer was the church. The revolution broke up the church's holdings and redistributed them in smaller units. French inheritance law also made its contribution. Instead of following primogeniture, in which the senior heir inherits the main share, Burgundian land was divided equally among all heirs. Plots became smaller and smaller, and alliances through marriage created domaines with plots often scattered through various vineyards.

The appellation system in Burgundy reflects the smallness of the holdings. Basically, the more geographically specific the appellation, the more prestigious the wine is meant to be. So the very highest ranked Burgundy, a grand cru (an equivalent status to premier grand cru classé in Bordeaux), does not even have to state which village it comes from; the appellation is the vineyard.

Here is the official ladder of excellence, starting with the most prestigious:

GRAND CRU. A grade established only in 1935, its intention was to protect prestige "brands" from imitation and adulteration. The vineyards occupy the best sites on the center of the premier slopes of the Côte d'Or and produce about 3 percent of the region's wine. Whether a wine deserves its status (and elevated price) depends on the quality and age of the vines (generally, the older *the better) and the skill of the winemaker. The magic words* grand cru *are not an automatic guarantee of success.*

PREMIER CRU. *Produce 10 to 15 percent of Burgundy from the best of the non-*grands crus *vineyards in the Côte d'Or and the best sites of the more southerly and less prestigious Côte Chalonnaise. Their label will carry the name of the village followed by the name of the vineyard. Many* premiers crus *are capable of outperforming some* grands crus *and they should be considered lesser, and more affordable, versions of* grands crus *rather than a superior* village, *the next rung down on the Burgundy ladder.*

VILLAGE. *On the Côte d'Or the vineyards sit either in the heavy soil at the bottom of the slopes or on the exposed tops. They account for 25 to 30 percent of the total crop.*

RÉGIONAL. *An appellation that covers several villages in specific areas—Bourgogne Côte Chalonnaise, Côte de Beaune-Villages, Côte de Nuits-Villages, Hautes Côtes de Beaune, Hautes Côtes de Nuits. This category accounts for about 20 percent of the crop.*

GENERIC BOURGOGNE ROUGE OR BOURGOGNE BLANC. *If it is red and comes from the Côte d'Or, it will be 100 percent Pinot Noir (Gamay if it comes from* crus *vineyards in Beaujolais) from vineyards on the plain rather than the prime-site slopes. It can offer excellent value for money and be a good introduction to a grower's style. If it is white, it must be Chardonnay and/or Pinot Noir. This category comprises 10 to 15 percent of the crop.*

BOURGOGNE PASSETOUTGRAINS. *Literally, "from any berry" (grain). A blend of Gamay and Pinot Noir that must be 30 percent the latter. The wine from this appellation, either red or rosé, will be light and fruity. It makes up 5 to 10 percent of the total output.*

BOURGOGNE ALIGOTÉ. *White wine made from the Aligoté grape, with or without the addition of Chardonnay. Can make sharp, characterful wine.*

BOURGOGNE GRAND ORDINAIRE. *Now almost a defunct appellation, with the emphasis very definitely on the* ordinaire. *Best avoided.*

GRANDS CRUS OF BURGUNDY

Red Wines

GEVREY-CHAMBERTIN: Chambertin; Chambertin Clos de Bèze; Latricières-Chambertin; Mazis-Chambertin; Charmes-Chambertin; Mazoyères-Chambertin (may also be called Charmes Chambertin); Griotte-Chambertin; Ruchottes-Chambertin; Chapelle-Chambertin

MOREY-SAINT-DENIS: Bonnes Mares; Clos de la Roche; Clos de Tart; Clos Saint-Denis; Clos des Lambrays

CHAMBOLLE-MUSIGNY: Musigny; Bonnes-Mares

VOUGEOT: Clos de Vougeot

FLAGEY-ECHÉZEAUX: Grands Echezeaux; Echezeaux

VOSNE-ROMANÉE: Romanée-Conti; La Tâche; Romanée-Saint-Vivant; Richebourg; La Romanée; La Grande Rue

ALOXE-CORTON: Corton; Any hyphenated name starting with Corton

White Wines

ALOXE-CORTON: Corton-Charlemagne; Corton Blanc

PULIGNY-MONTRACHET: Montrachet; Chevalier-Montrachet; Bâtard-Montrachet; Bienvenue-Bâtard-Monrachet

CHASSAGNE-MONTRACHET: Montrachet; Bâtard-Montrachet; Criots-Bâtard-Montrachet

• HOT SHOTS •
BURGUNDY (CÔTE D'OR)

GEVREY-CHAMBERTIN—Denis Bachelet; Domaine Geantet-Pansiot; Alain Burguet; Joseph Roty; Charles Rousseau; Bernard Maume; Pierre Bourée; Claude Dugat; Bernard Dugat; Georges Mugneret; Domaine Dujac; Domaine G. Roumier

MOREY-SAINT-DENIS—Domaine Dujac; Domaine Hubert Lignier; Domaine Ponsot

CHAMBOLLE-MUSIGNY—Domaine G. Roumier; Barthod-Noëllat; Hudelot-Noëllat; Domaine Comte de Vogüé; Jacques-Frédérique Mugnier; Robert Groffier

VOSNE-ROMANÉE—Jean Grivot; René Engel; Jean Gros; Gros Frère & Soeur; Forey Père & Fils; J. Confuron-Cotetidot; Henri Jayer; Jayer-Gilles; Georges Mugneret; Mongeard-Mugneret; Daniel Rion; Méo-Camuzet

NUITS-SAINT-GEORGES—Domaine de L'Arlot; Robert Chevillon; Henri Gouges; Méo-Camuzet; Georges Chicotot; Jean Grivot; Daniel Rion

ALOXE-CORTON—Chandon de Briailles; Dubeuil-Fontaine; Bonneau du Martray; Tollot-Beaut

PERNAND-VERGELESSES—Chandon de Briailles; Dubeuil-Fontaine

SAVIGNY-LÈS-BEAUNE—Simon Bize; Chandon de Briailles; Maurice Ecard; Tollot-Beaut; Albert Morot

BEAUNE—Louis Jadot; Joseph Drouhin; Albert Morot; Tollot-Beaut

POMMARD—Comte Armand; De Courcel; Hubert de Montille; Michel Lafarge; Domaine de la Pousse d'Or

VOLNAY—Comtes Lafon; Michel Lafarge; Marquis d'Angerville; Hubert De Montille; Domaine de la Pousse d'Or; J. F. Coche-Dury; Jean-Marc Boillot; Jacques Prieur

MONTHÉLIE—Paul Garaudet; Comtes Lafon; J. F. Coche-Dury

MEURSAULT—Jean-Marc Boillot; J. F. Coche-Dury; François Jobard; Comtes Lafon; Thierry Matrot; Patrick Javillier; Jacques Prieur; Guy Roulot; Verget

PULIGNY-MONTRACHET—Louis Carillon; Domaine Leflaive; Olivier Leflaive; Verget; Paul Pernot; Domaine Ramonet

CHASSAGNE-MONTRACHET—Jean-Noël Gagnard; Gagnard-Delagrange; Blain Gagnard; Fontaine-Gagnard; Georges Deleger; Michel Niellon; Domaine Ramonet; Marc Colin; Colin-Deleger

SAINT-AUBIN—Henri Prudhon; Marc Colin; Domaine Ramonet

SANTENAY—Marc Colin; Adrien Belland; Domaine de la Pousse d'Or

ᐯᐱ

FRENCH APPELLATIONS CONTRÔLÉES AND HOW THEY WORK

Created in 1935, the Institut National des Appellations d'Origine is officially authorized to regulate the French wine industry and ensure standards of quality that will not only safeguard the consumer from fraud but also the winemaker from unfair competition from inferior product. Even though there are loopholes aplenty (and even the periodic scandal), the system is a useful guide to quality and good value.

Stated simply, the appellation system is a quality pyramid based on the centuries-old understanding that certain sites in combination with certain climates, grape varieties, and winemaking techniques produce better wines than do others. The appellation regulations vary from region to region to take into account specific conditions and traditions, but in all regions they define and supervise core requirements. The geographical area covered by the appellation is defined; the variety of grape or grapes permitted is established; the amount of fruit harvested is controlled to prevent overcropping and the dilution of juice quality; the time of harvest is established; and the method of winemaking is regulated as is the addition of, for example, sugar or acid.

The base of the appellation pyramid covers wide geographical winemaking areas and applies the loosest regulations. The pinnacle is usually a village, or in the case of Burgundy sometimes a single vineyard, and the restrictions covering permitted grapes, yields, and what winemaking techniques must be followed are tougher than the wider-based appellations such as vin de pays.

Appellation status is not an automatic guarantee of quality or value for money (there are many wines waiting in the VDQS wings for the official nod to walk on to the full appellation contrôlée *stage) but it is a useful indicator.*

In addition to the appellation contrôlée *structure, many regions have a superimposed or parallel pyramid of local excellence. For example, Burgundy has its* grands *and* premiers crus *(see page 60), the Médoc its* crus classés *(see page 83).*

Starting with the pinnacle . . .

Appellation (d'Origine) Contrôlée (AC or AOC). *A strict control of geographic boundaries, grape varieties, alcoholic strength and quantity produced. Most AOC wines are limited to forty hectolitres per hectare (approximately two hundred cases), but there are complicated allowances for topping up and holding over wine that vary from year to year depending on the harvest. It can be as much as 20 percent more than the permitted yield if the growers' union can make a case to the authorities.*

The ceiling on harvest yields for the best wines within an appellation—the grands *and* premiers crus *in Burgundy, and* crus classés *in the Médoc, for example—is usually more restricted than the requirements of the appellation in order to prevent dilution of the juice. But it has to be said that it would take more supervision than can reasonably be expected to ensure that no topping up with inferior wine ever went on. A tasting test (amazingly, this is only a fairly recent introduction to appellation controls) is now meant to detect fraud, but there are simply not enough inspectors and not enough time for comprehensive taste testing.*

In the final analysis the best regulators of wine quality are the producers themselves. If they let standards fall and the consumer loses confidence in the authenticity and quality of the wine, it is the winemaker who suffers most in the long run.

Vin Délimité de Qualité Supérieure (VDQS). *Created in 1945, VDQS is really a waiting room or staging post between the lowly* vin de table *and the AOC category. About 1.5 percent of the annual harvest qualifies for VDQS status. The wines can be very good value indeed, especially when they come from tightly controlled regions—often as small as a village—and comply with the strict regulations covering grape varieties and yields per acre. VDQS is a great value-hunting ground.*

Vin de Pays. *An appellation established in 1981 and intended to give a bit of dignity (and some minimal quality guidelines) to what were otherwise anonymous local café wines. It covers wines with a definite regional flavor and identity—country wines—that come from specified areas. Producers of* vin de pays *have more freedom regarding the grape varieties they use. Many are experimenting with the popular Chardonnay and Cabernet Sauvignon—and as the only appellation category that can mention grape varieties on the label, it's a great marketing advantage. These can be as specific as a group of villages to as general as a region. The whole of the Loire valley, for example, is covered by the Vins de Pays du Jardin de France appellation. The appellation also stipulates levels of alcohol (as a rule of thumb, the higher, the better the wine) as well as the vineyard yield (the lower the better). These rules are meant to ensure that, say, a vin de pays from Corsica will be of a similar quality to, say, a vin de pays from the Loire. Whether one tastes better or worse will be a matter of personal preference, but at least they should be on the same quality playing field. There can be some remarkable values found within this category. Do not dismiss it because of its name.*

Vin de Table. *The base of the pyramid, which accounts for half of all the wine made in France. It can be made from more or less any grape or blend of grapes from any or a mix of regions. In France this is the casual daily drink, basic jug wine in plastic bottles, its price determined by its alcohol level.*

FRENCH WINE-SPEAK

(See also Champagne-Speak, page 169)

APPELLATION [D'ORIGINE] CONTRÔLÉE (AC OR AOC).
    An official specification of a wine according to such factors as grape variety or blends of different varieties, alcohol level, geographical area of production, yield level. Almost all AOCs are based on geographical areas and the practices within them. Some, though, are technique- rather than site-specific. For example,

crémant *is a type of sparkling wine made in the Loire, Alsace, and Burgundy, and its AC defines the acceptable techniques that must be used. To some extent the same goes for Champagne (although the area in which the specific* méthode champenoise *is employed is relatively small and coherent).*

BLANC DE BLANCS. Sparkling white wine made only from white wine grapes (as distinct from most Champagne, which is made from a mixture of white and black grapes). A Champagne that is Blanc de Blancs is made only from Chardonnay (usually only a constituent grape along with, for example, Pinot Noir).

BLANC DE NOIRS. Sparkling white (or "blush") wine made from red grapes.

CAVE. Cellar or winemaking establishment.

CÉPAGE. Grape variety.

CHAI. Cellar of a winery, with particular reference to Bordeaux.

CHAPTALIZATION. An approved practice, particularly in Burgundy, of adding sugar to wine must in order to increase its alcohol potential.

CLIMAT. A plot within a vineyard, especially in Burgundy.

CLOS. A vineyard (originally a walled pieced of land).

COMMUNE. An administrative district within a département.

CÔTE/COTEAUX. Hillside(s).

CRÉMANT. A sparkling wine made by traditional method, but not the same as Champagne. The fizz is milder than most Champagnes. Where Champagne has five to six atmospheres of pressure, crémant *has two to three.*

CRU. The dictionary defines it as a "growth," as in the produce of a particular vineyard (for example, the French expression boire du vin de son cru *means to drink the wine from one's own vineyard).*

CRU BOURGEOIS. A level of quality below that of Cru classé *(see below).*

CRU CLASSÉ. *A vineyard included in the 1855 Classification of the Médoc (see page 83) as well as a classed wine from other areas of the Bordeaux: Graves (page 86), Saint-Émilion (page 85), and Sauternes. Officially the best wines of the region.*

CUVAISON. *The period the juice spends macerating with the skins.*

CUVÉ DE FERMENTATION. *Vat.*

CUVÉ CLOSE. *A method for mass-producing sparkling wine. Also known as the "Charmat" or "tank" method. Unlike Champagne, where the second fermentation takes place in the bottle,* cuvé close *ferments in a stainless-steel tank (the sparkle will be less long-lasting than that of champagne).*

CUVÉE. *A slippery word to define, it can refer to the wine from a particular blend of vats, or to a special batch of wine.*

DEMI-SEC. *Half dry/sweet. When applied to Champagne it con-notes a wine definitely on the sweet side.*

DÉPARTEMENT. *An administrative area roughly equivalent to a state in the United States.*

DOUX. *Sweet.*

EN PRIMEUR. *Classic wines (particularly red Bordeaux) that are offered for sale before they have been blended and bottled.*

GOÛT DE TERROIR. *Literally "taste of the earth" but usually applied to a wine where soil, climate, grape variety, and method of winemaking all contribute to a unique and defining flavor and aroma. The opposite of anonymous, mass-produced wine.*

GRAND CRU. *The term has a specific and controlled meaning in Burgundy, Alsace, and Champagne, where it denotes a wine of the very highest quality. In Saint-Émilion it includes the third rank of châteaux. In other areas the term has been debased to sug-gest top quality when something far less is being palmed off.*

JEUNES VIGNES. *Recently planted vines.*

MARC. *The debris of skins, seeds, and stalks (also known as pomace) left after grapes have been pressed, and the clear, fiery liquor that is distilled from them. Marc de Bourgogne is the best.*

MIS EN BOUTEILLE (au château; dans nos caves; au domaine). *Bottled at the vineyard (not necessarily a guarantee of quality: very nasty wine can be bottled on site!).*

MOELLEUX. Semisweet.

MOUSSEUX. A sparkling wine, but not made by méthode champenoise.

MOÛT. Must: the juice of the freshly pressed grapes, with or without skins.

NÉGOTIANT/ÉLEVEUR. A trader, merchant, middleman. Sometimes they will own vineyards but essentially they are in the business of buying, maturing, blending, bottling, and selling wine.

NOUVEAU. New red wine that is meant to be drunk young.

PÉTILLANT. Slightly sparkling.

POURRITURE NOBLE. The fungal growth of the bacterium Botrytis cinerea, *which dehydrates grapes to produce sweet wine.*

PREMIER CRU. The highest level of the 1855 classification of the wines of the Médoc, and the second level (after grand cru*) of the wines of Burgundy.*

RÉCOLTE. Crop or vintage.

SEC. Dry, or low in sugar.

SÉLECTION DE GRAINS NOBLES. A term used in Alsace that is roughly equivalent to Trockenbeerenauslese *in Germany: late-picked selected grapes that have been allowed to ripen much longer than usual and may also be affected by* Botrytis cinerea *to produce a sweet dessert wine.*

SUR LIE. A wine that has been left to age in contact with the yeasty sediment (the lees) produced during fermentation. The resulting wine will have a nuttier, fuller flavor. The term Muscadet sur lie generally indicates a superior Muscadet.

SUPÉRIEUR(E). Indicates a higher degree of alcohol. For example, a Bordeaux Supérieur has 0.5 percent more alcohol than does the basic Appellation Contrôlée Bordeaux (10 percent).

TASTEVIN. A shallow metal cup used for tasting wine (now a largely ceremonial accessory particularly associated with Burgundy).

TÊTE DE CUVÉE. The first, and best, juice from newly pressed grapes.

VENDANGE. The grape harvest.

VENDANGE TARDIVE. Late harvest; a term used in Alsace, roughly equivalent to the German Auslese.

VIEILLES VIGNES. Old vines. The older the vine (assuming it is not diseased), the more intensely flavored the juice—in theory (a lousy old vine will produce lousy wine!).

VIGNERON. Vineyard worker.

VIN DE GARDE. Classic wine with aging potential.

VIN DÉLIMITÉ DE QUALITÉ SUPÉRIEUR (VDQS). An official quality level above vin de pays *but below* appellation contrôlée.

VIN DE PAILLE. A dessert wine made from grapes that have been allowed to dry on straw (paille) *mats. Particularly associated with the Jura region.*

VIN DE PAYS. An official designation for a "country" wine that has regional characteristics but is below VDQS.

VIN DE PRESSE. The wine resulting from the last and heaviest pressing of the grapes. It is often used to beef up lighter wine, especially at the low end of the market.

VIN DE TABLE/VIN ORDINAIRE. Everyday table wine not subject to quality controls.

VIN DOUX NATUREL (VDN). A wine fortified with wine alcohol before all the natural sugar has been fermented out, resulting in a sweet wine (from the residual sugar) with quite high alcohol levels. Popular in the Rhône and Languedoc-Roussillon. Well-known VDNs are Muscat de Beaumes-de-Venise, Muscat de Rivesaltes, Muscat de Frontignan, Maury, and Banyuls.

VIN GRIS. A pale rosé or blush wine made from the juice of red grapes before they have begun to ferment.

BURGUNDY'S
CÔTE CHALONNAISE

As you drive out of the southern tip of the Côte de Beaune into the Côte Chalonnaise at Chagny, you cross an invisible border that separates the Côte d'Or from the relatively neglected "Région de Mercurey," as the Chalonnaise is known locally. It's a fairly small area, about three thousand acres planted to grapes, with four main communes: Givry, Montagny, Mercurey, and Rully. In addition there is Aligoté de Bouzeron (a village given its own appellation in 1979 for the production of white wine from the Aligoté grape). Although the Côte Chalonnaise shares the same soil composition and grape varieties (Chardonnay, Pinot Noir) with the more illustrious Côte de Beaune to the north, the wines here tend to be a little lighter and perhaps a shade more rustic. The vineyards, although farther south, are often cooler and tend to need more time to ripen. On the whole the wines are leaner.

A combination of events has caused a minirevolution in the region, making it one of the sources for ultravalue wines in Burgundy. First, as wines from the Côte d'Or have skyrocketed, consumers have begun to look for alternatives, and a new generation of younger, perhaps better-educated, and more innovative winemakers are looking to fill the gap.

Mercurey produces mainly red (the best of which can give Pommard a run for its money) and a little white (barely 10 percent of total production) that's akin to Meursault. Givry, another red-wine commune, makes jammy, easy-drinking wine that, at its best, is similar to Pernand-Vergelesses. Montagny makes a slightly buttery, nutty, Chablis-like white (but watch out for *premier cru* designations; in a unique ruling it only has to reach a minimum alcohol level of 11.5 percent to achieve *premier cru* status, which is a bit unfair to other *premiers crus,* which have to meet much more stringent standards). From Rully comes plummy Pinot Noir, a Chablis-like Chardonnay, and the very good Crémant de Bourgogne.

•HOT SHOTS•

For Aligoté de Bouzeron: Aubert de Villaine. *For Rully:* Michel Briday; Domaine de la Folie; Olivier Leflaive; P. Ninot. *For Mercurey:* Château de Chamirey; Faiveley; Michel Juillot; Domaine Bertrand; Domaine de la Meix Foulot. *For Givry:* Clos Salomon; Joblot, René Bourgeon. *For Montagny:* Château de la Saule; Jean Vachet.

CHABLIS

Although Chablis is usually lumped with Burgundy, it is actually closer to Champagne and Sancerre. In fact what we see of Chablis today, about 7,500 acres, is only one-tenth of what used to be an enormous winemaking region that supplied the thirsty souls of Paris with their daily inexpensive wine. But with the advent in the 1850s of a rail system capable of transporting much cheaper wine from the Midi, and the arrival of the deadly phylloxera louse in 1887, Chablis fell on hard times. These days it's expanding again, but not without its critics, who believe that the inclusion of land that doesn't strictly conform to the traditional composition only harms the appellation.

Although Chablis, like the whites of Burgundy, is made from Chardonnay, the Côte de Beaune is more than one hundred miles away to the south, and the styles are very different. This is partly because of the cooler climate. On my first visit in the early spring of 1981 I remember seeing curious little lanterns throughout the vineyards. These oil-burning smudge pots were there to ward off spring frosts, which can be devastating to the newly sprouted buds. At the first warning of dropping temperatures the vigneron would run into his vineyard, often in the middle of the night, to light up the pots to warm the air down the rows of vines. Nowadays the same vigneron is much more likely to spray his vines with water to create a thin insulation of protective ice; a paradox maybe, but it works.

The soil is also a distinguishing factor. Chablis is part of a geological basin that was formed 180 million years ago from clay, limestone, and the compacted shells of tiny shellfish. This soil, known as Kimmeridgian, imparts the unique "gunflint" *(goût de pierre de fusil),* steely/minerally flavor and aroma that is Chablis's hallmark.

Worldwide, Chardonnay usually sees some sort of oak treatment, but not necessarily in Chablis. Until the 1960s the wine was aged in oak barrels, but with the advent of stainless steel most producers switched over because they wanted the true *goût de terroir* to be able to express itself without being masked by the vanillin flavors leached by the barrels. Today there are still two camps, and it's really a matter of one's personal preference.

There are four levels of Chablis (see box on p. 75). At the top are the *grands crus,* which sit together looking down on the town of Chablis across the river Serein. Next come the *premiers crus,* and with them a fair amount of controversy. In recent years the land that could be classified *grand cru* was extended into areas of Portland, rather than Kimmeridgian, limestone, and of course purists had conniptions. The third rank is generic Chablis, which encompasses many styles but tends to be more forward than *premier cru.* At the bottom of the ladder is *Petit Chablis,* a simple, crisp, and refreshing

---

• H O T   S H O T S •

Jean Collet; Jean Dauvissat; René et Vincent Dauvissat;
J. P. Drouhin; Domaine de la Maladière; Louis Michel;
Jean-Marie Ravenau; Billaud-Simon; F. Bachelier;
Michel Barat; Domaine Laroche, J. Moreau.

white without any great length or intensity. It's in these last two categories that most overproduction has taken place in recent years.

Not too long ago "Chablis" seemed to be the catchall name for any old glass of white jug wine produced in California or Australia. In fact I still get people in the restaurant asking for a glass of "Chablis," meaning a glass of dry white wine. Today the market for the real stuff has strengthened, and it now represents excellent value for those who like the pure expression of Chardonnay. True Chablis has a green-gold glint; a flinty, apple, and floral aroma; racy acidity followed by round, rich Chardonnay flavors, and a long, refreshing finish. Bring on the shellfish!

CHABLIS EXCELLENCE

At the top:

GRANDS CRUS. *Big, rich, and complex but leaner and more restrained than white Burgundy farther south. All Chablis* grands crus *are grown on the same southwest-facing slope underpinned by prized Kimmeridgian limestone. They are:*

> *Bougros; Blanchot; Les Clos; Grenouilles; Les Preuse; Valmur; Vaudésir; La Moutonne (an honorary* grand cru*)*

PREMIERS CRUS. *Also from the southwest slopes on the right bank of the Serein, above the village of Chablis. Technically there are forty, but only a dozen or so regularly appear on labels (the first two on the list are generally considered closest to* grand cru *status):*

> *Montée de Tonnerre; Monts de Milieu; Fourchaume; Vaucoupin; Les Fourneaux; Beauroy; Côte de Léchet; Vaillons; Mélinots; Montmains; Vosgros; Vaudevey*

CHABLIS. *The basic appellation. The simple* village *Chablis competes with Mâcon-Villages.*

PETIT CHABLIS. *The recent fast expansion of planting has resulted in a fair bit of controversy over whether* Petit Chablis *should be allowed to call itself Chablis at all.*

BEAUJOLAIS

Just thinking of Beaujolais makes my mouth water! It is one of the most succulent, juicy, thirst-quenching, and all-around delicious wines I know.

The Beaujolais region is a three-mile stretch that starts just south of Mâcon and extends down to just north of Lyons. About two-thirds of all the wine of the Burgundy (of which Beaujolais is considered a part) comes from here. The granite landscape is seriously hilly. (I remember once starting out on a jog with all the determination and pride one feels when making a determined effort to cleanse the system of the excesses of the previous evening. It only took fifty yards of one of those steep hills to convince me that I really ought to get on to my next appointment. After all, it's rude to be late!) The grape of the region is Gamay (or to be precise, Gamay à Jus Blanc).

There are essentially two areas of production and two distinct styles of wine. The southern end, or Bas Beaujolais, produces basic Beaujolais and Beaujolais Supérieur. The soil here has more clay, and the wines lack the zip and character of those farther north in the Haut Beaujolais. There thirty-nine villages are entitled to

the Beaujolais-Villages appellation, and ten communes—the
Cru Beaujolais—may use their
own name (see "Beaujolais Quality Ladder," page 78).

Two methods of vinification
produce wines of very different
styles. The first, and by far the
most popular, is carbonic maceration (see page 23), in which
bunches of uncrushed grapes are
blanketed with inert carbon dioxide, and fermentation starts
within the grape itself until the
grapes burst and fermentation is
finished in the conventional way.
Wines made by carbonic maceration are generally very fruity, low
in acid and tannin, and not meant
to be aged. The bouquet has a
distinctive "banana" accent.

The second method is the tra-
ditional one for red wines, in which the grapes are first crushed
and then fermented in open tanks. This results in wine of deeper
color and higher levels of tannin and phenolic compounds, which
make it suitable for aging. The oldest Beaujolais I have ever drunk
was a 1929 Moulin-à-Vent in 1994, and it was still a superb
wine—not youthfully fruity but full of rich, sweet fruit flavors and
balance that were amazing in a sixty-five-year-old Beaujolais.

The secret in finding traditional Beaujolais is to look for small
top producers, because most of the wine of the region—some of
which is very good indeed—is sold off to large *négociant* houses
and rarely aspires to the level of the small grower who estate-
bottles his own wine.

Beaujolais is the ultimate antisnob wine. One of my greatest

> *When I look for wine
> bargains, I go for
> the great wine regions:
> Bordeaux, Burgundy,
> California. Anyone can
> drink inexpensive wine from
> marginal areas; the trick is
> to find good buys from the
> best vineyards. Wonderful
> Bordeaux comes from lesser
> known Châteaux. But for
> good value, year in and
> year out, nothing beats
> Beaujolais. Whether it's
> from Georges Duboeuf,
> Louis Jadot, Château de
> Lachaize, or a dozen other
> producers, there is a
> Beaujolais to please every
> taste—and pocketbook.*
>
> —FRANK PRIAL,
> wine columnist,
> *New York Times*

wine experiences was in a simple bistro in Lyons, where, with Al Hotchkin, proprietor of The Burgundy Wine Company in New York City, we ordered the house charcuterie platter of homemade sausages *en croûte* followed by cheese, all washed down with pitcher after pitcher of the house Fleurie. For me this is the essence of dining and drinking. It can be a profound experience to drink an aged and noble Pauillac, but nothing comes close to the sheer joy of roll-up-your-sleeves full-tilt funloving Beaujolais.

• H O T   S H O T S •

For Beaujolais Villages: Domaine des Vissoux; *For Brouilly:* Alain Michaud; Chateau de la Chaize; *For Fleurie:* Michel Chignard; *For Julienas:* Michel Tête; *For Moulin à Vent:* Domaine Diochon; Jean-Pierre Bloud; Jacky Janodet; *For Morgon:* Jacky Janodet; Jean Foillard; Jean-Paul Thevenet; Marcel Lapierre; *For all regions mentioned above:* Georges Duboeuf

❦

BEAUJOLAIS QUALITY LADDER

From the top:

CRU BEAUJOLAIS. *Ten village communes in the north of the region (where the soil is more granite/clay/schist than in the south). Although there are no grand or premier cru distinctions officially made within each commune, they do exist on an unofficial level:*

Brouilly; Chénas; Côte de Brouilly; Fleurie; Chiroubles; Juliénas; Morgon; Moulin-à-Vent; Saint-Amour; Regnié

BEAUJOLAIS-VILLAGES. *Just to the south of the prestigious cru communes are thirty-nine well-sited communes that are capable, at the best, of giving some of the lordly crus a run for their money.*

BEAUJOLAIS SUPÉRIEURE. *Usually only distinguished from basic Beaujolais by one degree more alcohol.*

BEAUJOLAIS. *The basic appellation available to all growers in the Beaujolais as long as they are using Gamay and achieving a minimum of 9 percent alcohol. Although the appellation covers red, white, and rosé, the vast majority of wine is red and from the southern part of the region.*

BEAUJOLAIS NOUVEAU

There's probably never been a more successful wine-marketing campaign since the invention of Champagne. In the 1960s, taking advantage of a medieval law forbidding the release of Beaujolais before midnight November 14, a group of growers, journalists, and assorted PR executives concocted the idea of a race—the fastest bottle from picking to table. Nouveau *has been such a success that half of all Beaujolais is sold this way, and now we are seeing wineries across the world developing similar marketing techniques for fruity red grapes.*

Some Beaujolais had always been available en primeur *(straight from a quick fermentation and bottling) and, apart from the cynical marketing angle, there's some sense to it. The Gamay grape is full and fruity and not exactly overloaded with the tannins that make for longevity. A quick fermentation via carbonic maceration keeps skin and seed extract to a minimum, and what we are left with, only a few weeks after harvest, is an unpretentious, fruity quaffing wine. And there's nothing wrong with that, although we should not be led only by the rockiest of rock-bottom prices. Beaujolais-Villages makes better* nouveau *than plain old Beaujolais, and even some of the lesser wines from the prestigious* Crus Beaujolais *vineyards are released* en primeur *(although they have to wait until December 15, one month after their lowlier brethren have made their splashy debuts).*

Do you need to drink nouveau *before the clock tolls its sell-by date at midnight on New Year's Eve? No, most of it will be fine for six months, but after that it loses its brightness as the acid levels fade.*

BORDEAUX

Not only is Bordeaux the single most important wine region of France (almost five times larger than Burgundy, it accounts for 25 percent of all of France's *appellation* wine) but it is also seen as a bellwether for wine throughout the world. I remember watching the evening news one day in late August 1989 before the grapes had even been transformed into wine, and seeing the vintage proclaimed as the greatest of the century. The point was that Bordeaux was seen somehow as representative of all wine. In the popular imagination Bordeaux *is* wine. (Actually the 1989 vintage was horrible in many parts of the world, notably Tuscany and areas of California.)

Bordeaux has thirteen thousand growers, more than nine thousand châteaux (the region's catchall word for *domaine* or estate, although many don't have a building on them, much less a grand château beloved of fancy wine labels), and fifty-three appellations. Of the thousands of châteaux only sixty-one in the Médoc have the exalted status of *grand cru classé* (see page 83 for the 1855 classification of the Médoc), sixteen are classified in Graves and seventy-four in Saint-Émilion. But this isn't the end of the story;

> I t is absolutely not neces-
> sary to spend a lot of
> money in order to find a
> good wine. Price does not
> always indicate quality
> when it comes to fine wine.
>
> For red wines one should
> be looking at Bordeaux.
> The simple Bordeaux AC,
> regional AC wines such as
> Saint-Émilion AC or
> Pauillac AC, and the Crus
> Bourgeois are a great source
> of good-value reds.
>
> —KEVIN ZRALY,
> author, educator,
> and wine director,
> Windows on the World
> restaurant, New York

it's just the beginning as far as great Bordeaux values are concerned.

Some properties are too small, lack marketing clout, or are in unfashionable appellations and therefore do not get into the limelight. For example, *crus bourgeois* (see page 85) are for the most part smaller properties around the villages of Moulis and Listrac in the Médoc. Their wines are made to the same standards and with the same grape varieties as the classified châteaux and are well worth seeking out. In addition look for second-label wines made of lots the cellar master has rejected for the *grand vin*. They are not flawed wines in any way; they just don't have the richness, intensity, or structure that is needed for the premier label. Second labels—often more approachable in their youth than their more austere cousins—have been treated with the same care and come from the same sources but at half the cost. Many châteaux release a second label, but I think the best values are those from *cru classé* châteaux (see page 87).

Where in the region will you find good deals? I'm particularly keen on the delicious wines of the Entre-Deux-Mers, the area lying between the Dordogne and Garonne. Its light whites from the Sauvignon Blanc and Sémillon (the red can only be classified simply as Bordeaux Rouge or Bordeaux Supérieur) are clean and crisp, and those that have been barrel-fermented have a richer and fuller style.

With Merlot the hot varietal of the moment, I would also look at the area on the right bank of the Dordogne near the town of

Libourne (known as the Right Bank, or Libournais). Nearby is one of the most underrated appellations in Bordeaux, the Fron-

sac (including Canon-Fronsac). Until the 1800s the wines of Fronsac were much more highly regarded than those of their now much more prominent neighbors, Saint-Émilion and Pomerol. Fronsac wines have much more Cabernet Franc than Pomerol, which makes them a little more tannic and structured. Thus they are able to offer the aging potential associated with Médoc, allied with the soft Merlot-based palate of Pomerol. There has been a tremendous amount of activity in the area, with a new generation of eager winemakers and some serious investment (particularly by the Right Bank's leading house, Jean-Pierre Moueix) in machinery and barrels.

• HOT SHOTS •

In Fronsac and Canon-Fronsac: Canon de Brem; Cassagne-Haut-Canon-La Truffière; La Dauphine; Fontenil; Mazeris; Moulin-Haut-Laroque; La Vieille Cure. *Hot-Shot Crus Bourgeois:* Capbern-Gasqueton; Haut-Marbuzet; Les Ormes de Pez; de Marbuzet; Meyney; Phélan-Ségur; Château La Haye (all Saint-Estèphe); Chasse-Spleen (Moulis); Poujeaux (Moulis); Cissac (Cissac); Larose-Trintaudon (Saint-Laurent); Greysac (Begadan); Potensac (Potensac); Sociando-Mallet (Saint-Seurin-de-Cadourne); Château Charmail (Haut-Médoc).

THE 1855 CLASSIFICATION OF THE WINES OF THE MÉDOC

The Paris Exhibition of 1855 prompted members of the Bordeaux wine trade to give some official ranking to the wines of the Médoc (the most prestigious winemaking area of the Bordeaux region and made up of the appellations, *or approved and regulated wine areas, Médoc, Haut-Médoc, Saint-Estèphe, Saint-Julien, Pauillac, Moulis, Listrac, and Margaux; in addition they included one château, Haut-Brion, from Graves, just south of the Médoc). They did it quite simply on the basis of which wines at the time commanded the highest prices. The ranking has held up remarkably well (there has been only one substantial adjustment—the upgrading in 1973 of Château Mouton-Rothschild to the highest class—and many blind tastings have since provided a pretty consistent verification of the 1855 classification. Obviously, though, given the ups and downs of almost 140 years, some châteaux have improved and some declined. For example, a château that is included in the ranking (and is therefore entitled to call its wine* cru classé*) can buy up vineyards producing unclassed wine and ennoble it with its own* classé *status. The same is not true in reverse. Even a superb unclassed château such as Gloria, which is made up of parcels of land, some of which came from classed vineyards, cannot sell its wine as* cru classé. *Strictly speaking, it is* cru bourgeois *(the category below* cru classé*), although in the case of Château Gloria and a number of other super-*crus bourgeois *they disdain to use the designation* cru bourgeois *on their labels. (See page 85 for more on* cru bourgeois *and other "petits châteaux" great-value wines.)*

The order of listing within each class of the 1855 classification does not signify relative merit.

First Growths *(Premiers/1ers Crus):* Château Lafite-Rothschild *(Pauillac); Château Latour (Pauillac); Château Margaux (Margaux); Château Mouton-Rothschild (Pauillac); Château Haut-Brion (Graves)*

Second Growths *(Deuxièmes/2èmes Crus):* Château Rausan-Ségla *(Margaux); Château Rauzan-Gassies (Margaux); Château*

Léoville-Las-Cases (Saint-Julien); Château Léoville-Poyferré (Saint-Julien); Château Léoville-Barton (Saint-Julien); Château Durfort-Vivens (Margaux); Château Lascombes (Margaux); Château Gruaud-Larose (Saint-Julien); Château Brane-Cantenac (Margaux); Château Pichon-Longueville-Baron (Pauillac); Château Pichon-Longueville-Lalande (Pauillac); Château Ducru-Beaucaillou (Saint-Julien); Château Cos d'Estournel (Saint-Estèphe); Château Montrose (Saint-Estèphe)

Third Growths *(Troisième/3èmes Crus): Château Giscours (Margaux); Château Kirwan (Margaux); Château d'Issan (Margaux); Château Lagrange (Saint-Julien); Château Langoa-Barton (Saint-Julien); Château Malescot-Saint-Exupéry (Margaux); Château Cantenac-Brown (Margaux); Château Palmer (Margaux); Château La Lagune (Haut-Médoc); Château Desmirail (Margaux); Château Calon-Ségur (Saint-Estèphe); Château Marquis d'Alesme-Becker (Margaux); Château Boyd-Cantenac (Margaux); Château Ferrière (Margaux)*

Fourth Growths *(Quatrièmes/4èmes Crus): Château St. Pierre (Saint-Julien); Château Branaire-Ducru (Saint-Julien); Château Talbot (Saint-Julien); Château Duhart-Milon-Rothschild (Pauillac); Château Pouget (Margaux); Château La Tour-Carnet (Haut-Médoc); Château Lafon-Rochet (Saint-Estèphe); Château Beychevelle (Saint-Julien); Château Prieuré-Lichine (Margaux); Château Marquis-de-Terme (Margaux)*

Fifth Growths *(Cinquièmes/5èmes Crus): Château Pontet-Canet (Pauillac); Château Batailley (Pauillac); Château Grand-Puy-Lacoste (Pauillac); Château Grand-Puy-Ducasse (Pauillac); Château Haut-Batailley (Pauillac); Château Lynch-Bages (Pauillac); Château Lynch-Moussas (Pauillac); Château Dauzac (Margaux); Château Mouton-Baronne-Philippe (Pauillac); Château du Tertre (Margaux); Château Haut-Bages-Libéral (Pauillac); Château Pédesclaux (Pauillac); Château Belgrave (Haut-Médoc); Château de Camensac (Haut-Médoc); Château Cos-Labory (Saint-Estèphe); Château Clerc-Milon-Rothschild (Pauillac); Château Croizet-Bages (Pauillac); Château Cantermerle (Haut-Médoc)*

CLASSY SAINT-ÉMILION

Unlike the ranking of wines in neighboring Médoc, which has not changed substantially in 140 years, Saint-Émilion reviews its rankings periodically, and for some classes annually. Starting with the best:

Premiers Grands Crus Classés "A" *(Château Cheval Blanc and Château Ausone)*

Premiers Grands Crus Classés "B" *(roughly equivalent to second- or third-growth Médoc)*

Grands Crus Classés *(roughly equivalent to fourth- or fifth-growth Médoc)*

Grands Crus *(equivalent to cru bourgeois in the Médoc)*

However, the system is not quite such a good indicator of quality and value as it appears. The grades given to châteaux bob up and down in a confusing way, and at the lowest level, where you would expect to find good values, the grand-sounding title grand cru can lend indifferent wine a spurious prestige. At this level too many of the winemakers lack the resources that give larger establishments stability.

Just to complicate things further, there is an unofficial but very impressive-sounding Saint-Émilion Grand Cru classification that is open to any winemaker who submits wine to an annual tasting. To be sure you are getting officially graded Saint-Émilion, look for "Saint-Émilion Grand Cru Classé" on the label.

BOURGEOIS IS NOT A DIRTY WORD

Not among the wines of the Médoc it isn't. Nor to anyone who wants great value Bordeaux. Crus bourgeois were those left out of the 1855 league table of classed growths. But as happens with many aristocratic families, the bloodline can become diluted, the estate neglected by careless heirs.

Many of the best crus bourgeois wines have ambitions, but the problem is that, unlike their human counterparts, they cannot simply buy their way into the peerage. Even if they buy up parcels of vines from classed growths they cannot call themselves crus classés. *Ironically, existing* crus classés *are allowed to buy up inferior land and confer on the wine made from it their* classé *status. This apparent injustice is allowed because a classed château is seen not just as a piece of real estate but rather as a* marque, *or brand, its status the sum of tradition, expertise demonstrated over time, and the fact that in 1855 it was making high-priced wine.*

Membership in the Syndicate of Cru Bourgeois is voluntary, and some unclassed but exceptional châteaux have formed an unofficial elite holding themselves aloof from their fellow bourgeois in the hope of eventual elevation to the ranks of the nobility.

The Super-Bourgeoisie: *Château Gloria; Château d'Angludet; Château Bel-Air-Marquis-d'Aligre; Château La Couronne; Château Fonbadet; Château Labégorce; Château Labégorce-Zédé; Château Lanessan; Château Maucaillou; Château de Pez; Château Siran; Château La Tour de Mons; Château Villegeorge*

The syndicate has about 130 members, divided into three categories. Starting with the highest:

CRU GRAND BOURGEOIS EXCEPTIONNEL. *Eighteen châteaux from* cru classé *country between Ludon and Saint-Estèphe. Wine must be château-bottled.*

CRU GRAND BOURGEOIS. *Satisfies the basic requirements of* cru bourgeois *but also ages its wine in oak. Includes forty-one châteaux.*

CRU BOURGEOIS. *Covers almost seventy châteaux, with properties of a minimum of seventeen hectares (roughly seven acres), whose wine comes up to the syndicate's standards.*

"SECOND-LABEL" VALUES

Many of the classed-growth châteaux of the Médoc (see page 83) produce a second-string wine that, although not up to the highest standards of the château's grand vin, can offer good value and an introduction to the style of the château and commune. In the following list the grand vin is given in parentheses after its second-label sibling.

First Growths: *Moulin des Carruades (Lafite-Rothschild); Les Forts de Latour (Latour); Pavillon Rouge de Château Margaux (Margaux); Bahans-Haut-Brion (Haut-Brion)*

Second Growths: *Clos du Marquis (Léoville-Las-Cases); Moulin-Riche (Léoville-Poyferré); de Curebourse (Durfort-Vivens); La Gombaude (Lascombes); Sarget de Gruaud-Larose (Gruaud-Larose); de Fontarney and de Notton (Brane-Cantenac); Réserve de la Comtesse (Pichon-Longueville-Lalande); de Marbuzet (Cos d'Estournel); Demereaulemont (Montrose); La Croix (Beaucaillou)*

Third Growths: *Les Fiefs-de-Lagrange (Lagrange); Baudry (Desmirail)*

Fourth Growths: *Connétable Talbot (Talbot); Moulin de Duhart (Duhart-Milon-Rothschild); Sire de Camin (La Tour-Carnet); de Clairfont and Haut-Prieuré (Prieuré-Lichine)*

Fifth Growths: *Les Hauts de Pontet (Pontet-Canet); Lacoste-Borie (Grand-Puy-Lacoste); Artigues-Arnaud (Grand-Puy-Ducasse); La Tour d'Aspic (Haut-Batailley); Haut-Bages-Averous (Lynch-Bages); Grand-Duroc-Milon and Bellerose (Pédésclaux)*

LANGUEDOC-ROUSSILLON

The great arc of the Languedoc-Roussillon runs from the Rhône River in the east, around the Mediterranean, and down to the Spanish border in the west. It's really two areas—the Languedoc and Roussillon—and although they tend to get lumped together, they have distinctive characteristics. The Languedoc is very definitely French, while Roussillon has close ties with the Catalan culture just over the border in Spain. Where the Languedoc is mainly hilly, Roussillon is dominated by the Pyrénées. Not only is this one of the oldest viticultural areas of France (the Greeks started making wine around what is now Marseilles in the seventh century B.C. and the Romans extended it throughout the region) but it is also the largest. Within its boundaries lie one-third of all the vines in France (although it represents only 10 percent of the country's appellation-designated wines), and it traditionally was the supplier of that great sea of *gros rouge*—the everyday drink of French workers. But as consumption of cheap wine has dropped in France (from 177 liters per head in 1960 to 69 liters in 1993), the wine lake began to evaporate and the region adapted brilliantly to the increased demand for better-quality wine. Of all the "hot spots" of France, this is my contender for supersizzler.

The principal appellations in the region—Costières de Nîmes, Coteaux du Languedoc, Corbières, Minervois, Côtes du Roussillon, Côtes du Roussillon-Villages, Faugères, Saint-Chinian, and Fitou—are backed up by a terrific array of *vins de pays*. In fact the region produces 80 percent of France's *vins de pays*. The Vin de Pays d'Oc (*oc* means "yes" in the old language of the Languedoc) was created in 1987 in response to the needs of the international market (exports from the region run at about 70 percent, a far higher proportion than any other area in France). Not only do the *vin de pays* regulations (covering yields, alcohol and acidity levels, grape varieties, etc.) stimulate winemakers to improve the quality of their traditional blends but they also allow growers to use "international" grapes—"fighting varietals" or *vins de cépage,* such as Cabernet Sauvignon, Sauvignon Blanc, Merlot, and Chardonnay—that would not be allowed under appellation rules but are much in demand in export markets such as the United States. Although the appellation controls are tight, there's always a bit of leeway for producers to shift the emphasis from one grape to another. More and more quality-conscious growers are replanting the good-but-not-great Carignan with more elegant Syrah and Mourvèdre.

Red wines are what the region is known for and they, like the people, are warm and outgoing. Also keep an eye out for dessert wines—*vins doux naturels*—such

Frugal-minded Europeans have been gobbling up recent vintages from the Languedoc-Roussillon corridor. Enormous qualitative progress has been made, and the best wines from such once obscure viticultural regions as Corbières, Minervois, Faugères, Saint Chinian, Coteaux du Languedoc, Côtes de Roussillon, and the Vins de Pays d'Oc represent a treasure trove of bargain-priced wines for true consumers who drink wine, not prestigious labels.

—ROBERT M. PARKER, JR., publisher, *Wine Advocate*

as Muscat de Frontignan from the Languedoc, Banyuls, Maury, and Rivesaltes from the Roussillon; they can be superb. Whether it be aromatic and well-balanced refreshing whites, spicy rosés, or lusty, full-bodied reds, Languedoc-Roussillon scores high on flavor per dollar.

• H O T   S H O T S •

For Vin de Pays d'Oc: Domaine d'Aupilhac; L'Enclos d'Ormesson; Domaine de Capion; Mas de Daumas Gassac; Domaine Provenquière Chardonnay. *For Corbières:* Domaine Fontsainte; Château de Cabriac Étang des Colombes; Château Saint-Auriol. *For Coteaux du Languedoc:* Château Lascaux; Domaine L'Aiguilière; Mas Julien; Domaine Peyre Rose; Château Pech-Redon; Domaine de l'Ortus; Pic Saint-Loup. *For Faugères:* Gilbert Alquier. *For Saint-Chinian:* Château Maurel Fonselade. *For Minervois:* Château d'Oupia; Saint-Eulalie; La Tour Boisé; Château de Gourgazaud.

TOURAINE

The Touraine region is smack in the middle of the Loire Valley, running along both banks of that glorious river from Bourgueil in the east to Blois in the west. The gentle landscape of mixed agriculture and vineyards is dotted with the greatest châteaux in France—Amboise, Azay-le-Rideau, and Chenonceaux among them—to remind us that this was once the playground of French royalty and aristocracy. Today it is more the playground of Parisian weekenders and tourists, but it is also the home of some of the best reds and whites in the Loire—and anywhere in France, for that matter.

The best-known appellations of the region are Vouvray and Montlouis for whites made from Chenin Blanc (known locally as Pineau de la Loire), and Chinon, Bourgueil, and Saint-Nicolas-de-Bourgueil for reds made principally from Cabernet Franc (known locally as Breton).

Chenin Blanc has a rather unglamorous image in the United States, where for the most part it is used to make flabby semi-sweet or sweet jug wine. This notion couldn't be farther from the truth when it comes to the Chenins Blancs of the Loire. Here it has the aroma of quince, pear, apple, citrus, flowers, and honey, with a waxy richness on the palate that inspired Rabelais to compare it to taffeta. Quite high in acid, Chenins are balanced by their rich, round texture, and it is this balance that makes the wines so enticing and gives them a kind of energy that wine writers like to call "nervous." These wines go beautifully with lobster, scallops, poultry, and mild cheeses.

Located on the southern bank of the Loire, Montlouis doesn't have a bridge to the other side. When it was given its own appellation in 1935 (until then its wine had been known as Vouvray), the lack of a bridge made it difficult for buyers who had to make a determined detour, and Montlouis remained a backwater while its neighbor, Vouvray, took the limelight. A bridge is due to be completed in 1996.

Vouvray, on the north bank, makes Chenin in a variety of styles from the dry *(sec),* to the semisweet *(demi-sec),* sweet *(moelleux),* and sparkling *(crémant).* A good dry Vouvray has the rich, creamy texture of a Chardonnay with the fresh appley bite of the Chenin. And for a relatively light white wine its ability to age is incredible, matched only by German whites.

· H O T   S H O T S ·

For Montlouis: Domaine Chidaine. *For Vouvray:* Philippe
Foreau; Gaston Huet; Domaine des Aubuissières. *For Chinon:*
Charles Joguet; Domaine Jean Baudry; Olga Raffault.
For Saint-Nicolas-de-Bourgueil: Joel Taluau.
For Bourgueil: Pierre-Jacques Druet.

🍷

Chinon. This wine, named after the village about twenty kilometers east of Tours, was made famous by the early sixteenth-century writer Rabelais, who was from the region. Cabernet Franc takes on a terrific personality in these light- to medium-bodied wines, providing a fruity easy drinking profile along with a more serious structured style. The best ones have an aroma of roses, raspberries, and lead pencil (a positive term in tasting notes) with a great balance of fruit and acidity.

Bourgueil and Saint-Nicolas-de-Bourgueil. These wines are made on the north bank of the Loire and are essentially very similar to the wines of Chinon, yet are generally considered a bit more tannic and fuller bodied.

ALSACE

Maybe there's no smoke without fire, but Alsace seems to prove you can certainly have fire without smoke. This place is hot, but nobody seems to notice (not that Alsace lovers mind; they like to keep it that way so that prices won't go through the ceiling, like those of Chardonnay). Alsace wines may not be the cheapest in the world, but they deliver as much flavor per dollar as any. Do I like these wines? No, I love them! And I think they are more food-friendly than the wines of any region or country I know.

The best wines comes from the so-called noble grapes: Riesling, Gewürztraminer, Pinot Gris, and Muscat. Others are made from Sylvaner, Pinot

> For white wines, Alsace is a particularly good source, especially the dry ones. They're also very flexible with food. Another exciting area in France for whites are what I call new-wave white Bordeaux fermented with a bit of oak, coming from the Première Côtes de Bordeaux and Entre-Deux-Mers. For reds, American Zinfandel gives more bang for the buck than Cabernet Sauvignon.
>
> —CLIVE COATES, Master of Wine

Blanc, Pinot Noir (the only red or, more accurately a kind of darkish rosé), Chasselas, and Pinot Auxerrois. Styles range from light to full-bodied, from bone dry to intensely honeyed and sweet.

Much of the history of Alsace has been entwined with that of Germany. Right on the border, Alsace has been part of Germany at least twice; the regional dialect is Germanic; the bottle shape is German; the cuisine is Germanic; so it's no wonder that most people who are unfamiliar with the wines think that they too are German. The truth is, they are very different. For the most part Alsace wines are much drier than German ones, with alcohol levels of 11 to 13 percent. German wines tend to be much lighter—7 to 10 percent—but with more residual sugar. I find German wines great as an aperitif or, in sweeter style, with dessert, but Alsace wines strike a balance between richness and dryness, which makes them much more compatible with food.

> I'm a white-wine bargain hunter, and my favorite place to look is in off-vintage Alsace wines. The level of winemaking is so high there that hardly anyone puts out bad wines, and I actually prefer the less expensive "off-vintage" wines to the more-heralded "great vintages." While I love the fruit in the heralded wines, I'm continually finding residual sugar in these wines, something I don't want, expect, or enjoy in Alsace wines. The "off-vintage" wines are crisp and have plenty of flavor.
>
> —ALAN RICHMAN,
> food and wine critic,
> *GQ* magazine

It seems to me that the only obstacle to Alsace taking the market by storm is the public's unfamiliarity with the grape varieties used there. The wines are well priced; have clean, pure flavors (a minuscule percentage is fermented or aged in oak); and the labels are easy to read (which certainly cannot be said for German wines). In fact, Alsace has been using varietal labeling much longer than California.

Alsace was awarded its appellation in 1962. The appellation

> **F**or good value, I look to Alsace, particularly for Pinot Blanc, which I personally find to be the Chardonnay alternative, if Americans could just wake themselves up to the fact. Pinot Blancs from quality producers can be quite extracted and, with their silky, oily texture, even give the illusion of being kissed by oak.
>
> —MADELAINE TRIFFON, master sommelier

covers the whole region and not individual varietals as many people think, although the varietal—Gewürztraminer, Pinot Gris, Riesling, etc.—is added on the label. Crémant d'Alsace (a semisparkling wine) got its AOC in 1976, and a *grand cru* appellation was created in 1983 with more stringent conditions than those covering the main Alsace appellation. A *grand cru* (of which there are just over fifty) must be a wine from a single named vineyard, a single vintage of one of the four "noble" grapes, and with lower yields than the general appellation. If there's any criticism (and there's plenty!) it's that there are too many *grands crus* and not all of them make fine-enough wine.

Pinot Blanc and Riesling acreage has increased dramatically as growers realize that they can really challenge Chardonnay with their intensity, complexity, and downright drinkability.

• HOT SHOTS •

Zind-Humbrecht; Schoffit; Hugel et Fils; Kuentz-Bas; Domaine Weinbach; F. E. Trimbach; Marcel Deiss; André Ostertag; Marc Kreydenweiss; Dirler; Albert Boxler; Roland Schmitt; André Kientzler; Schleret; Albert Mann; Jos Meyer; Ernest Burn; Léon Béyer.

AUSTRIA

The Austrian wine scandal of 1985 (in which diethylene glycol—one of the components of antifreeze—was added to wine, causing the deaths of several people and leading to the prosecution of some of Austria's leading *négociants*) triggered an intensive soul-searching in the Austrian wine industry. The lessons of the past were learned and a new path was taken for the future. There's a new vigor and determination in the Austrian wine business these days, and as a result it is producing some of the best wines available from cool regions.

Riesling produces the most exciting wines, but in terms of land planted to it, it follows Grüner Veltliner, Müller-Thurgau, Welschriesling, and even the red wine variety, Zweigelt. The style of Austrian Riesling is a cross between those of Alsace and Germany. Austrian wines are generally drier than German but have the higher alcohol level, richness, and body that's characteristic of Alsace wine. Look to the Wachau region in the north-eastern part of the country for dry Riesling (locally the lightest—no more than 10.7 percent alcohol—is called *Stein-*

feder; the middle-bodied—up to 11.9 percent alcohol—*Feder-spiel;* the richest and most concentrated—at least 12 percent alcohol—*Smaragd*). While the Wachau, on the banks of the Danube, has the upper hand for Riesling and Müller-Thurgau, another important wine region is Neusiedlersee, in the Burgen-land district bordering Hungary. This region delivers rich Weiss-burgunders, Traminers, and Welschrieslings at all levels of sweetness. The most noteworthy characteristic of this area is its ability to produce sweet wines equal in quality and sometimes superior to those produced anywhere else in the world. The lake (Neusiedlersee) provides the perfect microclimate to enable the noble rot, *Botrytis cinera,* to develop. As in Burgundy, most of the top wines are available only in tiny quantities. This can be frustrating, but in the world of wine the hunt for the treasure is half the fun. And when you find the best of the Austrian whites you will be rewarded with some of the most exciting white wines available anywhere.

• H O T   S H O T S •

From the Wachau: F. X. Pichler; Franz Prager; Emmerich Knoll; Franz Hirtzberger; Nikolaihof; Nigl. *From Neusiedlersee:* Kracher. *Other regions:* Tement; Ing. Weininger; Bründlmayer.

AUSTRIAN WINE LAWS

As part of Austria's effort to rectify its image after the 1985 scandal, it has drawn up laws that are some of the strictest in the world.

The terms are the same as those used in Germany, but the standards are higher. Must weights (measured by Oechsle degrees) that qualify wines for specially designated categories are higher as well. All wines that are vintage-dated and carry the name of a grape variety must be composed of at least 85 percent of that vintage and grape. All Austrian wines have a red-and-white band that is a sort of registration system.

Starting with the top-quality wines:

Prädikatswein
All wines belonging to this category must come from a single district and from an authorized grape variety, have their must weights officially verified, be vintage-dated, and not be chaptalized or have Süssreserve added. Wines in this category are:

Spätlese: *Minimum must weight of 94 Oechsle.*
Auslese: *Minimum must weight of 105 Oechsle.*
Strohwein: *Wine made from overripe grapes and dried on straw mats. Minimum must weight of 127 Oechsle.*
Eiswein: *Wine made from grapes picked and pressed while still frozen. Minimum must weight of 127 Oechsle.*
Beerenauslese: *Overripe grapes affected by noble rot, with a minimum must weight of 127 Oechsle.*
Ausbruch: *A sweet wine from the town of Rust on the shores of Neusiedlersee in Burgenland. The grapes must be affected by noble rot and have a minimum must weight of 138 Oechsle.*
Trockenbeerenauslese: *A very sweet wine made from shriveled overripe grapes affected by noble rot, with a minimum must weight of 168 Oechsle.*

As noted earlier, the Wachau region has its own categories for describing the richness levels of its wines.

KABINETT: *These wines are part of the Qualitätswein category and follow the same guidelines except that they must have a minimum must weight of 84 Oechsle and residual sugar may not exceed 9 grams.*

QUALITÄTSWEIN: *This is its own category but includes the subcategory Kabinett. All wines in this category must come from a* single district specified on the label and from an authorized grape variety that displays its varietal characteristics. The must weight must reach 73 Oechsle and chaptalization is not permitted.

LANDWEIN: Made from specific grape varieties with a minimum must weight of 68 Oechsle. Alcoholic strength may not exceed 11.5 percent and residual sugar may not exceed 6 grams per liter.

TAFELWEIN: The greatest volume of wine falls into this category; it must have a minimum must weight of 63 Oechsle.

GERMANY

I practically have to beg people to try German Riesling. I remember an evening in the restaurant when a customer asked me which wines we had by the glass. When I told her that we had a Chardonnay and a German Riesling she unhesitatingly chose the Chardonnay. It's true that the Chardonnay we were offering was wonderful, but I wanted to see how she would react to a comparative tasting of both, so I brought a glass of each. She switched to the Riesling.

> The most interesting and totally under appreciated region of the world is the (Mosel) Saar-Ruwer region of Germany. Whoever wants to understand great white wine has to understand Riesling from here.
>
> —HOWARD GOLDBERG, *The New York Times*

The essence of good German wine is the balance between acid and sugar. It's something like the tension in a violin string: If it's too tight it will snap, if too loose it will play off key. Most people think of German wines as too sweet, and it's true that they do have some residual sugar. But this sugar is essential to balance the naturally high acid levels that develop in grapes that do not get a lot of sunshine (even with a lot of sun, Riesling is still high in acidity). It is neither too sweet nor too tart and low in alcohol (8 to 10 percent). And it is this sweet/sour contrast that makes Riesling so mouthwateringly good. Like green apples and firm apricots.

> For white wines, the Rieslings from Germany are the most undervalued wines in the world. You can buy the best wines from the top estates for the same price as average California Chardonnay.
>
> For reds, the best value is coming from the Languedoc region of France.
>
> —LARRY STONE, master sommelier, Rubicon restaurant, San Francisco

In my opinion Riesling is the only grape worth talking about in Germany. Rieslings make great aperitifs because they are so refreshing. Sometimes they have a difficult time standing up to food, although the semidry *(halbtrocken)* will be a better mealtime bet than the dry *(trocken)*.

Two areas that offer particularly good value are the Mosel (all elegance, flowers, apples, and pears) and the Pfalz (powerful, full-bodied, ripe summer fruit such as peaches and apricots). Which is not to say there aren't great values in other regions, but there just seem to be a very large number of good producers in the Mosel and Pfalz, which increases your odds of getting a good bottle. It's a cardinal rule anywhere, in fact, that the quality of the winemaker is more important than the status of the area or the reputation of the vintage.

The Germans are well aware of the problems of selling their wine in the United States and seem to be more willing to attack the thorny problem of the label. All that Gothic clutter is gradually giving way to a much clearer presentation. One importer in particular, Rudi Weist, has simplified the labels of many of the wineries he is working with, and shifted a lot of the verbiage that used to decorate the front label to the back label. Now you get a clear statement of the varietal and the vintage on the front. Dienhard is another house that favors a clear varietal front label. If any of this increases the number of people who will experiment with German wine, I raise my hat to them.

• H O T   S H O T S •

For the Mosel: Fritz Haag; K&H Lingenfelder; Egon Müller; J. J. Prum; Dr. Loosen; Selbach-Oster; G. Zilliken; Willi Schaefer; Schloss Lieser; Von Schubert; Milz. *For the Pfalz:* Lingenfelder; Müller-Catoir; Neckerauer; Bürklin-Wolf; Pfeffingen. *For the Rheingau:* Knyphausen; F. Kunstler; R. Weil. *Other:* Toni Jost (Mittelrhein); Dönnhof (Nahe); Gunderloch (Rheinhessen).

🍷

QMP, QBA, QED? GERMAN WINE LAWS

There's no doubt that German wine has been through a very rocky period in the last twenty years.

Under the rather eccentric German wine laws of 1971, almost all vineyards are created equal. Of course some sites are known to produce better wines than others but, unlike as in France, German legislation does not recognize them. The only criterion is ripeness. The more natural (as against added) sugar a grape contains, the higher the quality designation. Starting at the top of the pyramid:

Qualitätswein mit Prädikat (QmP). A difficult term to translate elegantly, it means that the quality of the wine assumes (literally, is "predicated by") a high level of natural as against added (in the form of sweetened wine called *süssreserve*) sugar as an indicator of ripeness and eventual alcoholic strength. The degree of ripeness is indicated on the label:

Kabinett: The earliest picked and lightest and driest of all QmPs. About 9.1 percent alcohol.

Spätlese: The second step on the QmP quality ladder, these wines are from "late-picked" grapes that give a fuller flavor balanced with good acidity. They are not necessarily sweet because the sugar can be fermented out into alcohol. About 10 percent alcohol.

Auslese: Made from grapes picked later than *spätlese,* these wines have more concentration. Again, although the grapes will have a higher sugar content because they have been allowed to ripen longer, they need not necessarily produce a sweet wine. They too may be fermented dry. Alcohol about 11.5 percent.

Beerenauslese: Wine from individually selected late-picked grapes. At around 16 percent alcohol, it will be sweet and concentrated in flavor.

Trockenbeerenauslese: The top of the pile! The grapes have been shriveled by *Botrytis cinerea* mold to produce *Edelfäule,* or

IS DRY BETTER?

"I want the driest wine you can give me." "I only like dry wine." It seems to be the current fashion. Even though everyone believes he or she only likes dry wine, the truth is most people love a little sweetness. Whenever I recommend a German wine to someone, their reaction is, "But I don't like sweet wine." It's true that most German wine has a little sweetness. But whenever I give someone a taste without telling them what it is, they tend to love it.

There is a definite place for sweet wines, either with or without food. Moreover, a wine's sweetness alone is not an indication of quality. Château d'Yquem, the great Sauternes, is an intensely sweet wine. Yet it happens to be one of the greatest and most expensive wines in the world. A mildly sweet wine with balancing acidity is great as an aperitif or as an accompaniment to slightly spicy foods. A medium-sweet wine goes well with fruit or fruit pastries for dessert. And an intensely sweet wine like Sauternes or Port is an excellent match with blue-veined cheeses or very sweet desserts, or on its own as dessert.

"noble rot." The potential alcohol level can be as much as 21.5 percent, although only 5.5 percent need be actual alcohol. The rest is residual sugar that produces an intense and complex wine with rich honey, raisin, and caramel flavors.

Eiswein: A kind of "super-*Beerenauslese*." The grapes are so late-picked (sometimes in January) that they have become frozen, thus separating the water from the concentrated sugars, acids, and flavors. It is more acidic than *Beerenauslese* and therefore has a tremendous potential for aging. Rare and expensive.

Qualitätswein bestimmter Anbaugebiete (QbA). "Quality wine from a designated area." The designated areas, however, are so large that they encompass practically all of Germany's vineyards. The qualification for QbA is ripeness (about 7 percent alcohol) but here, unlike the QmPs, sugar is added. About 80 percent of all German wine (including Liebfraumilch) is legally sold as QbA. In France, by comparison, less than 30 percent of a year's production can be sold as *appellation contrôlée* wine. The problem is that the German wine laws do not legislate grape varieties, only levels of ripeness. So, you can have inferior grapes such as Sylvaner or Müller-Thurgau in bad sites producing high yields, but ripening sufficiently to achieve QbA status.

Landwein. A relatively new category roughly equivalent to *vins de pays*. It denotes wine from one of fifteen approved areas. They will have been sweetened with added sugar but will be dry *(trocken)* or medium-dry *(halbtrocken)*. More style and regional flavor than the lowest category, *Tafelwein*.

Tafelwein. Low alcohol levels (5 percent) and few regulations. *Deutscher Tafelwein* has to be German in origin, whereas plain *Tafelwein* is made from a mix of European wines (although the labels are usually dripping with Gothic lettering to suggest German origin).

Amtliche Prüfungsnummer (AP number). Every wine of QmP and QbA quality has to be chemically tested and blind-tasted. The AP number thus awarded must be displayed on the label. It is worth bearing in mind, though, that 95 percent of all wines submitted are awarded an AP number and, as some past scandals have revealed, laws cannot absolutely guarantee quality.

GERMAN WINE-SPEAK

ABFÜLLUNG (OR ABZUG). Bottling.

AMTLICHE PRÜFUNG. The official number on the label which indicates the wine has passed statutory quality tests.

ANBAUGEBIET. A wine region, for example, Rheingau or Nahe.

AUSLESE. The third step up the QmP quality ladder (see page 104) describing wines with high natural sugar content when picked. They are usually intensely flavored and rich.

BEERENAUSLESE. Fourth step up the QmP quality ladder (see page 104). Wine made from individually picked overripe grapes (usually affected by Edelfäule, or "noble rot") with up to sixteen degrees of potential alcohol. These wines are rich and very sweet but have good enough acid to make for great aging.

BEREICH. A group of villages that make up a wine-producing district within an Anbaugebiet, or region.

BUNDESWEINPRÄMIERUNG. Official national wine award. Winners often display their awards on their wine labels.

DEUTSCHER. If seen on Tafelwein labels (as in Deutscher Tafelwein), it indicates that the grapes are from German vineyards and not some anonymous imported mix. The lowest grade of German wine.

DEUTSCHES WEINSIEGEL. A red neck label available to producers who have exceeded the minimum standards for wines of the region.

DOMÄNE. Estate.

EDELFÄULE. Noble rot (Botrytis cinerea).

EINZELLAGE. An individual vineyard, the smallest geographical wine-producing unit recognized in Germany by the EEC.

EISWEIN. Literally, "ice wine," from overripe grapes of B.A. level picked in the depth of winter when their water content is frozen and can be separated from the residual juice. A rare, expensive, superb wine with almost limitless aging potential.

ERZEUGERABFÜLLUNG. Bottled at the estate (equivalent to French mis au château).

ERZEUGERGEMEINSCHAFT. An association of producers created to promote and market its wine.

FLASCHE. Bottle.

GEMEINDE. Village, or commune.

GROSSLAGE. A group of adjoining Einzellagen *producing wines of similar style and character.*

HALBTROCKEN. Medium-dry.

HERB. Equivalent of brut.

JAHRGANG. The wine of a particular year or vintage.

KABINETT. First step on the QmP quality ladder (see page 103). No sugar has been added to these wines, and good examples should be light, dry, and delicate.

KELLEREI. Winery (particularly associated with a merchant's cellar rather than with a grower (Weingut).

LANDWEIN. A notch above Tafelwein *and roughly equivalent to French* vin de pays. *Can be dry* (trocken) *or medium-dry* (halbtrocken).

LIEBLICH. A medium-sweet wine equivalent to French moelleux.

OECHSLE. A system of measuring the specific gravity of grape juice to determine its alcoholic potential.

PERLWEIN. *Semisparkling wine.*

QUALITÄTSWEIN BESTIMMTER ANBAUGEBIETE (QBA). *The quality level below QmP (but above* Tafelwein *and* Landwein*) for
wines that meet certain official standards (such as area of origin)
but to which sugar has been added to bring up the alcohol level.*

QUALITÄTSWEIN MIT PRÄDIKAT (QMP). *The top quality division
of wines from grapes ripe enough not to need the helping hand of
added sugar. QmP wines are further subdivided into quality rat-
ings starting with* Kabinett, *then* Spätlese, *then* Auslese, Beerenauslese, *and, finally,* Trockenbeerenauslese.

ROTLING. *Rosé.*

SCHAUMWEIN. *Sparkling wine.*

SEKT. *Sparkling wine made by the* cuvé close *(see page 68)
method. Unless the label says "Deutscher," it can be made from
grapes grown outside Germany. Sometimes described as "quality" sparkling wine, most of it is, in fact, quite horrible.*

SPÄTLESE. *Second stage on the QmP quality ladder (above* Kabinett *but below* Auslese*). Literally means "late-picked." The wines
can be sweet or dry but should have a good acid/fruit balance that
will give them much more aging potential than* Kabinetts.

SPRITZ/SPRITZIG. *Lightly sparkling.*

SÜSS. *Sweet.*

SÜSSRESERVE. *Unfermented grape juice used to sweeten basic
wines.*

TAFELWEIN. *The lowest quality category, which, unless it states
"Deutscher" on the label, may be made from grapes from different EEC countries.*

TROCKEN. *Dry.*

TROCKENBEERENAUSLESE. *Fifth and highest subdivision among
the topflight QmP wines. The wine is made from individually
selected overripe grapes affected by botrytis rot. Because they are
so high in sugar, not all of it ferments out to alcohol (in fact they
are rarely more than 5 percent alcohol), so the wines are sweet,*

with intense honey/raisin/caramel accents. The residual sugar acts as a natural preservative, giving Trockenbeerenauslesen *great aging potential.*

WEINGUT. Wine estate. May be used only on labels where all the grapes were grown on that estate.

WEISSHERBST. A rosé of at least QbA quality produced from a single variety of red grape, the specialty of Baden-Württemberg.

WEISSWEIN. White wine.

WINZERGENOSSENSCHAFT. A growers' cooperative.

SPAIN

The history of Spanish winemaking goes back about two thousand years, but it wasn't until some thirty years ago that Spain emerged from its dark cloud of isolation. Today it is one of the hottest hot spots in the wine firmament.

The first step in improvement in fact goes way back to the end of the eighteenth century, when Bordelais winemakers whose vineyards had been devastated by phylloxera crossed the Pyrénées to their nearest Spanish neighbors in the Rioja, which had until then been unaffected by the dreaded louse. The French brought with them their tremendous experience, technology, and probably the single most important contribution: the *barricas,* the 225-liter oak barrels that would transform the taste of Rioja wine. By 1910 vineyards throughout Spain had followed France's lead and regrafted native varieties onto American rootstock.

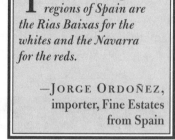

The end of Franco's reign and Spain's entry into the European Economic Community (EEC) in 1986 saw the end of isolationism and the beginning of great improvements in vineyards and wineries. Better grape varieties, lower yields, the replacement of the old clay fermentation pots, *tinajas,* with stainless-steel tanks that can be easily cleaned and temperature-controlled (particularly important in a country where many of the vine-growing regions are very hot indeed) are just some examples of countrywide improvement. And so from a sea of dark, highly alcoholic red wines and flabby oxidized whites, islands of excellence began to emerge.

Although Spain boasts more than six hundred grape varieties, only about twenty cover nearly 80 percent of vineyard land, and too many of the twenty make boring wine (for example, the Aíren is the most widely planted white grape variety in the world, but the wine produced from it is usually pretty dull stuff). But things are changing fast, and for the better. In Navarra, for example, the widely planted Garnacha (Grenache in the Rhône) was banned from new planting and replaced with the much classier Tempranillo (the main grape in Rioja reds), Cabernet Sauvignon, and Graciano. As a result Navarra now produces some of the most exciting wines in Spain. International "superstars" of the grape world such as Cabernet Sauvignon, Chardonnay, and Merlot are being used to replace prolific but dull native varieties. Miguel Torres in the Penedès region of Catalonia, for example, is one of the most astute marketers and winemakers in Spain and is credited with bringing Cabernet Sauvignon to the region after completing his studies in Bordeaux.

Look to the following regions for terrific values:

Rioja. This has long been a good source for aged, supple, earthy, and complex reds. The tradition of aging in oak casks and bottle until the wine is fully matured makes for tremendous value when compared to the price asked for mature Bordeaux or Burgundies, for example. Also look to the *crianzas* for fresher-tasting, fruitier, and less expensive wines.

• H O T   S H O T S •

Marqués de Cáceres; CVNE (Compañia Vinicola del Norte de España); Martinez Bujanda; Bodegas Montecillo; Bodegas Muga; Marqués de Murrieta; Granja Nuestra Señora de Remelluri; La Rioja Alta; Bodegas Sierra Cantabria; Breton y Cia (Loriñon); Marqués de Riscal; Contino; Bodegas Campo Viejo.

❧

Navarra. Next to Rioja and famous for its rosé (it's been called the best source for rosé anywhere in the world). The relatively small market for rosé has forced the wine industry of Navarra to innovate with red wine. The result has been spectacularly successful, especially with the Garnacha (France's Grenache) but also with "international" varieties such as Cabernet Sauvignon, Chardonnay, and Merlot. A lot of success can be attributed to Bodegas Juliàn Chivite, which has not only succeeded in marketing its own wines very effectively but has also been an ambassador for the whole region.

• H O T   S H O T S •

Juliàn Chivite; Magaña; Guelbenzu; Vega Sindoa; Palacio de Nuruzabel; Las Campañas; Alma

❧

Ribera del Duero. Located to the south and west of Rioja, the region is producing some of the most concentrated and full-bodied wines in Spain. The main grape is the Tempranillo (here called the Tinto del País) of Rioja fame. The climate in the Ribera del Duero is warmer than that of Rioja and this, together with modern technology and earlier bottling, results in a wine with more young, grapey fruit flavors and tannins than Rioja. Although Vega Sicilia is the region's most famous bodega (and probably the most internationally renowned Spanish wine), the driving force has been Alejandro Fernández of Pesquera, whose wine style is now being emulated by many others in the region.

• HOT SHOTS •

Alejandro Fernández (Pesquera); Hermanos Pérez; Pascuas (Viña Pedrosa); Ismael Arroyo (Messoneros de Castilla); Viña Mayor; Vega Sicilia (Alion).

Galicia. A great white wine area and the home of the Rias Baixas DO (for more on DOs see page 114). Some of the most seductive and delicious whites in Spain are being made from the Albariño grape. They are marked by a particularly exotic, floral, spicy character that makes me want to call them the Viognier of Spain. Many white wines are made in Spain, but none comes even close in quality. In fact these coastal whites can compete with the best in the world and also offer stunning values considering their quality.

• HOT SHOTS •

Adega Das Eiras; Terras Gauda Albariño; Morgadio Albariño; Vilariño-Cambados (Martin Codex Albariño); Lagar de Cervera; Granja Fillaboa S.A. (Fillaboa); Bodegas Chaves (Castel de Fornos)

SPANISH WINE-SPEAK

ABOCADO. Medium-sweet.

*AÑO. Year. It was common for labels to say "2 [or 3 or 4] Año" rather than state the year of vintage. This meant the wine had been aged for two, three, or four years before being bottled. This practice is now used more on wines from South America than from Spain, where the year of vintage (*cosecha *and* vendimia*) is given. See also "Crianza."*

BLANCO. White.

BODEGA. Can mean a wine store, a commercial wine cellar, or the maker/blender/shipper of wine; roughly equivalent to French négociant.

CAVA. A sparkling wine made from "traditional methods" (due to an EEC ruling it cannot say it is made by the méthode champenoise, *although it is), which carries its own* denominación de origen. *The* cava *business is massive—much bigger than the production of Champagne—but the wine cannot compete with Champagne because the varieties of grape used in Spain (mainly Xarel-lo, Macabeo, and Parellada) as well as the hotter climate work against the intense and light-footed elegance of true Champagne. This is not to say that* cava *is not a decent drink as long as it is not taken too seriously. And it certainly beats the bubbles out of Champagne in terms of price.*

CLARETE. Light red wine (a term now discouraged by the EEC).

COSECHA. Harvest, or vintage.

CRIANZA. Barrel-matured before bottling. For red, it cannot be sold before its third year with a minimum twelve months in oak casks.

DENOMINACIÓN DE ORIGEN (DO). Equivalent to France's appellation contrôlée.

DENOMINACIÓN DE ORIGEN CALIFICADA. A higher level than a DO. So far only Rioja qualifies.

DULCE. Sweet.

ESPUMOSA. Sparkling.

GARANTÍA DE ORIGEN. Simple wines guaranteed to be from the grapes of a defined area, but with little or no oak aging.

GRAN RESERVA. The top quality designation. Reds must have spent a minimum of two years in oak and three years in bottle before release. Whites must have been aged for four years, of which at least six months must have been spent in cask.

JOVEN. Young wine.

RESERVA. Reds must be matured for a minimum of three years, of which at least one must be spent in cask. Whites and rosadas *have to be aged for a minimum of two years with at least six months in cask.*

ROSADO. Rosé.

SECO. Dry.

SIN CRIANZA. No cask aging.

TINTO. Red.

VENDIMIA. Harvest, vintage.

VIEJO. Aged.

VIÑA/VIÑEDO. Vineyard.

VINO DE AGUJA. Slightly sparkling wine.

VINO DE MESA. Table wine.

VINO DE PASTA. Light red for inexpensive drinking.

VINO DE LA TERRA. Equivalent to French vin de pays, *a country wine with some regional character.*

SHERRY

Sherry is terrific and wildly underappreciated in this country. It runs the gamut from the very dry right up to the sweet, and all of them have an exotic, slightly musky sexiness that I think makes them one of the most exciting wines around.

Sherry comes from three towns that form what is known as the Sherry Triangle: Jerez de la Frontera, Puerto de Santa Maria, and Sanlucar de Barrameda. The main grape is the Palomino Fino, which accounts for about 95 percent of all the vineyards; next in volume—about 3 percent—comes the Moscatel, followed by the Pedro Ximénez, both of which are used to produce sweeter styles of sherry.

Sherry starts its vinicultural life in much the same way as any dry white wine. After fermentation, though, it goes into cask and is fortified with wine alcohol to bring it up to 15 to 20 percent, depending the style of sherry being made. Now something quite unique happens. The yeasts in the wine bloom to create a cap— the "flower," hence *"flor"*—that covers the surface of the wine. The *flor* protects the wine from oxidizing and imparts its own wonderfully yeasty aroma. The wine is now blended in the *solera* system, made up of a series of casks. The bottom rank of casks is called the *solera* and this is where the oldest wine is kept and periodically drawn off for shipping. Whenever the *solera* is drawn off (no more than a third at any time) it is topped up by younger wine from the casks above, called *criaderas* (nurseries). When the cask holding the youngest wine is drawn off, it is replenished with the wine of the vintage, or *añada*.

• H O T   S H O T S •

For Fino: González Byass "Tio Pepe"; Pedro Domecq "La Ina"; A. R. Valdespino "Inocente"; Emilio Lustau "Jarana." *For Manzanilla:* Vinicola Hidalgo "La Gitana." *For Amontillado:* Emilio Lustau "Los Arcos"; González Byass "Amontillado del Duque." *For dry Olorosos:* Vinicola Hidalgo. *For sweet Olorosos:* Osborne & Cia "Oloroso Abocado; Vinicola Hidalgo "Cream." *For other sweet Sherries:* Emilio Lustau "East India Solera Reserva" and "Pedro Ximénez Reserva San Emilio"; González Byass "Pedro Ximénez Noe."

SHERRY STYLES
(FROM DRY TO SWEET)

FINO: Made in Jerez, usually from 100 percent Palomino grapes. Very pale, delicate, with a yeasty accent. Alcoholic strength: 15 to 18 percent. Drink young and well chilled.

MANZANILLA. From Sanlucar de Barrameda. Lighter, saltier, with slightly bitterer tang than fino. Drink chilled.

AMONTILLADO. A fino that has been aged for more than eight years until it has become darker and developed a dry, nutty flavor. Fuller bodied (16 to 18 percent alcohol). Drink chilled.

OLOROSO. The darkest, richest, and fullest bodied of the natural sherries (as compared to the "concocted" styles, such as cream). The word means fragrant, and although the wine is dry it has a nutty/caramel/raisin softness that is the result of controlled oxidation and fortification (18 percent alcohol). Drink cool.

CREAM. Nothing whatsoever to do with cream. This style was manufactured to suit a British and North American market with a sweet tooth. Pale creams (created by Croft in the 1970s) are usually made of poor-quality finos that have been sweetened. Dark creams are made from sweetened Oloroso. Higher-quality creams are made from blending Oloroso with Pedro Ximénez or Moscatel. Pedro Ximénez is sometimes bottled by itself, making an ultra-rich, sweet drink that might be best served with ice cream.

PORTUGAL

Lancers and Port. Aren't these what most of us think of when we think of Portuguese wines? In fact, both were created for export (only 6 percent of Portuguese wine production is Port, and it's not a particularly popular drink in its homeland) and are not really representative of the terrific potential of the country. For one thing, Portugal has more grape varieties than Spain. It's the world's seventh largest wine producer and the third largest wine consumer. Portugal had established a regulatory system twenty-five years before France did; and in a way that has been a problem. Until their relatively recent membership in the EEC, Portugal was stuck with an outmoded appellation system and a wine industry as backward as any in Europe. Now there are more than thirty newly recognized wine regions or IPRs *(indicação de proveniencia regulamentado)* and a breakaway from the old-fashioned practices of cooperatives, which previously had a stranglehold on winemaking.

> I look for wines from obscure regions from reputable producers.
>
> —ROGER DAGORN, master sommelier

Independent and innovative estates are now popping up all over the country. Also, there's a change of styles. The Portuguese have traditionally valued alcoholic strength, deep color, and heavyweight tannins: red wines that need aging for decades to soften. Now there's much more emphasis on fruit and even flirtations with such "international" grapes as Cabernet Sauvignon. But the great thing is that Portuguese winemakers haven't thrown over their native grapes and fallen neatly into step with Merlot, Cabernet, and Chardonnay. It is to be hoped that their natural conservatism will keep alive the wide range of indigenous grape varieties that give Portuguese wines their unique character.

HOT SHOTS

In Alenquer: Quinta de Pancas; Quinta de Parrotes. *In Alentejo:* José Maria da Fonseca, Succs.; Garrafeira AP; Portalegre; José Sousa; Rosado Fernandes Garrafeira. *In Douro:* Quinta da Cotto; Quinta da Aveleda; Charamba. *In Dão:* Casal de Tonda; Terra Altas. *In Terras do Sado:* Periquita. *In Bairrada:* Caves São Jáo; Frei Jão Bairrada Reserva. *In Ribatéjo:* Quinta da Lagoalva.

PORTUGUESE WINE-SPEAK

ADAMADO. Sweet.

ADEGA. Cellar, winery.

BRANCO. White.

CARVALHO. Oak.

CLARETE. Light red wine.

COLHEITA. Vintage.

DENOMINAÇÃO DE ORIGEM CONTROLADA *(DOC). Official wine region.*

DOCE. *Sweet.*

ENGARRAFADO NA ORIGEM. *Estate-bottled.*

ESPUMANTE. *Sparkling.*

GARRAFEIRA. *Designates a superior wine (a* reserva*) that (if red) has been aged for three years, including one year in bottle; if white, aged for one year, of which six months will have been spent in bottle.* Garrafeira *wines must bear a vintage date and have 0.5 percent more alcohol than the minimum.*

INDICAÇÃO DE PROVENIENCIA REGULAMENTADA. *A group of newly created wine regions that are on probation for DOC status.*

LICOROSO. *Sweet, fortified wines.*

MADURO. *Aged in barrel and bottle.*

QUINTA. *Wine-producing estate.*

REGIÕES DEMARCARDAS. *Equivalent to French* appellations contrôlées.

RESERVA. *Wine from grapes of one or several regions made during an outstanding vintage.*

ROSADO. *Rosé.*

SECO. *Dry.*

TINTO. *Red.*

VELHO. *Old. Reds must be over three years old; whites over two.*

VERDE. *Young, "green" wine as in* vinho verde, *a term now reserved for wines from the northern province of Minho.*

VINHO CONSUMO. Vin ordinaire.

VINHO GENEROSO. *Fortified aperitif/dessert wine.*

VINHO DE MESA. *Table wine.*

VINHOS REGIONÃOS. *Roughly equivalent to French* vin de pays.

ITALY

The ancient Greeks called Italy *Oenotria,* or "land of the vine," and we all know that the Roman legions spread their viticulture throughout the lands they conquered, particularly France and Spain. Today Italy is the world's largest producer of wine, and second to France as the world's greatest consumer (France averages sixty-seven liters per head per year; Italy, sixty; the United States, seven). The quantity has always been impressive, but the quality has been a problem. The confusions of local tradition, the complicated but often ineffective wine laws, chaotic labeling, and what might be called an "integrity factor" leave many of us feeling bewildered and a bit intimidated.

Because wine was such a staple of the Italian diet, much more emphasis, historically, was placed on the quantity of production. The result was a crude, basic wine that lacked both character and depth. Because Italy came late to industrialization, it didn't have a middle class, as in France, Germany, and the United States, that drove the market for quality wine (of course, fine wine has always been available in Italy, but I'm talking about a wine industry generally devoted to the finer points of winemaking). Nor was there a significant export business, as there was for French and, to a lesser extent, German wines. Italy has been a nation only since 1861, and until then (and in fact for decades after), it was feudal. It's amazing to remember that Italy's premier wine, Brunello, didn't exist before the end of the nineteenth century.

After World War II the Italian economy improved, but the emphasis was still on quantity because that was where desperately needed export earnings lay. So, bulk wine high in acidity and tannin was shipped off to France and Germany for blending (a trend accelerated by Italy's membership in the EEC, with its generous agricultural subsidies). Italian politicians also knew that it was advantageous to secure the maximum number of jobs in high-volume wine production, and that's not an incentive to rationalize the industry. The 1980s saw improvements: stainless steel, better temperature control, lower yields, better cloning, pumping-over rather than punching down the must, and so on.

Italian wine laws (see page 125 for more details) have tried to set guidelines, but the problem is that they have more holes than a gopher's backyard. The shenanigans of local, regional, and national politicos and bureaucrats have undermined consumers' faith in the product, and it's going to be interesting to see if the revised wine law of 1992 will be able to establish some integrity.

Depressing? Well, at times it has been, but there are always individual winemakers and winemaking areas that know they can produce something superb. They may have to battle the serpentine coils of red tape or, more likely, just ignore them. But they also represent something that's central to the Italian tradition—a maverick's contempt for the mediocre.

As in all winemaking regions of the world, one must look to top producers for the best value. Italy is no different. And because of this, there are pockets of exciting wine from all regions of Italy. Because of more modern winemaking equipment and techniques, the southern peninsula, and more specifically Apulia, is offering intensely flavored wines at very reasonable prices. This region is not only the leader in overall wine production in Italy but also holds the title of number two in number of DOCs, with twenty-four after Piedmont's thirty-seven. Although these wines may deliver great flavor for your dollar, I look to the noble regions of Tuscany and Piedmont for wines with more finesse and complexity. Those regions are home to the two greatest red grape varieties in Italy, Sangiovese in Tuscany and Nebbiolo in Piedmont. In Tuscany, Chianti may be the most famous of the DOCs but it is also the one that is the most inconsistent. The best wine of the region for your money is Rosso di Montalcino. This DOC (1984) is an outstanding alternative to the more backward and

---

• H O T S H O T S •

In Tuscany—For Rosso di Montalcino: Altesino; Cacci Piccolomini; Costanti; Col D'Orcia; Fattoria dei Barbi; II Poggione; Lisini; Pertimali; Poggio Antico; Tenuta Caparzo; La Torre. *For Chianti:* Badia a Coltibuono; Castello dei Rampolla; Castello di Ama; Castello di Volpaia; Fontodi; II Palazzino; Isole e Olena; Le Corti; Monte Grosso; Monte Vertine; Peppoli; San Giusto Terrabianca; Viticcio; Marchese L. & P. Antinori. *For Carmignano:* Fattoria Ambra; Tenuta di Capezzana. *In Piedmont:* Silvio Grasso; Elio Altare; Bruno Giacosa; Bruno Ceretto; Aldo Conterno; Produttori di Barbaresco; Vietti; Giacom Conterno; Roberto Voerzio; Clerico; Sandrone; Angelo Gaja; Scavino; Rocca; R. Fenocchio; Moccagatta; Carretta; Renato Corino; Brovia. *From other regions:* Vie di Romans, Franco Furlan, Jermann, Livio Feluga (all from Friuli); Anselmi (Soave); Alois Lageder (Alto Adige); Palazzone (Orvieto); Puiatti (Collio); Conti Martini (Trentino); Bisci (Le Marche); Mazzi (Valpolicella, Amarone); Quintarelli (Amarone); Dal Forno (Valpolicella, Amarone); Dr. Cosimo Taurino (Salice Salentino); Mastroberardino (Taurasi); Barone Cornacchia (Abruzzi); Lungarotti (Umbria).

〰

expensive Brunello di Montalcino. The wine is made from a selection of grapes and/or vats destined to make Brunello and is sold after only one year as opposed to three and a half for the "Grand Vin." It is softer and more enjoyable in its youth, but made by top winemakers it is a wine with depth, concentration, and class.

In Piedmont, I look at what one might call the second wines from top producers of Barolo and Barbaresco. Although these DOCGs are two of the greatest in all of Italy, the wines generally need many years in the bottle before they shed their hard tannins and reveal elegant and complex fruit flavors. I therefore look for Nebbiolos, Dolcettos, and Barberas from the region's Hot Shots.

WHAT'S UP, DOC?: A GUIDE THROUGH THE ITALIAN MAZE

The rules that govern Italian winemaking (the equivalent of the French appellation contrôlée system, see page 64) have an ancient history but all too often they resemble a carabiniere in full-dress uniform bedecked with epaulets and gold spaghetti— impressive to look at but not always as effective as one might wish.

In 1415 Chianti became the first wine region in Italy to be controlled by wine regulations. More than five hundred years later, in 1924, regional regulations—the denominazione di origine controllata (DOC)—began to be laid down to give Italy, it was hoped, a logical categorization of its wines. In 1966 the first DOC was issued (to the Tuscan white wine Vernaccia di San Gimignano). In 1992, law 164 was passed in an attempt to tighten up the regulations.

Starting with the best:

Denominazione di Origine Controllata e Garantita (DOCG)

In 1980 an elite level of wines, designated as denominazione di origine controllata (DOCG), was added to the DOCs. The first four areas elevated to the aristocracy—Barolo, Barbaresco,

*Brunello di Montalcino, and Vino Nobile di Montelpulciano—
seemed fair enough, as did the elevation, in 1984, of Chianti
Classico. But when Albana di Romagna became the first white
DOCG in 1988 everyone knew that the system was open to
manipulation by local pressure groups. Nevertheless DOCGs still
carry much more authority than DOCs. Permitted varieties,
alcohol, extract and acidity levels, yields, aging, and viticultural
practices are strictly controlled. DOCG wines must also undergo
analysis and tasting tests. An official tag marks the capsule and
the bottles are often numbered.*
  Current red wine DOCGs:

  *Barolo; Barbaresco; Chianti; Brunello di Montalcino; Vino
  Nobile di Montepulciano; Torgiano; Carmignano; Gattinara; Sagrantino di Montefalco; Taurasi Riserva*

  Current white wine DOCGs:

  *Albana di Romagna; Vernaccia di San Gimignano; Asti
  Spumante; Moscato d'Asti*

Denominazione di Origine Controllata (DOC)
*A DOC governs such factors as the approved area, yield levels,
grape varieties, alcoholic strength, production techniques, and
aging in barrel and bottle. Since 1966 around 250 DOCs have
been issued, and it is generally acknowledged that some were
issued too generously (Soave and Lambrusco, for example). Only
about 13.5 percent of Italy's wine is recognized as DOC (compared to 30 percent in France), not because it's an impossibly
hard club to join but because producers and consumers didn't
believe in it nor feel it was worth the extra cost. DOC wines are
more expensive. Because of the tighter restrictions on producing
DOC wines, they are costlier to make and to buy.*
  *One of the problems with the DOC system was that it tried to
freeze traditional characteristics of Italian wines and make them
conform to inflexible standards during a time of tremendous
change in Italian winemaking. The pressures of local politics and
tradition (DOCs are run by regional bodies working within a fed-
eral framework) rather than quality and common sense have too
often dictated the way Italian wine is made. In Chianti, for*

example, if they want to be able to use the DOC on their label, winemakers are forced to add white grapes to their red wine according to traditional practice. There is nothing intrinsically wrong with mixing white and red grapes, of course. In the northern Rhône, the winemakers of Côte Rôtie can add white Viognier grapes to their Syrah—but they are not forced to if they believe that the wine would be better without them. In Chianti, even the best-made wine will have to be sold as vino da tavola *if it does not strictly adhere to the letter of the law. Then there were the other problems of seemingly strict regulations that were not rigidly enforced; too generous boundaries that embraced areas of very marginal quality; and the usual old business of creating DOCs for political rather than viticultural reasons.*

The 1992 revision of the law has scrapped about fifty low-achieving DOCs. Aspiring wines are considered for acceptance after five consecutive years of quality production (and for election to DOCG after another five). It also recognizes smaller subzones, townships, villages, individual estates, and even vineyards that are willing to register and define their geographical area. Quality is now going to be based primarily on topography, and producers can opt for a more geographically extended or more specific DOC when they are weighing the quality of the vintage.

Indicazione Geographica Tipica (IGT)
Equivalent to France's vin de pays, *the IGT classification is looser than DOC and allows use of a geographical provenance as well as a varietal identification.*

Vino da Tavola
Technically the lowest rung on the ladder, it also embraces many of the best and most expensive wines in Italy. It's true that masses of vino da tavola *never even see the inside of a bottle, but if even a very good wine fails to conform to DOC or DOCG rules (see below), it can only be classified as a* vino da tavola. *Many of the great "super-Tuscans," for example, favor Cabernet Sauvignon, which is not a grape recognized in the official regulations, and so they must be sold, somewhat ignominiously, as* vino da tavola. *The label can only proclaim a brand name without reference to provenance or varietal character.*

ITALIAN WINE-SPEAK

ABBOCCATO. Semisweet.

AMABILE. The next step up in sweetness from abboccato.

AMARO. Bitter; but sometimes used of a dry wine such as the powerful Amarone *of Veneto. See also* "Recioto."

ANNATA. Year. The expression vino all'annata *means young wine to be drunk during the year following the harvest.*

ASCIUTTO. Bone dry.

BIANCO. White.

BOTTIGLIA. Bottle.

CANTINA. Wine cellar.

CANTINA SOCIALE (OR COOPERATIVA). Wine cooperative.

CHIARETTO. Somewhere between a rosé and a light red.

CLASSICO. One of the seven zones in which Chianti can be made.

COLLI. Hilly area, as, for example, in Colli Albani, (the wine from) the hills near Rome.

CONSORZIO. An organization of producers from the same area who band together to market and promote their wines.

DENOMINAZIONE DI ORIGINE CONTROLLATA (DOC). Roughly equivalent to a French appellation contrôllée. *(See page 126 for more details.)*

DENOMINAZIONE DI ORIGINE CONTROLLATA E GARANTITA (DOCG). The elite grade. (See page 125 for more details.)

DOLCE. Sweet.

FATTORIA. Literally a farm, but used to mean a wine-producing estate, particularly in Tuscany.

FIASCO (FIASCHI, PLURAL). A wine flask, particularly the straw-covered one associated with Chianti.

FRIZZANTE. Slightly sparkling. Frizzantino *is even less fizzy.*

IMBOTTIGLIATO. Bottled; as in imbottiglio del produttore all' origine—*that is, estate bottled.*

INDICAZIONE GEOGRAPHICA TIPICA (IGT). Equivalent to French vin de pays. *(See page 127 for more details.)*

LIQUOROSO. A strongly alcoholic wine, often but not exclusively sweet.

LOCALITÀ. Single vineyard (also ronco *and* vigneto*).*

METODO CLASSICO. Méthode champenoise.

NERO. Very dark red, "black," wine.

PASSITO. Strong sweet wine made from semidried grapes. Similar to the vin de paille *of the French Jura.*

PASTOSO. Medium-sweet.

PODERE. Small farm or estate.

RAMATO. Golden-colored wine made from Pinot Grigio grapes left to macerate briefly with their skins.

RECIOTO. Wine made from late-picked grapes from the Veneto. It can be dry (amarone) *or sweet* (amabile). *All share strong, intense flavors and high levels of alcohol.*

RISERVA/RISERVA SPECIALE. Wines aged in barrel for longer than the DOC requirement (the speciale *even longer than regular* riserva*).*

ROSATO. Rosé.

ROSSO. Red.

SECCO. Dry.

SUPERIORE. Wines aged longer than the regular DOC standards, plus 1 percent more alcohol.

UVAGGIO. Wine blended from a number of grape varieties.

UVA. Grape.

VECCHIO. Old (use of the term is controlled under DOC regulations).

VENDEMMIA. Vintage, or harvest.

VIN SANTO/VINO SANTO. A Tuscan sweet dessert-style wine (although a dry version is available). It is made from semidried (passito) *Trebbiano and Malvasia grapes. As the name suggests, the wine has religious associations and was traditionally racked off its cask during Holy Week.*

VINO DA ARROSTO. A red wine robust enough to match roast meat.

VINO DA PASTO. Vin ordinaire.

VINO DA TAVOLA. Equivalent to French vin de table. *(See page 127 for more details.)*

VINO NOVELLO. "Nouveau"-style red wines.

CENTRAL COAST

For most people the Napa Valley *is* American wine, and it's undoubtedly true that Napa represents the heart of American viticulture, where its world-class reputation was founded, and is still home to some of the very best wine being made in the country, indeed the world. But the Napa region is not the beginning and end of the story. One of the real hotbeds of winemaking in the United States is the Central Coast of California.

"Central Coast" is a catchall that embraces several counties and several important AVAs (for more on AVAs, see page 137). Although one could talk of the North Central Coast, including Monterey and San Benito counties, the real excitement, as far as I'm concerned, is in the South Central Coast counties of San Luis Obispo and Santa Clara, and in the Santa Maria and Santa Ynez valleys in Santa Barbara County.

Although we know that grapes were introduced into Arroyo Grande in 1772, vineyards did not appear in the Santa Maria and Santa Ynez valleys until the late 1960s, and it's only now that we are beginning to see some of the best Chardonnays and Pinot Noirs in California coming from the region. It is true that

> **W**ithout doubt the
> greatest values in
> wine today are found in the
> premium varietal category
> in the six-to-eight-dollar
> range. I favor the wines of
> California's Central Coast,
> particularly Monterey
> County, and France's
> Pays d'Oc.
>
> —FRED DAME,
> MASTER SOMMELIER

Chardonnay and Pinot Noir are the area's strong suit, but there are also some very successful Sauvignon Blancs and Sémillons as well as such Rhône varieties as Viognier, Marsanne, and Roussanne for the whites and Syrah for the reds. Some very interesting experiments are also going on with Nebbiolo, the noble grape of Barolo and Barbaresco, as well as Sangiovese, the Tuscan grape used for Chianti and Brunello di Montalcino. The major grape missing from the area is Cabernet Sauvignon, because although the region is several hundred miles south of the Napa and Sonoma valleys, the ocean breezes and fogs that roll over the vineyards keep the climate much cooler than those of Napa and Sonoma. On the Winkler/Amerine heat-summation system (see page 134), Napa is Region III while the Arroyo Grande Valley is a chilly Region I, a climate that has more in common with the long growing season of Burgundy, where Chardonnay and Pinot Noir are the grapes of choice.

The willingness to experiment, added to its already impressive track record, makes the Central Coast one of the most exciting wine regions of California.

• HOT SHOTS •

Talley Vineyards; Au Bon Climat; Byron Vineyard; Qupé Cellars; Vita Nova; Babcock Vineyards; Sanford Winery.

OREGON

Although Oregon is by no means an unknown wine region, it doesn't seem to get the exposure it deserves. This may be due to the fact that it doesn't have an industry advocate as effective as Robert Mondavi has been for California and that its output is pretty small. But what it lacks in quantity it makes up in quality.

Lying on the western side of the Cascade Mountains, Oregon has a Pacific maritime climate that makes for cool summers; very often it's downright wet. For a long time many experts flatly refused to believe that wine could be made here at all until pioneers such as David Lett of Eyrie Vineyards saw the connection between the "marginal" climate of Oregon and that of Burgundy. In this type of climate grapes have to struggle to ripen, and this "stress" can produce wine of much greater complexity. The cool summers also mean the grapes have a much longer growing season—all of which is good news for Pinot Noir, *the* grape of Oregon. And climate isn't the only connection with Burgundy. Both places are made up of small holdings—the average in Oregon is twenty-five acres—that put a lot of emphasis on experiment, character, and quality rather than on blandness and volume.

The early success of David Lett in the 1970s was followed by such great winemakers as Dick Ponzi, David Adelsheim, and Dick Erath, who demonstrated that Oregon was capable of making very fine Pinot Noir indeed; in fact so fine that in a blind tasting in France that compared New World Pinot Noir with French, Eyrie Vineyard took the honors. This so impressed Beaune's top *négociant,* Robert Drouhin, that he bought land in the Dundee Hills, as did Laurent-Perrier of Champagne. The influential wine critic Robert Parker Jr. has also invested here by becoming a partner in Beaux Frères.

• H O T   S H O T S •

Ponzi Vineyards; Adelsheim Vineyards; Beaux Frères; Cristom Vineyards; Domaine Drouhin; Evesham Wood; Domaine Serene; Erath Vineyards; Benton Lane; Oak Knoll; Bethel Heights Vineyard; Sokol Blosser Winery.

TEMPERATURE-SUMMATION DAYS

In 1944 two U.C. Berkeley biologists, A. J. Winkler and Maynard A. Amerine, published their classic viticulture climate map of California. By measuring the difference between the lowest temperature (fifty degrees Fahrenheit) that vines need to start growing and the mean temperature for each day aggregated as monthly totals spread over the seven months of a vine's productive cycle (April to October), they came up with a classification of areas ranked by their temperature status. Every degree Fahrenheit over fifty equals a degree-summation day. For example, if the average temperature for twenty days had been eighty-two, you would deduct fifty, leaving thirty-two, and multiply that by the twenty-day period. This gives you 640 degree-summation days.

Although the system has been criticized because, for example, it doesn't take into account the vine's reaction to temperature fluctuations during the day or the fact that a vine will "close down" to minimize dehydration when the temperature gets over ninety-seven Fahrenheit, it's still pretty useful as a broad-based guide. It laid out five regions according to their overall temperature profile:

	DEGREE SUMMATION DAYS
Region I	*fewer than 2,500*
Region II	*2,501–3,000*
Region III	*3,001–3,500*
Region IV	*3,501–4,000*
Region V	*4,001–4,500*

WASHINGTON STATE

As late as 1969 there were only two commercial wineries in the state of Washington. Today there are more than eighty, and their number is climbing rapidly. The cost of real estate is a fraction of what it costs in, say, the Napa Valley, so it can price its wines very competitively. But it's not all about price. The wines of Washington can offer superb quality, which, combined with their great value, make them some of the country's supersizzlers.

The defining geographic feature is the Cascade mountain range, which dramatically divides west and east (*so* dramatically it's like having Maine next to Algeria!). On the Pacific side there's a good deal of rain, but on the eastern side, where most of the winemaking takes place, there're barely ten inches a year and the landscape is semidesert. Luckily there is plenty of irrigation from the Columbia River, which is delivered to the vines through half-mile-long rotating sprinkler booms. This is the home of the Columbia Valley AVA, which encompasses the AVAs of Yakima Valley and Walla Walla. The hot days promote reliable ripening while the chill desert nights ensure good acid levels, intensity, and length of flavor.

The state's first commercial wines were Riesling (the late great wine consultant André Tchelistcheff thought that they were about the best he had ever tasted), both dry and sweet, but it also produces some very compelling Sémillons and Sauvignons Blancs. Chenin Blanc and Gewürztraminer also do well. Merlot and Cabernet Sauvignon are clearly the leading red wine grapes and produce richly fruity, intense, and well-structured wines. Merlot is the star, however, and has become the state's signature varietal in the same way as Pinot Noir has in Oregon. And for my money Washington State Merlot offers one of the best flavor-for-dollar deals in the world.

• H O T   S H O T S •

Andrew Will Cellars; Quilceda Creek Vintners; Chateau Ste. Michelle; Columbia Winery; Hedges Cellars; Hogue Winery; Leonetti Cellars; Delille Cellars; Woodward Canyon Winery; Columbia Hills.

🍷

AVAs

Although AVA stands for Approved Viticultural Area, it shouldn't be taken to mean the American equivalent of a French appellation contrôlée *or its Italian, Spanish, or German counterparts. When the AVA system was started by the Bureau of Alcohol, Tobacco, and Firearms (BATF) in 1978 in California it went to great lengths to stress that the granting of an AVA did not imply any kind of quality control or approval of the wine. It was simply recognizing that certain areas were distinct from surrounding areas but not necessarily better, and that the proposed AVA was already locally or nationally known as a viticulturally distinct entity. Unlike the European systems BATF does not stipulate per-*

mitted grape varieties or lay down the law about yields or production methods. It does insist, though, that 85 percent of a wine must come from within the AVA and that if a wine uses a vineyard designation (Martha's Vineyard, for example), then 95 percent of the wine must come from that vineyard.

One of the problems is that in its zeal to please everybody, BATF drew the AVA boundaries too widely to make viticultural sense, often including chunks of land of such different character and climate as to make nonsense of the whole business (Napa AVAs, for example, conveniently coincide with county boundaries that have nothing to do with viticulture). If a vineyard had been excluded from a proposed AVA, BATF invariably bent over backward to include the outsider. There are even overlapping AVAs, where a winery can choose which one to join. The winemaker and writer James Halliday makes the point that if a winery was just east of the town of Sonoma it could choose from California/ Sonoma County/Northern Sonoma/Sonoma Coast/Russian River Valley/Chalk Hill (Wine Atlas of California, *Viking, 1993*).

As time goes by AVAs will probably get smaller and more focused, as they are in France. If winemakers are going to break out of selling varietal wine where there's so much emphasis on competitive pricing, they will have to advertise—and protect— their distinctive terroirs, because it's terroir, as the French have found, that gives quality wine its distinction and lasting "brand" image. To some extent this is already happening in some AVAs— Napa's Stag's Leap, for example, where there's a concentration on certain grapes or blends (in the case of Stag's Leap's, the Bordelais classic blend of Cabernet Sauvignon, Merlot, and Cabernet Franc) that have proved successful.

PINOT NOIR

It's called Burgundac, Crni, Nagyburgundi, Rouci, Pignola, Blauburgunder, Spätburgunder, and Pinot Nero. We call it Pinot Noir and almost immediately associate it with Burgundy. In 1395 Philippe the Bold, one of the great dukes of Burgundy, banned the more productive but lowly Gamay from the Côte d'Or (and Georges Duboeuf blesses him every day!). Pinot Noir is a capricious grape with a myriad strains, clones, and genetic mutations and if you add the multitude of climates and soil compositions you begin to see the dizzying complexity of producing the perfect formula for Pinot Noir. It's the Holy Grail of winemaking and has defeated many vignerons who have had to rip out their Pinot Noir and replant with much more amenable varieties such as Merlot or Cabernet Sauvignon. Anything is better than being told that your Pinot Noir is good but it's not Burgundy.

I believe the best Pinot Noir being made outside Burgundy comes from America's West Coast. Specifically I would look at Oregon's Willamette Valley and California's South Central Coast Santa Maria Valley, Santa Ynez of Santa Barbara, Sonoma's Russian River Valley, and to a lesser extent, Napa's Carneros. Santa

---

• H O T   S H O T S •

From Oregon: Ponzi Vineyards; Adelsheim Vineyard; Beaux
Frères; Cristom Vineyards; Domaine Drouhin; Evesham Wood;
Domaine Serene; Erath Vineyards; Benton Lane; Oak Knoll;
Sokol Blosser Winery; Bethel Heights Vineyard; Willamette
Valley Vineyards. *From Central Coast:* Talley Vineyards; Au
Bon Climat; Byron Vineyard and Winery; Ojai; Sanford
Winery; Foxen Vineyards; Calera. *From Sonoma:* Williams-
Seylem; Marcassin; Kalin Cellars; Olivet Lane; Kistler; J.
Rochioli; Iron Horse Vineyards; Gary Farrell. *From Carneros:*
Saintsbury; Acacia Winery; Kent Rasmussen; Étude.

❧

Barbara leads the pack in California, and I would buy almost anything from the vineyards of Bien Nacido, Sanford & Benedict,
and Talley. Although each winery will have its own fingerprint,
their wines seem to share a heady aroma, pure, intense fruit, and
perhaps a touch of that wildness that gives Pinot Noir such an
exotic and complex palate. All the areas I've mentioned have a
relatively cool and long growing season that enables the grape to
ripen fully and develop its wonderful aromas. Pinot Noir grown
in warmer climates usually produces coarse wines high in alcohol, with jammy, candied flavors.

Pinot Noir can be deceptive. Somehow its relatively light col-
oring and soft tannins don't seem "serious" enough to carry the
profound depth of flavor that you find in good mature wines. A
young Pinot typically has an enticing aroma of freshly crushed
strawberries, black cherries, or plums with smoky spiciness and a
rich, thoroughly seductive, texture.

ZINFANDEL

"You mean they make red Zinfandel too?" asked the man who ordered a Ridge Zinfandel the other night. Yes, they do make red Zinfandel, but let's also give thanks for the makers of white Zinfandel, which has taken a bit of a bashing recently as being very unchic. Without them, though, we could have lost a lot of old Zinfandel vines that would have gone under the plow in order to make room from Cabernet Sauvignon or Merlot. Some of these old vines are at least one hundred years old and are part of our great viticultural heritage, and tastings confirm that wine from old vines is much more intense and complex than wine from young vines.

Zinfandel is America's own grape variety. Its origins are bit vague (some ampelographers—those who study vines and grape types—think there may be a link with the Primitivo of southern Italy, although it's still a hotly debated issue), but we do know it was widely planted in the late 1800s and a favorite of Italian immigrants to California.

Zinfandel suffered from an inferiority complex through the 1970s and 1980s but seems to be emerging with its head held high. White Zinfandel (actually a light rosé) was created in the early 1970s almost singlehandedly by Bob Trinchero of Sutter Home, and as a marketing coup it ranks alongside Georges Duboeuf's brainchild, Beaujolais Nouveau. White Zin took the country by storm but was never taken seriously by confirmed wine drinkers. Red Zinfandel was also a bit of a problem. The swings in style can be extreme, ranging from light quaffable table wine to very thick, heavy, and alcoholic reds. Even late-harvest Zinfandels that were pruny and sweet were available. In the 1970s Ridge Vineyards were the first to bottle their wines using site-specific names, and this has pretty much now become the norm. Although there are stylistic differences from winery to winery and microclimate to microclimate, the top producers go for pure, concentrated flavors with balance and integrity.

Zinfandel is not as tannic as Cabernet Sauvignon but fuller bodied than Pinot Noir. Raspberry is the fruit most evoked in tastings, together with cranberry, plum, currant, smoke, mint, spice, and bramble. The texture is rich and the tannins moderate.

• HOT SHOTS •

St. Francis Old Vines; Elyse; Morisoli Vineyard; Ridge Vineyards; Ravenswood; Martinelli Vineyards; Turley Wine Cellars; Nalle; Topolos; Storybrook; Robert Mondavi; Lytton Springs; Rosenblum Cellars; Deux Amis.

CHILE

Miguel Torres, Spain's most innovative winemaker, has described Chile as a "viticultural paradise." The climate is great, especially in the Central Valley, which runs south from Santiago and is the best winemaking territory in the country. It's dry, frost free, and sunny, with plenty of runoff water from the Andes to the west, and although it is on the same latitude as North Africa and southern Spain, it's cooled by Pacific breezes. This makes it climatically more like Napa or Bordeaux, which may explain the strong connection—going back to the 1880s—with France, and the Bordeaux in particular: There is no phylloxera or mildew, so the grapes grow healthily without much chemical interference.

The winemaking tradition in Chile goes back a long time, to the conquistadores of the mid-sixteenth century. By the eigh-

> I *look to Chile for good value. Especially for the Cabernet Sauvignons and Sauvignon Blancs. For seven dollars you can get a really tasty bottle of wine that's ready to drink.*
>
> —THOMAS MATTHEWS,
> New York bureau chief,
> *Wine Spectator*

teenth century the quality, quantity, and cheapness of Chilean
wines had Spain worried (are we seeing history repeating itself?).
After independence from Spain in the nineteenth century, Chile
laid the foundations of its wine industry along European—particularly French—lines. The largest company today, Concha y Toro,
was founded in the last century.

In 1980 the Chilean government and wine industry realized
that modernization was essential if Chile was to become an international wine player. The old methods too often produced faded
reds and oxidized whites; but the introduction, for example, of
pneumatic presses, stainless-steel fermentation, oak barrels, filtration, and cold storage now produces wine that is notable for its
approachable softness and fresh fruitiness ("tender elegance,"
Bruno Prats calls it). They are wines to be drunk young, and they
are terrific value. So far they do not have great body or the sort of
structural tannins that make for aging, but this will change as the
Chilean wine industry matures.

In 1994 the *Wine Specta-
tor* commented: "If anyone
ever figures out how to get
more intensity out of those
vineyards, watch out." Well,
some very heavy hitters
from France and Spain are
investing in Chile's poten-
tial. Bruno Prats of Cos d'Estournel and Paul Pontallier of
Château Margaux have put in more than two million dollars to
create Domaine Paul Bruno. Jacques Lurton of Bordeaux and
Henri Marionnet of the Loire are also there. Château Lafite-Rothschild is a partner in Los Vascos. Miguel Torres is experimenting
in his Chilean bodega on intensity and depth of flavor, and
Michel Roland of Pomerol's Le Bon-Pasteur has invested twelve
million dollars in conjunction with the Marnier-Lapostolle family
(owners of Cognac's Grand Marnier liqueur) to make Cabernet
Sauvignon, Merlot, Chardonnay, and Sauvignon Blanc. Roland is

convinced about what the future holds: "Chile has extraordinary potential. It hasn't been realized, in my opinion, but it's coming. In three or four years wine quality will explode."

HOT SHOTS

Casa Lapostolle; Santa Rita Reserva; Santa Carolina Reserva; Los Vascos Cabernet Sauvignon; Concho y Toro; Errazuriz; Cousino Macul Cabernet Suvignon Antiguas Reservas; Domaine Paul Bruno.

ARGENTINA

Although Argentina is easily the largest producer and consumer of wine in South America (in fact it's the fifth largest consumer—fifty-two liters per head per year compared to about seven liters in the U.S.A.—and fifth largest producer in the world), it has not been as market savvy as its next-door neighbor Chile. Part of the reason for the neglect of Argentinean wines is that the home market was so huge that there was no great incentive to move away from the blockbusting alcoholic reds and heavy oxidized whites favored domestically. And until relatively recently the political climate was not conducive to the sort of foreign investment in the wine industry that is enjoyed by Chile, for example. But, realizing that it was being left behind in the lucrative international market for premium wines, the Argentinean wine industry has begun to turn itself around. My most recent tastings have convinced me that Argentina is not only a hot spot, it's positively sizzling with potential.

Mendoza province is by far the most important for wine production (on its own it has two-and-a-half times as many vines as the whole of Chile and accounts for about one-half of all the out-

---

• H O T S H O T S •

Bodegas Weinert; Flichman; Catena; Navarro Correa;
Etchart; Trapiche.

❦

put of South America). Within Mendoza the subregion of Maipù is the leader. Neuquen and Rio Negro are south of Mendoza and have a cooler, more European climate particularly suitable for crisp Chardonnays. Some think that these southerly regions may well prove to be the stars of South American winemaking.

Traditionally red wines were made from the high-yielding Criolla Grande, whites from Palomino and the Torrontes; but now the impact of such "international" grapes as Chardonnay, Sémillon, and Sauvignon Blanc for whites is manifesting itself. However, Argentina's real achievement is with red wine.

There's been a strong Italian influence for more than one hundred years, from the time immigrants brought Barbera, Lambrusco, Nebbiolo, and Sangiovese. There's also an increasing use of Cabernet Sauvignon, Merlot, Syrah, and Pinot Noir, but perhaps the most successful grape is the Malbec (a classic Bordelais blending grape, used with Cabernet Sauvignon and Merlot), which produces a deeply colored, richly flavored, robust, and complex wine.

AUSTRALIA

Thirty years ago Australians were beer drinkers with a side taste for fortified wines such as Australian "Port." Even when they drank table wine it was so alcoholic it tasted like fortified wine.

Where once fortified wine represented 80 percent of all wine drunk, it now represents only 15. Australia has become a wine-drinking nation with a passion (the per capita annual consumption is about twice as much as in the United States), and a discerning one at that: Although Australia has a population of only 16 million (compared to America's 270 million), even quite specialized wine books will outsell books of more general interest, such as those on Bordeaux or Californian wine, in the whole of the United States. The production of wine in Australia, however, is small compared to California's, and the Australians have been slow to market it internationally, perhaps because their home base is so strong. There seem to be two opposing factors here. On the one hand it's true that 75 percent of the wine drunk in Australia is mass-produced "box" wine (sold in gallon-size plastic containers packaged in a box with a plastic faucet in the side), but on the other there is tremendous interest and sophistication at both the production and consumer ends (Australian wines regularly score higher than Californian and European wines in blind tastings). Although Australian wine drinkers don't go much by hype (they want great flavor and value for money), they are probably more educated about their wines than are their American counterparts.

The system of wine competitions is a reflection of Aussie competitiveness in general. Wines cannot succeed there without having garnered some kind of award in state or regional tastings, and the standards are very high. Whereas in France almost any producer will be welcome on a tasting panel, in Australia tasters have to undergo grueling apprenticeships that can last for seven years. These competitions matter. A winner of one of the most prestigious awards—the Jimmy Watson Trophy, for example—can reckon on selling an additional million dollars' worth of wine.

Perhaps the greatest compliment being paid to the Australian wine industry these days is the invitations from many vineyards in France, California, and eastern

For red wine, you can't do better than France's Languedoc-Roussillon region, which produces a sea of ripe, flavorful wine that retails here for under ten dollars. Other sources of good cheap reds include Portuguese wines made by forward-thinking producers from indigenous grape varieties and Rioja crianza wines from good vintages. For inexpensive whites I look to Washington State for subtle, food-friendly bottles with fresh acidity, and to Australia for fat, generous Chardonnays with immediate appeal. Australia is also a very good source of inexpensive, uncomplicated Cabernet Sauvignon and Shiraz.

—STEPHEN TANZER,
editor and publisher,
International Wine Cellar

Europe, for example, to Australian winemakers to act as consultants and inject a bit of that Aussie pizzazz into their winemaking. The "Flying Aussie" is a phenomenon, so when you drink a Sauvignon Blanc from the Languedoc these days, you are probably getting a good dose of Wagga Wagga wine wizardry.

• H O T   S H O T°S •

Lindemans; Rosemount Estate; Redbank; Mitchelton; Normans; Mountadam; Penfolds; Orlando; Wynns; Yalumba; Brown Brothers; Chateau Reynella; Wolf Blass; Seaview.

🐏

SWEET WINES

Most people call them dessert wines. Most restaurants list them as dessert wines. And indeed they can be served with, or instead of, dessert, but to do so is to miss the versatility of these underappreciated and often excellently priced wines.

I remember my first taste of Muscat de Beaumes-de-Venise, a naturally sweet wine made from the Muscat grape of the Rhône Valley. I was visiting some friends in a small village in Provence. It was a warm summer's day and we were about to sit down to lunch on the terrace. Our host came out with a tray of glasses and a chilled bottle of Muscat de Beaumes-de-Venise. Its sweetness was beautifully balanced by its acidity, which made it refreshing. It made a wonderful aperitif, not a role one normally associates with sweet wines. The aroma—ripe melon, apricots, and peaches—reminded me of the market we had visited that morning and certainly stimulated my appetite for the meal to come. There's something slightly decadent about serving sweet wine before or with a meal, as anyone who has had Sauternes with foie gras can testify. Here are some of my favorites.

FRANCE

Loire Valley

The land of the Chenin Blanc grape. Here it can manifest itself as a racy, perfectly dry wine; or as a demisec that is slightly fruity but dry in the finish because of the balancing acidity; or perhaps once or twice in a decade as an intensely sweet, honeyed wine made from grapes infected with botrytis, the "noble rot" or *pourriture noble*.

The best sweet wines of the Loire come from the Anjou area, which encompasses the appellations of Coteaux du Layon, Coteaux du Layon-Villages, Quarts de Chaumes, and Bonnezeaux. Coteaux du Layon, by far the largest of these appellations, produces the finest sweet wine in the Loire. The valley of the river Layon is particularly well suited to *pourriture noble,* and on my first visit there I was shown how these sweet wines could be served with every course of a meal. I was first given a mildly sweet demisec as an aperitif; then a fuller, more intense one with a platter of pâté, rillettes, and other assorted charcuterie. The wine would have worked equally well with foie gras or freshwater fish or crayfish garnished with a light cream sauce, for example. The meal finished with an intensely honeyed wine from an exceptional vintage, served with an apple tart.

Favorite producers: Pierre-Yves Tijou; Domaine Beaumard; Domaine de la Guimonières.

Bordeaux

Of all the sweet wines in the world the most famous is Sauternes, with Château d'Yquem its star. Less famous but of equal quality are the sweet wines of Barsac, which has its own appellation but because it is a commune of Sauternes may also carry that of Sauternes. Both wines are made from Sémillon, Sauvignon Blanc, and a small amount of Muscadelle in varying proportions.

•TOP TEN SWEET WINES•

*(These wines, made by consistently reliable producers,
are within the $15 to $45 range.)*

1. Château St. Jean, Johannisberg Riesling,
Belle Terre Vineyards, Special Select Late Harvest
(Alexander Valley, California)

2. Bonny Doon, Muscat Canelli "Vin de Glacière"
(Santa Cruz, California)

3. Domaine de Coyeux, Muscat de Beaumes-de-Venise
(Rhône, France)

4. Château Doisy-Védrines (Sauternes, France)

5. Château de Fargues (Sauternes, France)

6. Château Lafaurie-Peyraguey (Sauternes, France)

7. Domaine Disnókó, Tokaji Aszu 6 Puttonyos (Hungary)

8. Graham's Port (Douro, Portugal)

9. Blandy's Madeira 15 Year Old Malmsey (Madeira, Portugal)

10. Château de Jau, Banyuls (Roussillon, France)

Those looking for the grandest of all Sauternes must be willing to pay the price for something that is rare and labor intensive to produce (botrytized grapes have to be handpicked). However, Sauternes lookalikes are available from such nearby appellations as Cérons, Loupiac, Sainte-Croix-du-Mont, and Cadillac. But keep in mind that these wines are lighter in style and do not undergo the rigorous selection involved in Sauternes. They're cheaper, of course, but only in the very best vintages can they compare to Sauternes. All these wines are great with fruit-based desserts, but they also make terrific accompaniments to blue-veined cheeses such as Roquefort.

Favorite producers: *For Sauternes:* Château d'Yquem; Château Lafaurie-Peyraguey; Château Coutet; Château Climens; Château de Fargues; Château Rieussec; Château Suduirat; Château Raymond-Lafon; Château Doisy-Dubroca; Château Doisy-Daëne; Château Doisy-Védrines. *For Loupiac:* Château du Cros; Château de Ricaud; Château Loupiac-Gaudiet; Château Clos Jean. *For Sainte Croix-du-Mont:* Château de Tastes.

Southwest France

A large area with many small wines of great interest and value. It starts east of Bordeaux at Bergerac and extends down through Cahors, Gaillac, and Madiran to the base of the Pyrénées on the Atlantic Coast. The best sweet wine comes from Jurançon and is made from Petit Mensang, Gros Mensang, and Corbu. The style is a little less rich than Sauternes but full-flavored and unctuous nonetheless. They have a distinctive tangy apple and exotic fruit quality that makes them a creative alternative to Sauternes.

Favorite producers: Domaine Cahupé; Cru Lamouroux; Clos Uroulat.

Vin Doux Naturel (VDN)

Describes a whole category of wines from the Rhône Valley and Languedoc-Roussillon. The grape's natural sweetness is captured by arresting fermentation with the addition of a neutral grape spirit. The resulting wine is rich in natural grape sugar and will have 15 to 16 percent alcohol. There are two styles: a white which is in fact golden and made from the Muscat grape, and a red made from Grenache. The most famous and best white VDN is Muscat de Beaumes-de-Venise but others worth exploring are Muscat de Frontignan, Muscat de Lunel, Muscat de Miravel, and Saint-Jean de Minervois. The red VDNs are Banyuls, Maury, Rivesaltes, and Rasteau (the latter two may also be made from

Muscat). The whites are great as an aperitif or with melon and prosciutto, or with apricot and peach desserts, or with almond cookies. The reds are a great solution to the problem of what wine to serve with chocolate desserts.

Favorite producers: *For Muscat de Beaumes-de-Venise:* Domaine de Coyeux; Domaine de Fenouillet; Jaboulet; Guigal. *For Banyuls:* Domaine de la Rectorie; Domaine du Mas Blanc.

Alsace

Most Alsace wine is dry, but a small amount of sweet wine is labeled *vendange tardive* (late-harvested) and *sélection de grains nobles* (individually picked grapes that have been subjected to noble rot). These wines can be made from Riesling, Gewürztraminer, Pinot Gris, and Muscat. *Vendanges tardives* are quite rich but not necessarily supersweet (in fact some are dry to semisweet but powerful), whereas the *sélection de grains nobles* are among the sweetest wines available anywhere (they are not made every year because it takes a very specific combination of climatic conditions to promote noble rot, so there is never a big supply and prices are high; however, a little goes a long way and makes a truly glorious finale to a meal).

Favorite producers: Zind-Humbrecht; Schoffit; Hugel et Fils; Kuentz-Bas; Domaine Weinbach; F. E. Trimbach; Marcel Deiss; André Ostertag; Marc Kreydenweiss; Dirler; Albert Boxler; Roland Schmitt.

SPAIN

Sherry

Although I have dealt with sherry more comprehensively on page 116, here I just want to highlight the sweet styles. Oloroso Sherries are basically dry but can be blended with varying amounts of Pedro Ximénez, a sweet grape. The amount of sweetness added will vary from producer to producer. The sweetest Sherries of all are made from either the Pedro Ximénez or Moscatel grape, which has been dried to produce dark, syrupy, raisiny wines low in alcohol.

Favorite producers: See "Sherry Hot Shots," page 117.

PORTUGAL

Port

Known worldwide as one of the greatest sweet wines, Port is a fortified wine like Sherry, Madeira, and the VDNs mentioned above. It grew out of the need to preserve wines on long sea voyages, particularly between Britain and its then colonies (Britain, always the biggest market for Port, is Portugal's oldest ally, and the trade in wine between the two countries is centuries old). Of the different styles (see page 161) my favorites are aged tawny and vintage and single quinta vintages. Not as sweet as vintage Ports, the tawnys make great aperitifs, especially if served slightly cool. They also work well with chocolate-based desserts. For my money, nothing can top a mature vintage or single quinta vintage Port as the grand finale to a meal.

Favorite producers: Taylor, Fladgate & Yeatman (Vintage, ten-, twenty-, thirty-year Tawny, Quinta de Vargellas); Dow (Vintage—a drier style—and Tawny); Fonseca Guimaraens (Vintage and Tawny; the Guimaraens label is used for wines for lesser years and great value); W & J Graham (Vintage in a fat, sweet style, and Quinta de Malvedos, which is a second-level wine); Quinta do Infantado (a privately owned single estate producing elegant, drier wine); Quinta do Noval Vintage; Ramos Pintos Tawnys; Warre (Vintage and Tawny—drier than Graham's, sweeter than Dow's).

Madeira

The island of Madeira, which is part of Portugal, lies midway between Portugal and North Africa. The fortified wine it produces is truly unique but unfortunately seems to have fallen out of fashion partly due to the low-grade stuff that ends up in dishes such as "Veal Madeira." Good Madeira is great wine with a fascinating tradition. Colonial America accounted for one quarter of all Madeira produced; the signing of the Declaration of Independence was toasted with Madeira, and George Washington was known to drink a pint a day. Of all the styles of Madeira (see page 160), Bual and Malmsey go well with desserts such as fruitcake, nut pastries, or chocolate. The high acidity characteristic of Madeiras refreshes the palate and makes them a superb foil for desserts.

Favorite producers: Blandys; Cossart Gordon; Leacock.

GERMANY

Any QmP wines at the Spätlese level and above (Beerenauslese, and so on; see page 103 for more details) have varying degrees of residual sugar and are sweet though not strictly dessert wines. They have so much balancing acidity that the finish or aftertaste is actually dry for the Spätlese. The Auslese and above are sweeter but never have a heavy, sticky, candy-like sweetness. Drink Spätlese as an aperitif or with a light fish dish. The others are delicious on their own or with apple, pear, and citrus-based desserts.

Favorite producers: Fritz Haag; K & H Lingenfelder; Egon Müller; Müller-Catoir; J. J. Prum; Dr Loosen; Pfeffingen; Selbach-Oster; Gunderloch; G. Zilliken; Milz-Laurentiushof; Von Simmern; Von Schubert-Maximin; Grunhaus; Willi Schaefer.

AUSTRALIA

There are basically four styles of sweet white wine in Australia. The first in importance is a German-style nonoaked Riesling. Next come a botrytized Sauternes-style Sémillon and Sauvignon Blanc. Both styles can be good but play different roles at the table. The late-harvest Rieslings are lighter and fresher tasting— ideal as aperitifs or to drink with fruit desserts. The others are good Sauternes substitutes. Then there is Australian "Port," which is made in the same way as Port in Portugal but from indigenous grapes such as Shiraz and Cabernet Sauvignon. (The best are Tawnys, which are superb values.) Finally, it is also worth seeking out sweet Muscats.

Favorite producers: Peter Lehmann Sémillon Sauternes; Henschke Late Harvest Sémillon; Rosemount Botrytis Affected Sémillon; Heggies Botrytis Affected Late Harvest Rhine Riesling; Pewsey Vale Botrytis Rhine Riesling; Seppelt Trafford Port; Yalumba Clocktower Tawny Port; Yalumba Museum Show Reserve Muscat; Brown Brothers Late Harvest Muscat.

HUNGARY

In the northwest of Hungary lies a little known but historic wine-producing area—Tokaj-Hegyalja—from which comes one of the jewels of all wine: Tokay (or if you prefer, Tokaji). Legend has it that Tokay was the first wine to be made from botrytized grapes more than four hundred years ago. It was regarded as one of the world's greatest sweet wines but practically disappeared during the Communist era, when land and wineries were under central government control. The end of Communism has seen a renewed interest and effort in reviving the great Tokay tradition. There are already some Tokays available but with big investment being made, especially by the French, more of this glorious nectar will come onto the market.

Tokay is made predominantly from the Furmint grape, blended with a small amount of Hárslevelü and an even smaller amount of Muscat Blanc. First a base wine *(szamorodni)* is made from grapes unaffected by botrytis and stored in 140-liter tanks. Second, shriveled, botrytized grapes, called Aszú, are kneaded into a paste and stored in twenty-liter barrels called *puttonyos.* The paste is added, one *puttonyos* at a time, to bring the base wine up to the required level of sweetness. The wine finishes its fermentation, which can take anything from months to years. A wine with three *puttonyos* is the equivalent of a German *Auslese;* four or five *puttonyos* would be the equivalent of a *Beerenauslese;* six, of a *Trockenbeerenauslese.* Pure Aszú is known as Essencia, which can live almost indefinitely. Although rare, a two-hundred-year-old Tokay Aszú would still be young today. The wine has a fresh peach, grape-juice flavor in its youth but develops raisiny, honeyed flavors as it ages.

Favorite producers: Chateau Pajzos; Diszjnókó, Royal Tokaji Wine Co.

MADEIRA

HOW MADEIRA IS MADE

The soil of the island of Madeira is richly volcanic and the climate is warm and wet, so the vines grow prolifically (one of them, Esgana Cão, translates as "dog strangler"!). Madeira turns normal winemaking practices on their head. Where most winemakers are concerned to reduce temperatures during fermentation and limit the wine's exposure to air, the winemakers of Madeira do the opposite. They "cook" their wine in tanks known as estufas *(hence the term "maderized" to describe wine with a burnt-caramel flavor caused by oxidation), in which temperatures can rise as high as 120 degrees Fahrenheit. Cheaper Madeiras are fermented in concrete tanks known as* cubas de calor *through which* run stainless-steel hot-water pipes. The wine is heated between 100 and 120 degrees for three months before fermentation is arrested by the addition of highly alcoholic grape spirit. Better-quality Madeiras are fermented at lower temperatures in wooden casks stored in warm rooms at about 35 to 100 degrees for six months to a year.

This quixotic, not to say downright bizarre, method of production is rooted in a fascinating history. During the age of Europe's colonial expansion, roughly from the sixteenth to the nineteenth century, ships from Portugal, Holland, and especially Britain (which had very strong ties with Portugal) would call at Madeira, pick up wine that had been fortified with spirit alcohol to help preserve it, and ship it off to their far-flung colonies in India, Africa, Australia, and so on. During these voyages the wine would slosh around in wooden holding tanks, often exposed to air and very high temperatures. So popular did Madeira become that ships were actually employed solely to cart it round the world and bring it back, nicely cooked up. Estufas were developed as a way to replicate the result without the expense of shipping.

One thing you can count on with Madeira is that wine that can survive this kind of treatment can survive anything. It will keep in sealed bottles for decades (a vintage Madeira will last for one hundred years without any trouble) and, unlike Sherry, doesn't deteriorate much even when you have opened a bottle and forgotten it.

MADEIRA STYLES

The higher the vineyards up the island's steep slopes, the cooler the climate, and the higher acidity and lower natural sugar levels there will be in the grapes. So, the higher the vineyard, the drier the wine. Starting with the driest:

SERCIAL. Pale and perfumed. After about ten years in cask (it's blisteringly astringent when young) the wine develops a nutty/almond aroma and subtle, mellow flavor. Serve chilled as a great aperitif alternative to dry sherry.

VERDELHO. Slightly richer than Sercial. Medium dry, with a darker color and a nutty, full flavor with a hint of lime, which is the characteristic of the grape variety. Serve chilled as an aperitif.

BUAL. Dark and raisiny but not cloyingly sweet. Smoky and complex with a slightly acidic marmaladey tang. Serve at room temperature.

MALMSEY. Dark, full-bodied, and concentrated with toffee and coffee notes. Sweet but not "sticky sweet" because it is balanced by high levels of acid in the grape. Serve at room temperature as an alternative to Port.

MADEIRA QUALITY LADDER

A lot of inferior bulk wine (granel) is made that has been quickly fermented and colored with caramel. It's coarse and stewed and will be labeled something like "Sercial-style," or "Bual-style," or perhaps sold under a brand name with descriptions such as "dry" or "medium-dry." Avoid!

FINEST. Does not mean that it is the finest but rather that it has been made from blended three-year-old wine that has been aged in a tank rather than a wooden cask.

RESERVE. Blended five-year-old, some of which will have been aged in cask.

SPECIAL RESERVE. Ten-year-old wine aged in cask. Made from at least 85 percent of the grape mentioned on the label.

EXTRA RESERVE. Fifteen-year-old wine aged in cask.

VINTAGE. Wine made from a single year's vintage and aged for at least twenty years in cask followed by two years in bottle.

PORT STYLES

VINTAGE. There are basically two ways of making Port: aging in wooden casks or aging in bottle. Vintage Port is aged in bottle and takes a great deal longer to mature than does wood-aged Port.

Vintage Port is made only in exceptionally good years when, after dozens of tastings, producers and the Instituto do Vinho do Porto declare a vintage. There have been only twenty-eight vintages declared since 1900, and on only three occasions have back-to-back vintages been declared: 1934/35, 1947/48, and 1991/92. The wine of the declared vintage will be bottled after only two years in barrel but will mature in bottle for twenty years or more (the longevity of Port is amazing; the 1955 vintage, for example, is drinking beautifully now). All vintage Ports will have a sediment and require decanting. Vintage Port should have a dark color, concentrated fruit, and a good tannin bite at the finish (known as "grip" in the trade).

TAWNY. Port aged in wooden barrels rather than bottles. A good tawny will have been aged in wood for twenty years or more until it darkens to its characteristic "tawny" brown and takes on a tangy, nutty flavor. Cheap tawny is merely a blend of red and white port and is often sold with fancy names such as "Superior Old Tawny" or "Fine Old Tawny." Usually a higher price and a specific statement of age—ten or twenty years—ensures that you are getting the real thing. In the Douro (the river valley in the north of Portugal from which Port comes), they drink it chilled. A twenty- or thirty-year-old tawny is very elegant and complex—a sophisticated drink.

LATE BOTTLED VINTAGE (LBV). A vintage Port that has been kept in wood for about five years. It is usually filtered and is consequently lighter, less powerful, and has less aging potential than vintage Port.

CRUSTED PORT. The result of blending several vintages, which can be a good, and cheaper, alternative to vintage Port. Like all vintage Ports it develops a sediment ("crust") as it picks up bottle age, and will need to be decanted.

SINGLE QUINTA. Wine made from one estate (quinta) as compared to most vintage Port, which is made from a blend of several quintas. Unlike vintage Port, though, it usually comes from an "undeclared" year. It is bottled young and is aged like vintage Port.

SPARKLING WINES
AND
CHAMPAGNE

Probably more mystery, misinformation, and misunderstanding surrounds sparkling wine than almost any other wine. The problem is that although it can take a good chunk out of our pocketbook, we hardly ever take it seriously. It is an occasional wine, the occasion being the focus rather than the wine.

The first thing to be said is that Champagne can come only from that area of northern France—*the* Champagne. Sparkling wine made by the Champagne method can, and does, come from almost anywhere and everywhere in the winemaking world (the most recent new producer is, rather improbably, India). Among wines it is unique, not least because its production involves the most complex, time-consuming (and therefore costly) techniques of any wine. Unlike other wines that identify quality by association with identifiable and named vineyards (Burgundy *grands crus* and

Bordeaux châteaux gain their prestige from the individual village, commune, or vineyard in which their grapes are grown), Champagne is a blend of wines from a range of sites, even a range of years (Krug, for example, has twenty-year-old wine kept for blending with the most recent harvest). The art of Champagne is in the balancing and harmonizing (the *assemblage*) of twenty or thirty or more wines to create a *cuvée*.

GRANDS AND PREMIERS CRUS VINEYARDS

In Champagne communes are graded according to the quality of the grapes they produce. Every year the Comité Interprofessionel du Vin de Champagne, an organization that represents both the growers and the Champagne houses (roughly equivalent to *négociants* in Burgundy and Bordeaux; they may have considerable landholdings themselves, but also buy in grapes on a contract basis), grades the wine-growing communes. This *échelle* ("scale," or "ladder") sets the price the growers can expect for their grapes. If a commune is ranked as a *grand cru* it can expect to get the full 100 percent of the price set that year. There are seventeen *grand cru* villages producing about 15 percent of the total crop. A *premier cru* commune is rated 90 to 99 percent (the percentage of the kilo price they can expect) and will represent about 18 percent of the crop. The rest, mainly in the Aube region, come in at 80 to 89 percent (nothing below 80 percent is included in the classification).

The best houses will use grapes mainly from *grand* and *premier cru* sites, but sometimes the *cru* of a commune can be misleading because the commune is made up of a number of vineyards, some better, or worse, than others. So in a *premier cru* commune you might find individual growers who beat the average (and vice versa in a *grand cru* commune, where someone can slip below the standard automatically enjoyed by all the growers in the commune).

• C H A M P A G N E   B E S T   B U Y S •

Nonvintage ($15 to $25): Laurent-Perrier Brut; Louis Roederer Brut Premier; Perrier-Jouët Grand Brut; Veuve Clicquot Yellow Label Brut; Taittinger Brut La Française; Drappier Carte d'Or Brut; Drappier Signature Blanc de Blancs; Jacquesson Perfection Brut; Mumm Cordon Rouge Brut; Joseph Perrier Brut; Paul Barra Brut; Cattier 1er Cru Brut.

Prestige Cuvée and Vintage ($35 to $75): Mumm René Lalou; Taittinger Comtes de Champagne Blanc de Blancs; Taittinger Comtes de Champagne Rosé; Pol Roger Blanc de Chardonnay; Veuve Clicquot Vintage; Veuve Clicquot La Grande Dame; Jacquesson Signature; Krug Grande Cuvée; Bollinger RD; Bollinger Grande Année; Moët & Chandon Dom Perignon; Heidseck Monopole Diamant Bleu; Laurent-Perrier Grande Siècle; Louis Roederer Cristal.

CUVÉE DE PRESTIGE

The first *cuvée de prestige* or super-Champagne was the 1921 "Dom Pérignon" from Moët et Chandon, released in 1937. After World War II Roederer came in with "Cristal," and since then most houses have had their own version. Some can be sublime (apart from "Dom Pérignon" and "Cristal," Taittinger's "Comtes de Champagne," Bollinger's "Grande Année Rare," Veuve Clicquot's "Grande Dame," Mumm's "Grand Cordon," Jacquesson's "Vintage Signature," Perrier-Jouët's "Fleur de Champagne," Pol Roger's "Cuvée Sir Winston Churchill," and Heidseck Monopole's "Diamant Bleu" are superb). But as wine expert/writer Hugh Johnson says, "Fabulously good though most of them are there is a strong argument for two bottles of non-vintage for the price of one *cuvée de prestige*."

RÉCEMMENT DÉGORGÉ

If Champagne is left in bottle in contact with its lees it will grow in stature, mellow, and fill out. Once it has been disgorged (the sedimented lees expelled) and recorked, a slow deterioration takes place. Bollinger was the first to market the idea of delayed disgorging (in fact the term *récemment dégorgé*, or RD, is a Bollinger trademark) and created another premium style to join vintage and *cuvée de prestige* Champagne. A fallacy one sometimes hears about RD Champagne is that it "goes off" quickly. This is nonsense. Other things being equal, a fifty-year-old Champagne disgorged ten years ago will be fresher and brighter than a fifty-year-old disgorged and recorked forty-seven years ago, after the more usual three-year disgorging period.

VINTAGE CHAMPAGNE

Vintage in most winemaking areas simply means the wine made every year from the grapes of that year. But in Champagne the word "vintage" takes on a special prestige meaning because a vintage Champagne is made only when the harvest warrants it—and that is not all that often (although some small domaines may declare a vintage every year because they do not have the reserves of previous years' wines from which to make blends). Some great houses, such as Krug, put as much emphasis on their nonvintage as vintage Champagne (Krug prefers the term "multivintage"), so "vintage" Champagne cannot be *guaranteed* to be better than nonvintage (although it can certainly be guaranteed to be more expensive). However, it must have been aged on its lees for at least thirty-six months, and usually from four to five years (nonvintage must stay on lees for a minimum of twelve months, although it too is often kept for three years) and is usually kept in bottle another three to four years after disgorging (a process that allows the sediment, or lees, to be blown out when the bottle is briefly uncorked; the wine is then topped up and recorked). Vintage Champagne should taste fuller, nuttier, and yeastier than nonvintage.

NONVINTAGE (N.V.) CHAMPAGNE

A great deal of care goes into the creation of nonvintage Champagne. It can be made from a blend of Pinot Noir, Pinot Meunier, and Chardonnay from several vintages. A *cuvée* can have as many as fifty wines—the product of different growers, grapes, and years. It must be allowed to stay on its lees for a minimum of one year, although the better houses extend that important maturing process for three.

GRANDS MARQUES

The Syndicat des Grandes Marques de Champagne was established in 1964 (*marque* means "brand"). It is basically a club, and its members are considered to be the elite of Champagne producers. The consistent quality of their nonvintage *cuvées* has been remarkable when compared to those of other wine regions. The members are:

Ayala & Montebello
Billecart-Salmon
Bollinger
Canard-Duchêne
Deutz & Gelderman
Charles Heidsieck
Heidsieck Monopole
Henriot
Krug
Lanson
Laurent-Perrier
Massé

Mercier
Moët & Chandon
Mumm
Joseph Perrier
Perrier-Jouët
Piper Heidsieck
Pol Roger
Pommery & Greno
Ch & A Prieur
Louis Roederer
Ruinart
Salon
Taittinger
Veuve Clicquot-Ponsardin

WHEN "EXTRA DRY" IS NOT THE DRIEST

When Champagne is disgorged some wine is lost and is replaced with a sugar-sweetened wine called the *dosage.* The percentage of *dosage* that is sugar will determine the dryness/sweetness of the wine.

Brut zéro/sauvage. No added sugar. Bone dry.
Brut. 0.5–1.5 percent sugar. Very dry.
Extra dry. 1.5–2.5 percent sugar. Dry.
Sec. 2–4 percent sugar. Slightly sweet.
Demisec. 4–6 percent sugar. Medium sweet.
Doux/Riche. More than 6 percent sugar. Very sweet.

CHAMPAGNE-SPEAK

ASSEMBLAGE. *The mixing of base wines to create the desired blend, or* cuvée. *The skill that goes into the* assemblage *is at the heart of fine Champagne making.*

BEAD. *The size of the bubbles.*

BLANC DE BLANCS. *Champagne made from 100 percent Chardonnay (rather than a mix of, usually, Chardonnay, Pinot Noir, and Pinot Meunier).*

BLANC DE NOIRS. *A white Champagne made from the black grapes Pinot Noir and Pinot Meunier.*

BRUT. *Dry but not bone dry. The most common style of Champagne.*

BRUT ZÉRO/BRUT SAUVAGE. *Completely unsweetened.*

CRÉMANT. *A less bubbly style (it has less than two-thirds the pressure of regular Champagne). Since 1975* crémant *has been synonymous with an* appellation contrôlée *method of making quality sparkling wine in Alsace, Limoux, Burgundy, the Loire, and most recently, Bordeaux.*

CUVÉE. *A blended Champagne.*

DÉGORGEMENT. *Removal of the plug of yeast lees by uncorking the bottle after the wine has finished its second fermentation. The natural pressure in the bottle blows out the lees. The bottle is then topped up and recorked.*

DOSAGE. *The topping-up wine and sugar solution* (liqueur d'expédition) *added to the disgorged Champagne.*

ÉCHELLE DES CRUS. *A ladder (échelle) of quality that grades vineyards in the Champagne from 88 to 100 percent. The very best wines are made from grapes from 100 percent vineyards.*

GIROPALETTE. *Machine that automatically shakes and tips the bottles during their second fermentation to bring the yeast deposit into the neck of the bottle. A mechanical* remuage.

GRANDE MARQUE. *A group or "club" of top producers.*

LIQUEUR DE TIRAGE. *Solution of sugar, yeast, and wine added to the Champagne after its first fermentation in order to start a second.*

MATRICULATION NUMBER. *Legal requirement on all Champagne labels. The initials preceding the number indicate the source of the wine. NM=négociant-manipulant; wine from the whole region has been bought and blended by the Champagne house. CM=coopérative-manipulant; a group of growers share their grapes to produce a blend. RM=récoltant-manipulant; a grower who makes and sells his or her own wine. MA=marque auxiliare; a brand name owned by the producer.*

MOUSSE. *The fizz of Champagne.*

NONDOSAGE. *A Champagne that has not been sweetened. Very dry indeed and sometimes called* brut zéro *or* brut sauvage.

NONVINTAGE. *Covers the majority of Champagne drunk. A blend of many wines (Krug, for example, will use as many as fifty for its Grande Cuvée) to create the "signature" style of any particular house.*

RÉCEMMENT DÉGORGÉ. *Something of a buzz phrase, meaning Champagne that has been kept on its lees for years before being disgorged. Now in general use, the expression was originally a Bollinger trademark.*

REMUAGE. *The "riddling" or periodic turning of Champagne bottles during their second fermentation so that they gradually move from the horizontal to the vertical (*sur pointes, *or on their necks) in order to allow the yeast sediment to settle around the cork and be expelled during disgorging. The skilled worker who makes these adjustments by hand over several months is called a* remueur.

VINTAGE. *As with Port, a vintage Champagne is "declared" only when the harvest is exceptional. It must have been aged longer on its lees and should be fuller bodied and tastier than nonvintage. No more than 80 percent of a harvest can be sold as vintage.*

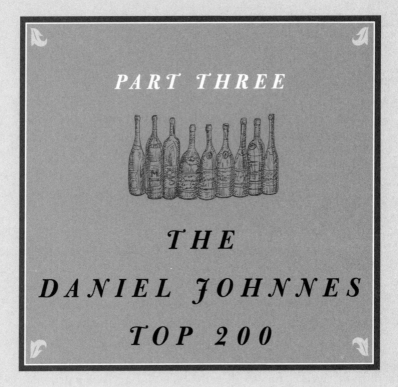

PART THREE

THE DANIEL JOHNNES TOP 200

AUTHOR'S NOTE

It is important to note that the wines tasted and written about here are examples of some of the great values I have found in the world of wine. I have written about them for several reasons:

They are representative of wines from the "Hot Spots" mentioned in the previous chapters; they are domaines, châteaux, or wineries that I have tracked and found to be consistent and reliable year after year. The style may change according to vintage variations but the quality/price ratio is constant. They are wines that I just simply love.

In setting up the following lists and tasting notes, I have avoided categorizing them by country. The emphasis is on the style, flavor, and expressiveness of the wines—criteria that transcend national boundaries altogether. When people are looking for a wine, they understand the style of wine they want better than the appellation or region they want it from. It is much more common for people to ask for a full-bodied red for eight to ten dollars than it is for them to ask for a wine from the Douro or the Languedoc, for that matter. With this in mind, I have therefore listed them according to style (full-, medium-, and light-bodied red and white wines, rosés, and sparkling wines). In listing the wines by style, I tried to make it easier to use this book as a reference for food matches, suggestions for which follow every tasting note.

If you can't find some of these wines, look for other wines from the "Hot Shot" regions in which they were produced and consult the listing of producers; talk to a wine merchant you trust and ask for a wine in a similar style; consult my list of reliable importers and look for wines they import from the same appellations as the one you're looking for.

Happy tasting! Happy hunting!

FULL-BODIED REDS

This is a checklist of wines for which tasting notes follow.

Alain Graillot, Crozes-Hermitage 1994, Rhône, France, $15 (p. 176)

Alma 1994, Navarra, Spain, $7 (p. 177)

Andrew Will, Merlot 1992, Washington State, U.S.A., $28 (p. 177)

Araujo Estate, Eisele Vineyard Cabernet Sauvignon 1992, Napa Valley, California, U.S.A., $40 (p. 178)

Arthus, Côtes de Castillon 1993, Bordeaux, France, $12 (p. 178)

Bodegas Agapito Rico, Carchello Monastrell 1995, Jumilla, Spain, $6 (p. 179)

Bodegas Ismael Arroyo, Mesoñeros de Castilla Crianza 1990, Ribera del Duero, Spain, $18 (p. 180)

Bodegas Magaña, Viña Magaña Reserva 1989, Navarra, Spain, $15 (p. 180)

Bodegas Nekeas, Vega Sindoa 1993, Navarra, Spain, $9
(p. 181)

Bonny Doon, Syrah 1992, Santa Cruz Mountains, California,
U.S.A., $28 (p. 182)

Château Cassagne-Haut-Canon, La Truffière 1990, Canon-
Fronsac, Bordeaux, France, $16 (p. 183)

Château d'Oupia, Cuvée des Barons 1990, Minervois, France,
$11 (p. 184)

Château La Vieille Curé, Fronsac 1990, Bordeaux, France, $20
(p. 185)

Chateau Montelena, Cabernet Sauvignon 1992, Napa Valley,
California, U.S.A., $30 (p. 185)

Château Saint-Auriol, Corbières 1991, Languedoc, France, $9
(p. 186)

Chateau Ste Michelle, Chateau Reserve Estate Red 1991,
Columbia Valley, Washington State, U.S.A., $19 (p. 187)

Château Sociando-Mallet, Haut-Médoc 1989, Bordeaux, France,
$23 (p. 187)

Corison Cabernet Sauvignon 1992, Napa Valley, California,
U.S.A., $28 (p. 188)

Delille Cellars, Chaleur Estate 1992, Yakima Valley, Washington
State, U.S.A, $27 (p. 188)

Domaine d'Aupilhac, Coteaux du Languedoc Montpeyroux
1992, Languedoc, France, $12 (p. 189)

Domaine Belle Père et Fils, Crozes-Hermitage Les Pierrelles
1991, Rhône, France, $17 (p. 190)

Domaine du Mas Cremat, Côtes du Roussillon 1991, Roussillon,
France, $8 (p. 190)

Domaines Rothschild, Quinta do Carmo 1987, Alentejo, Portugal, $20 (p. 191)

Francesco Candido, Salice Salentino Riserva 1989, Apulia, Italy, $7 (p. 191)

Henri Bonneau, Châteauneuf-du-Pape Cuvée des Celestins 1990, Rhône, France, $25 (p. 192)

Jade Mountain, Mourvèdre 1990, Napa Valley, California, U.S.A., $15 (p. 193)

M. Chapoutier, Saint-Joseph Rouge 1990, Rhône, France, $20 (p. 193)

Marietta, Old Vine Red Lot No. 16, Sonoma County N.V., Sonoma, California, U.S.A., $9 (p. 194)

Martinelli, Zinfandel Jackass Hill Reserve 1993, Russian River, California, U.S.A., $19 (p. 194)

Penfolds, Cabernet Sauvignon Shiraz Bin 389 1990, South Australia, $15 (p. 195)

Pesquera, Ribera del Duero Crianza 1991, Ribera del Duero, Spain, $20 (p. 195)

Quilceda Creek Vintners, Cabernet Sauvignon 1991, Washington State, U.S.A., $30 (p. 196)

Quinta da Aveleda, Charamba 1992, Douro, Portugal, $6 (p. 197)

Quinta de Lagoalva de Cima 1992, Ribatejo, Portugal, $9 (p. 197)

Qupé, Santa Barbara County Syrah, Bien Nacido Vineyard 1992, California, U.S.A., $23 (p. 198)

Ravenswood, Zinfandel 1993, Sonoma, California, U.S.A., $14 (p. 198)

Ridge Vineyards, Geyserville 1992, Santa Cruz Mountains, California, U.S.A., $22 (p. 199)

Sequoia Grove, Cabernet Sauvignon 1991, Napa Valley, California, U.S.A., $18 (p. 200)

Shafer, Cabernet Sauvignon Stag's Leap District Hillside Select 1989, Napa Valley, California, U.S.A., $35 (p. 200)

Sociedad Cooperativa Agricola Limitada de Borja, Borsao 1994, Campo de Borja, Spain, $5 (p. 201)

Steltzner, Cabernet Sauvignon Stag's Leap District 1990, Napa Valley, California, U.S.A., $19 (p. 202)

Vallana, Spanna del Piemonte 1983, Italy, $10 (p. 202)

Whitehall Lane, Merlot Knights Valley 1992, Sonoma County, California, U.S.A., $17 (p. 203)

ALAIN GRAILLOT, CROZES-HERMITAGE 1994, RHÔNE, FRANCE, $15

There are winemakers who rely on generations of tradition to determine their methods of tending their vines and making their wine. And then there is the new generation of winemakers, who have studied and traveled and drawn from their experiences. One type is not necessarily better than the other, just different; Alain Graillot is the second. He can be found on biking excursions with his colleagues from Burgundy, or lecturing on Syrah at the University of California at Davis. Wherever he is he shares ideas and applies them to his vineyard. The purpose is to try techniques that may help extract more flavor while retaining integrity in the appellation.

His 1994 is a resounding success. It is deeply colored with an explosive nose of black fruit jam, smoke, and spice. Richly textured and full bodied, it delivers layers of flavor and a well-balanced smooth mouth-feel that is powerful with youth yet not rough. Delicious.

Food match: Saddle of lamb stuffed with mushrooms and herbs

ALMA 1994, NAVARRA, SPAIN, $7

This winery is owned by Thelmo Rodriguez, who can more often be found at his family winery, Remelluri, in the Rioja. Thelmo is one of the "young Turks" of Spanish winemaking who has traveled and studied and is taking up the reins from the previous generation with one eye on tradition and the other on innovation. The fact that he would venture into a region outside his home territory, Rioja, speaks volumes of his modern-day vision of winemaking and his belief in the potential of the Navarra as a region capable of producing world-class wines.

Made from 100 percent Grenache, the purple core and crimson rim betray the youthfulness of this wine. It smells of violets, Kirsch, and strawberry jam. It has an exuberant, freshly crushed berry flavor, good concentration, balance, and chewy texture with a soft pleasant finish.

Food match: Stuffed cornish hen; grilled fish; soft-ripened cheese

ANDREW WILL, MERLOT 1992, WASHINGTON STATE, U.S.A., $28

In 1989 Chris Camara decided to quit his job waiting tables and start his own winery on Vashon Island, about fifteen minutes from Seattle. The vagaries of the economics of winemaking mean that Chris can still be found occasionally waiting tables at Pike Place Market in Seattle to support himself and his family until he can increase his production beyond its present one thousand cases. His production is split between Cabernet Sauvignon and Merlot, and although he has been at it only a short time he is capable of producing some of the most exciting Merlot and Cabernet Sauvignon in the country.

The first thing that impressed me was the deep red/purple hue and then the nose, suggesting spice, anise, ripe plums, and chocolate. Its full, luscious palate has a complexity uncommon in such a young wine, revealing layers of flavor. A wine of great class.

Food match: Roast lamb; prime ribs of beef

ARAUJO ESTATE, EISELE VINEYARD CABERNET SAUVIGNON 1992, NAPA VALLEY, CALIFORNIA, U.S.A., $40

The Eisele vineyard is famous for the Cabernets of the Joseph Phelps winery. Since 1991 it has been under new ownership, and this is the first wine of the new label. The winemaker is Tony Soter of Spottswoode and Etude fame, and the wine really shows the class combination of great vineyard and expert winemaker. It's an expensive wine, but as one of the best on anyone's list of great Californian Cabernets it's well worth the price.

Deep ruby with an intense classic Cabernet Sauvignon nose of cassis and spice. Although still a youthful wine, it has fantastic focus and concentration on the palate with great depth and length. Although it is delicious to drink now, it will hold well and should develop beautifully over the next ten to fifteen years.

Food match: Rack of lamb with natural juices; sirloin steak

ARTHUS, CÔTES DE CASTILLON 1993, BORDEAUX, FRANCE, $12

The Côtes de Castillon is one of those satellite appellations of Bordeaux that is worth taking a look at for its serious *petits châteaux.* Located east of the village of Saint-Émilion, Castillon has a historical significance that goes back to the fifteenth century.

In 1453 the English commander John Talbot, the earl of Shrewsbury, was killed in battle at Castillon and the English army was thrown out of France. In addition to being the site of many battles, this is one of the oldest viticultural regions of France.

The Arthus vineyard (which is owned by two enologist brothers who also have an estate in Saint-Émilion) is on clay-and-chalk soil that is an extension of the slopes producing Saint-Émilion *grand crus classés*. It is planted with Merlot and Cabernet Sauvignon, with the finished wine containing 70 percent Merlot. The aroma is an appetizing one of ripe, plummy fruit, roasted nuts, chocolate, and toasted oak. The taste is sweet and full with good concentration and intensity, while its finish is long and quite tannic.

Food match: The tannins would be served well by a grilled steak.

BODEGAS AGAPITO RICO, CARCHELLO MONASTRELL 1995, JUMILLA, SPAIN, $6

Jumilla is in the Levante, a region of central eastern Spain stretching along the Mediterranean coast with Valencia (the capital of paella) as its largest city. The Monastrell (known as the Mourvèdre in France) is the main grape variety here, and in fact is second only to Garnacha for red wine as the most widely planted grape in Spain.

The Rico family established their bodega in 1983 with existing old vineyards to which they added new parcels planted with Merlot, Cabernet Sauvignon, and Tempranillo. Low yields produce a deeply colored ruby wine with a nose of ripe black fruit, plums, and blackberry, with a nuance of anise and herbs. This is a wonderfully exotic-tasting wine (and at the price a real steal) with big fruit balanced by ripe, soft tannins. Give the wine a little air before serving. Decant or leave it in the glass for fifteen to twenty minutes to let all that flavor and aroma blossom.

Food match: Hearty meat or vegetable stews; roast lamb

BODEGAS ISMAEL ARROYO,
MESOÑEROS DE CASTILLA CRIANZA 1990,
RIBERA DEL DUERO, SPAIN, $18

This bodega provides strong evidence that the region of Ribera del Duero is producing world-class wines of great character. The Castilla y Léon region shares with its neighbor to the north, Rioja, a taste for the Tempranillo grape (called the Tinta del País locally) but here it yields deeper-hued and more powerful wine.

The *crianza* designation is a bit misleading. Although *crianzas* (see page 114) have less prerelease aging than *reservas* (see page 115), they are not necessarily inferior wines. They often retain more of their grapey, fresh flavors.

This wine is made from 100 percent Tinta del País and is aged fourteen months in oak barrels. It's deep ruby, almost opaque, with a nose marked by oak, smoke, and roasted aromas intermingled with seductive black cherry and chocolate. There's substantial mouth-feel, with full, soft flavors, ripe tannins, and a pleasingly long finish.

Food match: Barbecued duck; game dishes; full-flavored meats

BODEGAS MAGAÑA, VIÑA MAGAÑA
RESERVA 1989, NAVARRA, SPAIN, $15

Navarra has traditionally been seen as Rioja's Cinderella sister. Until 1980 most of the grapes were Garnacha with Tempranillo a poor second. Since then, though, the authorities have barred further planting of Garnacha, and this, along with modern machinery, has catapulted the region's wines into the quality that will cause many Rioja producers to look nervously over their shoulders.

Bodegas Magaña bucks the traditional grape varieties of the region in favor of the Bordelais classics: Cabernet Sauvignon, Merlot, and Cabernet Franc. And to reinforce the French influence the wines are aged in French rather than the American oak favored by most Spanish bodegas.

It's not surprising that the relatively high percentage of Merlot in the wine evokes comparisons with Pomerol and Saint-Émilion, but what I like about this *reserva* is that it has retained a rustic character that gives it great charm and individuality. The aroma is eucalyptus and roasted nuts. On the palate it is quite dense and concentrated, with real body and texture. A meaty and firm mouthful.

Food match: Game dishes such as venison; maigret of duck; veal stew

BODEGAS NEKEAS, VEGA SINDOA 1993, NAVARRA, SPAIN, $9

Here's yet another reason to keep an eye on Navarra as a source of terrific Spanish wines.

Although close to Rioja, the wines of Navarra might well be from another continent. Where Rioja is rooted in tradition, Navarra is dedicated to innovation. Garnacha is the primary red wine grape here, but many bodegas are keen on Tempranillo as well as "international" varieties such as Cabernet Sauvignon and Merlot.

This wine is a blend of Tempranillo and Cabernet Sauvignon which in many ways reminds me of the "super-Tuscan" blends of Sangiovese and Cabernet Sauvignon. It may be "international" but it's not anonymous—it's delicious! The color is a deep ruby/purple and the nose is infused with plums, black cherry, anise, and eucalyptus. It is full and rich on the palate with dense fruit and a balancing acidity. Very classy. Very polished. A deal at twice the price.

Food match: Minute steak; lamb chops

BONNY DOON, SYRAH 1992, SANTA CRUZ
MOUNTAINS, CALIFORNIA, U.S.A., $28

Randall Grahm, philosophical enologist and one of the wine world's true originals, founded Boony Doon in 1983. His original intention was to plant Pinot Noir and Chardonnay, but both were dropped as Grahm moved on to explore such Rhône varieties as Grenache, Marsanne, Roussanne, Viognier, Mourvèdre, and Syrah. Grahm describes himself as a Rhône Ranger and has done more to promote these wines than anyone in the country. Not only does he make fine wine, but he also has a tremendous flair for marketing and promotion with a wit that is often imitated but rarely matched. Whether it be his Le Cigare Volant (which is

•TOP TEN REDS FOR
GRAND OCCASIONS•

(These wines, made by consistently reliable producers,
are within the $25 to $50 range.)

1. Domaine G. Roumier, Chambolle-Musigny-les
   Amoureuses (Burgundy, France)

2. Michel Lafarge, Volnay Clos des Chênes (Burgundy, France)

3. Ponzi, Pinot Noir Willamette Valley Reserve 1992 (Oregon)

4. Cune Imperial Gran Reserva (Rioja, Spain)

5. Ridge Zinfandel Lytton Springs (Sonoma, California)

6. Château Pichon-Baron-Longueville (Pauillac, France)

7. Château l'Angélus (Saint Émilion, France)

8. Cain Cellars, Cain Five Meritage (Napa Valley, California)

9. E. Guigal, Côte Rôtie (Rhône, France)

10. Jean Louis Chave, Hermitage (Rhône, France)

🍇🍷

French for a UFO and was prompted by a 1950 ordinance of the town council of Châteauneuf-du-Pape forbidding UFOs from landing in its bailiwick), Le Sophiste, or Old Telegram (a play on Châteauneuf-du-Pape's famous Domaine Le Vieux Télégraphe), he has humor, personality—and great wine.

Unlike Le Cigare Volant and Old Telegram, which are Rhône-like blends, this wine, as its name makes clear, is 100 percent Syrah and the quality stands as proof that the California climate is capable of producing fruit that will, in the hands of an inspired winemaker such as Randall Grahm, produce wines up to the standards of their French counterparts. This Syrah is a deep ruby/purple—almost opaque—with a herbal and peppery nose cut through with bright raspberry tones. There's satisfying, full-bodied, and mouthfilling richness on the palate, with soft, luscious fruit and ripe, velvet tannins. One of the best Syrahs ever to come out of California!

Food match: Prime ribs of beef; daube provençale

CHÂTEAU CASSAGNE-HAUT-CANON, LA TRUFFIÈRE 1990, CANON-FRONSAC, BORDEAUX, FRANCE, $16

In the eighteenth and nineteenth centuries the wines of the hilly and wooded area of Fronsac (just to the west of Pomerol with the river Dordogne as its southern boundary) were more greatly esteemed than those of Saint-Émilion and Pomerol. Having fallen out of favor, the area's wines are now making a comeback, especially those of the Côtes de Canon-Fronsac, which are considered better than those of their larger neighbor, Fronsac. This resurgence is partly due to the ownership of some of the more notable châteaux by proprietors of the caliber of Christian Moueix of Château Pétrus, and consultants such as Michel Roland, together with updated technology. The grapes used in the region are the classic Bordelais Cabernet Sauvignon, Cabernet Franc, Merlot, and Malbec, but with a greater emphasis on Cabernet Franc, whose "grassy" edge helps to distinguish the wines of Fronsac from the plummy Pomerols next door.

Château Cassagne-Haut-Canon is planted with 60 percent Merlot and 40 percent Cabernet Franc to create a dense wine with plenty of power and drive. It's a deep, inky color with a ripe, fruity, and slightly gamey nose that gives it a touch of exotic wildness. Just the job on a winter's night with something hearty in the pot.

Food match: Venison casserole; duck confit; roast goose

CHÂTEAU D'OUPIA, CUVÉE DES BARONS 1990, MINERVOIS, FRANCE, $11

This gusty red comes from the Languedoc in southern France. The Minervois, one of the prettiest areas of France, lies amid rolling hills about twenty miles from the Mediterranean, where the preferred grapes are Carignan and Grenache. Although the wines of the area are often considered merely "country wines" (comparison to the great French vineyards of the Bordeaux and Burgundy, for example), they are undergoing a minirevolution that is fast establishing them as some of the most dynamic, flavorful, and best-value wines in France. In fact, the whole region of Languedoc-Roussillon is rapidly shedding its old reputation as a mass producer of deeply colored jug wine.

Château d'Oupia is a great example of the benefits of this turnaround. The wine is indeed a deep ruby, but it also has a nose rich and ripe with aromas of the *garrigue* (the aromatic wild brush found in the plains of the Languedoc) together with concentrated fruit and a spiciness that certainly lifts it out of the ordinary.

Food match: Hearty winter stews, or game dishes with red-wine sauce

CHÂTEAU LA VIEILLE CURÉ, FRONSAC 1990, BORDEAUX, FRANCE, $20

Fronsac lies on the right bank of the Dordogne just west of Saint-Émilion and Pomerol and, like them, is dominated by the Merlot grape. Although today the wines of Fronsac and Canon-Fronsac are less expensive than their better-known neighbors, it wasn't always so. A couple hundred years ago they commanded higher prices, and today we are seeing a definite  swing back in their direction as many Fronsac châteaux outperform their counterparts in Saint-Émilion and Pomerol.

Château La Vieille Curé is one of the leaders in the appellation. Most of its vines are about twenty-five years old, and the blend is the classic Merlot/Cabernet Franc/Cabernet Sauvignon. The 1990 is deep garnet with an inviting and warm aroma of plum and black currants. This warmth continues with a soft, thick palate of ripe, concentrated fruit and luscious, mouth-filling flavors and silky tannins.

Food match: Truffled scrambled eggs; shell steak

CHATEAU MONTELENA, CABERNET SAUVIGNON 1992, NAPA VALLEY, CALIFORNIA, U.S.A., $30

The origin of this winery can be traced back to 1882, when Alfred L. Tubbs purchased 250 acres of land in Napa Valley just north of Calistoga. But the real story begins under the current ownership of James Barrett, who produced his first vintage here in 1972 after a fifty-year interruption.

In a tasting held in New York in 1994 that featured every major vintage from 1974 to the present, I was struck by the remarkable consistency of style and level of excellence. These wines have grace, power, and complexity, which is something not always found in California winemaking.

The 1992 is no different. It has all the attributes of a great Montelena, with aromas of cedar, cassis, and berries. It fills the mouth with rich, luscious, spicy fruit and finishes with soft ripe tannins. Although it is wonderful for current drinking, it will continue to evolve for the future.

Food match: Lamb shanks or maybe a fine shell steak

CHÂTEAU SAINT-AURIOL, CORBIÈRES 1991, LANGUEDOC, FRANCE, $9

Château Saint-Auriol lies deep in the heart of Corbières country surrounded by rolling hills and brush. It is an extraordinary landscape with a past rich in history. On the Saint-Auriol estate there are traces of three first-century B.C. Roman villas (nearby Narbonne was the first great Roman city of Gaul), and it was near Saint-Auriol that Charlemagne engaged the Moors in battle in the eighth century. The history may be ancient and the winemaking techniques traditional, but this is not a domaine mired in the past. The present owners have their eyes on both today and tomorrow in their determination to produce high-quality wine.

As with many of the vineyards in the Languedoc, tradition is tempered by innovation to produce better wines. In this case the old reliance on Carignan (the grape responsible for that vast sea of *gros rouge* for which the Midi was the main source) has shifted to an emphasis on the more interesting Mourvèdre, Grenache, and Syrah. The grapes are fermented in whole clusters by carbonic maceration (see page 23), yielding a wine of intense grapiness with a spicy, peppery nose. Its maturation in Bordelais oak barrels adds aromatic nuance and helps develop its chewy texture. A wonderfully seductive wine for a cold night!

Food match: Game birds (quail, pheasant, goose, squab); hearty lamb or beef stews

CHATEAU STE MICHELLE, CHATEAU RESERVE ESTATE RED 1991, COLUMBIA VALLEY, WASHINGTON STATE, U.S.A., $19

Reasonably priced good-quality wines make Washington State one of the most exciting wine-producing areas in the United States today. Chateau Ste Michelle can trace its roots back to 1934, but the present-day winery dates from 1967 and is owned by U.S. Tobacco's wine-and-spirits holding company, Stimson Lane. This megabuck group owns other Washington State wineries, but Ste Michelle is the jewel in their crown. Mike Januik, the winemaker, is dedicated to keeping up the highest standards.

The Reserve Estate Red has a Bordelais quality with a mineral, cedary nose that reminds me of a Saint-Julien. On the palate it has a certain tension, energy, and backbone. There's concentration and richness here, with layers of flavor and good length.

Food match: Broiled lamb chops; roast goose; soft cheeses

CHÂTEAU SOCIANDO-MALLET, HAUT-MÉDOC 1989, BORDEAUX, FRANCE, $23

Although this wine isn't a *cru classé* (see page 83) it does rank in the highest echelons of the *crus bourgeois* (see page 85), which makes it a great value. In fact Sociando-Mallet regularly outguns classed-growth Médocs in comparative tastings. The one-hundred-acre vineyard is predominantly Cabernet Sauvignon (60 percent), with 30 percent Merlot and 10 percent Cabernet Franc; the goal of the owner, Jean Gautreau, is to make a classic Médoc with long aging potential.

The fruit from Sociando-Mallet (a château that prides itself on the quality of its *terroir*) is always full-powered and the '89 is wonderfully round and sweet with great impact on the palate and a forceful, concentrated finish. The nose is classy, toasty, and refined, and the Merlot helps give the wine its soft texture. Great balance and length.

Food match: Roast leg of lamb

CORISON CABERNET SAUVIGNON 1992, NAPA VALLEY, CALIFORNIA, U.S.A., $28

Cathy Corison is the owner and winemaker at Corison Wines. As a little-known winery she may not have a public relations office and a large promotional budget, but she gets the word out on her wines by putting the message in the bottle. She has had plenty of experience with about twenty vintages behind her, twelve of which were spent at Chappellet Vineyards as the chief winemaker.

The grapes come from the best sites in the Rutherford area and her goal is to fashion wines with lush supple flavors for early enjoyment yet with enough structure to allow aging. The wine is aged in 50 percent new French oak barrels.

This wine is maybe her best to date. It has a saturated ruby robe and an aroma of ripe black plums, cassis, and spice. On the palate it has deep flavors of ripe fruit, soft texture, and a long, layered, complex finish.

Food match: Steaks on the grill or under the broiler

DELILLE CELLARS, CHALEUR ESTATE 1992, YAKIMA VALLEY, WASHINGTON STATE, U.S.A., $27

Here is another wine that proves that the wines from Washington State are not just good value but, combined with their quality and low prices, some of the most exciting wines in the United States today. This little-known winery is dedicated to producing high-quality wines and should soon be better known.

The Chateau Reserve Estate Red has a Bordelais, even Saint-Julien-like quality with its mineral, lead-pencil nose. On the palate it has defined flavors, explosive fruit, and structure. The wine is concentrated and rich, with layers of flavor and length.

Food match: Grilled lamb chops; prime ribs of beef

DOMAINE D'AUPILHAC, COTEAUX DU LANGUEDOC MONTPEYROUX 1992, LANGUEDOC, FRANCE, $12

Sylvain Fadat, the owner of Domaine d'Aupilhac, is representative of a younger generation of winemakers who are now in charge of family estates. Although he loves the wines and traditions of his region, his study of viticulture and enology, and his years spent working in Burgundy and the Côtes-du-Rhône, have given him a wider perspective. His domaine, like most of those in the Langue-doc, is planted with Carignan, Grenache, Syrah, Mourvèdre, and Cinsault. He uses no herbicides and keeps his yields low in order to maximize the concentration in the wine. All the grapes are harvested by hand and then destemmed to eliminate harsh tannins. Although this kind of pampering is more common in the great estates of Bordeaux and Burgundy, producers such as Fadat in the south now have that confidence in their wines to apply the same diligence.

A deep purple, almost black hue is matched by a rich black-berry/cigar-tobacco/spice nose. In the mouth it is dense and chewy, with great concentration and elegance—a really exceptional wine for the price.

Food match: Grilled sausages or hamburgers

DOMAINE BELLE PÈRE ET FILS, CROZES-HERMITAGE LES PIERRELLES 1991, RHÔNE, FRANCE, $17

Crozes-Hermitage benefits from the fame of Hermitage, its neighbor just to the north, much in the same way the villages of Puligny and Chassagne hitched their wagons to their most famous vineyard, Montrachet. The wines of Hermitage were probably the most respected in all of France in the eighteenth and nineteenth centuries, to such an extent that in Bordeaux it was considered necessary to beef up the local wine with a liberal dose of Hermitage so that they could be promoted as "Hermitage." The wines from Crozes are a scaled-down version of Hermitage, although the winemaking rules that govern them are the same. But from a conscientious grower with good hillside vineyards you can get terrific value.

Domaine Belle is a rising star of the appellation, and this wine has an intense, peppery nose with hints of coffee and woodsy undergrowth. It tastes lush, with ripe berry fruit and moderate tannins for a soft but persistent finish.

Food match: Hearty winter dishes such as ragout of venison or beef

DOMAINE DU MAS CREMAT, CÔTES DU ROUSSILLON 1991, ROUSSILLON, FRANCE, $8

Mas Cremat is owned by the daughter of the famed Jean Mongeard of Domaine Mongeard-Mugneret in Vosne-Romanée, and her husband, Jean-Marc Jeannin. They have brought their expertise to the production of natural, handcrafted wines. Although it is no surprise to see good wine coming from the Roussillon, the success of Mas Cremat may encourage other vignerons from more famous appellations to set up shop and exploit the potential of this region.

With its blend of about 60 percent Syrah and 20 percent each of Mourvèdre and Grenache, this wine is like a small-framed Châteauneuf-du-Pape with a peppery, earthy, slightly leathery nose. There's density, with ripe concentrated fruit on the palate, which, together with a moderately long finish, make for delicious drinking now as well as over the next five years.

Food match: Red-wine stews; hamburgers

DOMAINES ROTHSCHILD, QUINTA DO CARMO 1987, ALENTEJO, PORTUGAL, $20

The most famous winemaking areas of Portugal tend to be in the north, but Alentejo is in the southern region, where wine is still made by the ancient method of fermenting in earthenware pots known as amphorae. This certainly isn't true of Quinta do Carmo since Domaines Rothschild bought it in 1991. The winery is modern with fermentation in tanks and aging in French oak.

The grapes grown here are the Alicante Bouschet, Periquita, and Tempranillo (also known as the Aragon), and although the Alicante is seen as a lowly grape in France, where it is used primarily for adding color, in the climate of Alentejo it produces very good wine indeed.

Quinta do Carmo is deep ruby with a spicy, leathery nose with hints of currants and chocolate—a real mouthful of full, concentrated fruit.

Food match: Roasted dark-fleshed birds such as goose or duck

FRANCESCO CANDIDO, SALICE SALENTINO RISERVA 1989, APULIA, ITALY, $7

Apulia is the heel in the Italian boot. It's also the largest wine producer in Italy, surpassing Sicily. The vine has made a home here since the time of the Phoenicians and the Greeks and along with the production of olive oil, this is what makes the economy turn. Among the many grape varieties found here is the most widely planted Negroamaro, and the Primitivo, which is also thought to be a cousin to the American Zinfandel. As expected, these two varieties produce wines of color and strength.

The Salice Salentino DOC was created in 1976 and is considered to produce some of the most stylish wines. This one, made from the Negroamaro with a touch of Malvasia Nera, is inky black in color with a ripe black fruit and a jammy, somewhat rural quality. It is a big, powerful wine with intense deep flavors, yet remains classy with southern Italian flair.

Food match: Meat loaf; beef stews; hard sheep's-milk cheeses like Pyrénées, Manchego

HENRI BONNEAU, CHÂTEAUNEUF-DU-PAPE CUVÉE DES CELESTINS 1990, RHÔNE, FRANCE, $25

Châteauneuf-du-Pape, named for a charming village in the Vaucluse, about twenty-five kilometers north of Avignon, was the first wine to be awarded an *appellation contrôlée* when the system was introduced in 1935. It's the home of some of the most compelling red wines in France and is governed by some of the country's most stringent wine regulations. For example, the minimum acceptable level of alcohol is 12.5 percent, the highest minimum in the country. A bizarre regulation stipulates that 5 percent of the crop must be discarded before fermentation to ensure good juice concentration. Although Châteauneuf may be made from up to thirteen different grapes, the principal blend is Grenache, Syrah, Mourvèdre, and Cinsault.

The color is a deep purple, almost black, with red highlights as though lit from within. There's a huge nose of earth, leather, flowers, and raspberry—a very exciting aroma. On the palate it is penetrating, with sweet, full fruit that has great intensity and length.

Although it's big bodied, it manages not to be heavy. Beautiful balance. A wonderful wine on a winter's night.

Food match: Salmis de pigeon; steak with marchand de vin sauce

JADE MOUNTAIN, MOURVÈDRE 1990, NAPA VALLEY, CALIFORNIA, U.S.A., $15

Jade Mountain in the Mount Veeder AVA began production in 1984 with Cabernet Sauvignon and Sauvignon Blanc. They were short-lived, and in 1988 the focus shifted to the grape varieties of the Rhône Valley. And what a brilliant decision that was! Now Jade Mountain is making wines of real distinction that in blind tastings can easily be mistaken for Rhône originals.

This Rhône/Bandol lookalike is made from seventy-year-old Mourvèdre vines that produce a saturated purple/black color and an intense aroma of lavender, spice, and leather reminiscent of the Provençal countryside—warm and slightly wild. It is soft-textured and plump with luscious fruit and great balance. And there's enough acidity to keep the concentration of flavor from becoming too heavy. Jade Mountain's La Provençale, made from a blend of Mourvèdre and Syrah, is also worth trying.

Food match: Civet de sanglier (casserole of wild boar); shell steak

M. CHAPOUTIER, SAINT-JOSEPH ROUGE 1990, RHÔNE, FRANCE, $20

Saint-Joseph is the second largest appellation in the northern Rhône after Crozes-Hermitages, covering an area on the west side of the Rhône from just south of Condrieu to about thirty miles south of Cornas. The reds are made from Syrah (as at Hermitage, Côte Rôtie, and the other great reds of the northern Rhône); in fact Saint-Joseph is a more rustic and lighter version of Hermitage.

Chapoutier, founded in 1808, is one of the largest vineyards in the northern Rhône, but in spite of its illustrious past it's one of the most progressive domaines, thanks largely to Michel and Marc Chapoutier, who have taken over the business from their father, Max. They farm their vineyards organically and are very concerned with biodynamic viticulture.

This wine is deep purple, almost black. The nose promises a mouthful of rich, full-bodied, chewy wine with its aromas of jam, spice, and herbs. It doesn't disappoint. In a blind tasting I could have mistaken it for a Hermitage.

Food match: Venison or lamb stew

MARIETTA, OLD VINE RED LOT NO. 16, SONOMA COUNTY N.V., SONOMA COUNTY, CALIFORNIA, U.S.A., $9

If you like chunky, mouth-filling wines that make up for their lack of finesse with truckloads of rich, ripe juicy wine and a punch of alcohol, then this is for you. It is a melange of everything growing in the vineyard, in this case Cabernet Sauvignon, Zinfandel, and Petite Sirah. The color is garnet and the nose is full of spicy, jammy, blackberry fruit. In the mouth it is sweet and plummy, bursting with flavor. There is not much length to the finish but so much wallop up front that you probably won't care too much.

Food match: Beef stew; lamb steaks

MARTINELLI, ZINFANDEL JACKASS HILL RESERVE 1993, RUSSIAN RIVER, CALIFORNIA, U.S.A., $19

Jackass Hill? Well, you would have to be a jackass to attempt farming on the steep slopes of this Russian River property. In fact practically no one is foolhardy enough even to try driving a tractor here!

Old man Martinelli will do it, but then he knows that this is the source of some of the best Zinfandel in California. The old vines and dry soil result in minuscule yields but also wines of extraordinary concentration and intensity. The winemaker is Helen Turley of Marcassin fame, one of the hottest consultants in California.

The wine is almost black with purple highlights. The nose is dense and smoky, with hints of ripe mulberry, plums, anise, and pepper. The palate is equally intense, but the balancing acidity keeps it from going over the top.

Food match: Stuffed shoulder of lamb

PENFOLDS, CABERNET SAUVIGNON SHIRAZ BIN 389 1990, SOUTH AUSTRALIA, $15

Established in 1844, Penfolds is not only one of Australia's oldest wineries but probably its most famous. Their Grange Hermitage Bin 95 (created by Max Schubert in the 1950s) has been called the only Australian Cabernet to match the *premiers crus classés* of Bordeaux. Schubert died in 1994, and his mantle has passed to the current winemaker, John Duval.

The blend of this Cabernet/Shiraz (Shiraz is the Syrah of Rhône fame) varies each year, but Cabernet is always the dominant partner. The 1990 is a 70/30 percent blend. It has a deep, almost opaque color with a saturated nose of cassis, jam, pepper, and chocolate. A sumptuous wine, richly textured, satisfying, and classy.

Food match: Roast leg of lamb; filet mignon

PESQUERA, RIBERA DEL DUERO CRIANZA 1991, RIBERA DEL DUERO, SPAIN, $20

The owner of Pesquera, Alejandro Fernandez, has been making outstanding wines with great concentrated flavor since the early

1980s, when he introduced such techniques as partial destemming and aging in French as well as American oak barrels. He, along with Vega Sicilia, has made Ribera del Duero one of the hottest wine-producing regions of Spain.

The 1991 *crianza* (denoting red wine at least two years old, of which one year is spent in barrel) is made from 100 percent Tempranillo, and is probably one of the best *crianzas* you can buy. It has a deep color (almost black) with a smoky, roasted cocoa nose that shows immense concentration and a dense, chewy palate, well structured yet supple. A big wine, definitely not for the faint-hearted!

Food match: Grilled steak and grilled lamb chops; blue-veined cheeses, like Roquefort or Forme d'Ambert

QUILCEDA CREEK VINTNERS, CABERNET SAUVIGNON 1991, WASHINGTON STATE, U.S.A., $30

Those unfamiliar with the wines of Washington State have a wonderful journey of exploration ahead of them. Some of the best Cabernet Sauvignons and Merlots in the nation are being made here, with most of the wineries located along the Yakima and Columbia River valleys. There is also some very exciting Sauvignon Blanc and Sémillon to be found.

Quilceda Creek Vintners (about twenty-five miles north of Seattle overlooking the Cascade Mountains) was founded by the Golitzen family in 1978, and they have dedicated their entire production to Cabernet Sauvignon. With output limited to only one thousand cases per year, this is a rare wine but well worth the effort to find it.

The saturated opaque purple hue suggests a wine of great concentration and power. The rich, full palate is delineated and focused by intense, pure, concentrated fruit and ripe, firm tannins, and its mineral nose is nuanced with hints of cassis and currants. In brief, this is a world-class Cabernet that can go against the best of California and Bordeaux.

Food match: A great cut of grilled steak or roast duck

QUINTA DA AVELEDA, CHARAMBA 1992, DOURO, PORTUGAL, $6

The Douro region of northern Portugal takes its name from the great river along whose banks are the vineyards that produce the country's most famous wine, Port. At their best, Douro red table wines can be packed with red berry flavors, as though a ruby Port had been crossed with a young Bordeaux. This dry red uses three of the classic grapes found in Port (which can be a blend of up to ninety varieties): Tinta Roriz (the Tempranillo of Spain, particularly Rioja), Tinta Barroca (which contributes a robust, earthy character), and Touriga Francesa (smooth and aromatic). This wine is obviously made in a modern style, in which it is bottled early to maintain the freshness of the fruit. (So many Portuguese and Spanish wines dry out from overaging in wood.)

Charamba is a deep garnet/ruby with an aroma of roasted nuts, coffee, anise, and plum pudding. It is thick and full on the palate with a round, velvety texture and real character. This is a luscious wine, and if Charamba doesn't make you wanna rumba, nothing will.

Food match: Oxtail stew; hamburgers

QUINTA DE LAGOALVA DE CIMA 1992, RIBATEJO, PORTUGAL, $9

The magic touch is applied once again by consulting enologist João Portugal Ramos (Casal da Tonda, Quinta de Pancas). The vineyards are in the Ribatejo region in east central Portugal, just south of the Tagus river. The grapes in this blend are Periquita and Touriga Naçional, one of the primary grapes found in Port wine. Like many of the new-style dry Portuguese wines, this one emphasizes rich ripe fruit flavors and balance but with its own varietal and regional personality.

This wine has a black-currant mulberry aroma with hints of smoke and cocoa. On the palate it is ripe and sweet tasting with dense chewy texture and a soft rounded finish.

Food match: Roasted flavorful fowl such as duck, goose, and quail

QUPÉ, SANTA BARBARA COUNTY SYRAH, BIEN NACIDO VINEYARD 1992, CALIFORNIA, U.S.A., $23

Qupé is owned by Bob Lindquist, one of the original "Rhône Rangers," a group of Californian winemakers, including Randall Grahm of Bonny Doon and Steve Edmunds of Edmund St. John, who specialize in classic Rhône grapes: principally Syrah, Grenache, Mourvèdre, Marsanne, Roussane, and Viognier. Bob Lindquist founded the winery in 1982 and is a close friend and collaborator of Jim Clendenon of Au Bon Climat in the Vita Nova Winery.

The best of Qupé's Syrah comes from the Bien Nacido Vineyard, Santa Barbara County, and this 1992 has an explosive, spicy, peppery, and herbal nose. The fruit is rich, full, and satisfying. Although it is ready to drink now, and very pleasurably so, a few years more in bottle would certainly be rewarded.

Food match: Grilled sausages; lamb steaks

RAVENSWOOD, ZINFANDEL 1993, SONOMA, CALIFORNIA, U.S.A., $14

Ampelographers (those who trace the origins of grapes) are a bit stumped by the origin of Zinfandel, suggesting that it may have come from the Primitivo grape of Apulia in Italy. It appears to have been first planted in California around the middle of the last century by the great Hungarian winemaker Count Agoston Haraszthy, who was responsible for introducing many of the European vinifera varietals to the New World.

Zinfandel can produce wines of incredible value because it does not have the cachet of Cabernet or Merlot yet can deliver almost equal quality. It is also very versatile, manifesting itself in the rosé of "white" Zinfandel, as well as straight red wine. The best examples, such as this Ravenswood, are deep red with a blackberry bramble nose and rich, spicy fruit bolstered with moderate tannins.

Food match: Grilled meat such as shell steak, marinated butterflied leg of lamb

RIDGE VINEYARDS, GEYSERVILLE 1993, SANTA CRUZ MOUNTAINS, CALIFORNIA, U.S.A., $22

A little-known fact is that the Santa Cruz area has some of the oldest vineyards in the state. The Monte Bello Ridge was terraced in 1885, and until Prohibition there were thirty-nine wineries in the area. By repeal, though, few had managed to survive and it wasn't until the 1950s that the success of the Martin Ray winery began to attract attention to the area. Ridge Vineyards was founded in 1962 and is now ranked one of California's best.

Paul Draper, CEO and chief winemaker at Ridge, makes some of the most intesely flavored wines in the state. His Ridge Monte Bello Cabernet Sauvignon is justly famous, but he also has a big reputation for his other wines, notably Zinfandel. Although the Geyserville tasted here is mostly Zinfandel, it doesn't have the necessary 75 percent to allow it to be sold as a varietal. It's a blend of about 65 percent Zinfandel, 20 percent Carignan, and 15 percent Petite Sirah. More than half of the vineyard that supplied the grapes is planted with vines 113 years old, and the concentration and intensity of flavor from their juice is fabulous.

This wine is a deep saturated purple, almost black. The nose bursts with grape, pepper, chocolate, and cassis aromas. It is lush and full on the palate and simply oozing with ripe, concentrated, spicy fruit. This is so wickedly delicious it's probably illegal in twenty-five states!

Food match: Roast kidneys à la Bordelaise; steak with marchand du vin sauce

SEQUOIA GROVE, CABERNET SAUVIGNON 1991, NAPA VALLEY, CALIFORNIA, U.S.A., $18

Sequoia Grove, close to Napa's famed Rutherford Bench, the heart of California's Cabernet country, was founded in 1980 by brothers Jim and Steve Allen (they also bought a 138-acre plot in Carneros for Chardonnay and Pinot Noir, now owned by the French Champagne house of Taittinger, which uses it to make sparkling wine).

The Allens' specialty is Cabernet Sauvignon, and one taste of this wine proves why this is so. It is a deep ruby purple with beautiful red reflections. The nose is of ripe black cherries with toasty, chocolate nuances. The palate is full and lush with a soft, comforting finish—like a warm blanket!

Food match: Roasted lamb chops; roast duck

SHAFER, CABERNET SAUVIGNON STAG'S LEAP DISTRICT HILLSIDE SELECT 1989, NAPA VALLEY, CALIFORNIA, U.S.A., $35

Shafer vineyards was established in 1979, although Shafer had been making wines elsewhere since 1972. Of their two Cabernet offerings (regular Stag's Leap District being the other, less intensely flavored), the Hillside Select comes, as you might expect, from the hills above the Napa Valley in its cooler southern third. Possibly because of the better drainage and drier soil of these slopes and/or the lower yields, the wines have a firm structure.

The Hillside Select has a saturated ruby/black color with a brooding nose of black fruit, licorice, and smoke. On the palate it is intense with ripe, sweet fruit, great concentration, and focused flavors.

Food match: Grilled shell steak

SOCIEDAD COOPERATIVA AGRICOLA LIMITADA DE BORJA, BORSAO 1994, CAMPO DE BORJA, SPAIN, $5

Campo de Borja is a small DO in northern Spain west of Zaragoza and near Navarra. The red grape of favor is Garnacha but its plantings are being reduced in favor of the more elegant Tempranillo. This wine produced at the Coop is proof that not only estate-grown wines are the best quality and value. And often Coop wines are less expensive because they produce greater volumes and have the financial support from an entire community and not just one winemaker.

This wine is a blend of Garnacha (50 percent), Tempranillo (30 percent), and Cabernet Sauvignon (20 percent). This remarkable wine for the money is a youthful black purple (partly due to a partial carbonic maceration), and has the aroma of crushed ripe strawberries and black cherries. It has crunchy, ripe, sweet-tasting fruit with full, deep, earthy flavors.

Food match: Roast kidneys; grilled sausages; strong-flavored cheeses

STELTZNER, CABERNET SAUVIGNON STAG'S LEAP DISTRICT 1990, NAPA VALLEY, CALIFORNIA, U.S.A., $19

In 1966 Dick Steltzner was one of the first to plant grapes in the Stag's Leap District, although he didn't start making wine until 1977. The area is one mile long and three miles wide on the Silverado Trail, and it's committed Cabernet country. In fact, in two famous (infamous if you're a Bordeaux winemaker) blind-tasting competitions (1976 and 1986) Stag's Leap Cabernet outperformed topflight Bordeaux.

Because the vines are some of the oldest in Stag's Leap, the wine has an amazing richness and complexity. There's ripe, black fruit, plumminess, and a lusciousness wrapped up in velvet-soft, ripe tannins.

Food match: Veal chops; sauté of wild mushrooms

VALLANA, SPANNA DEL PIEMONTE 1983, PIEDMONT, ITALY, $10

Spanna is the name given to the Nebbiolo grape in northern Piedmont. The vineyards in the provinces of Vercelli and Novara are the home of seven small DOCs, the most famous of which are Ghemme and Gattinara. In the middle of the last century, Gattinara was considered better and longer lived than Barolo. So the potential is there, yet as trends go, the glamour is now in Barolo. Perhaps because of this shifting fashion, the wines of northern Piedmont can offer terrific value.

This one from Vallana doesn't come from one of the DOCs. It is simply a red table wine. It has a table wine price tag but a more noble appellation's character. It has all the smoky, leathery aroma of a well-aged Nebbiolo. Slightly raisiny and earthy. On the palate it is fully mature with fully resolved tannins and a forceful, deeply flavored finish.

Food match: Osso buco; roast leg of lamb; roast duck

WHITEHALL LANE,
MERLOT KNIGHTS VALLEY 1992,
SONOMA COUNTY, CALIFORNIA, U.S.A., $17

Merlot is definitely gaining in popularity with wine drinkers. Its softer tannins and lush, supple flavors make it more accessible in its youth and more versatile with food than harder, larger-structured Cabernet Sauvignon.

Gary Galleron (who is also the talented winemaker of one of California's most-sought-after Cabernets at the tiny Grace Family Vineyards in the Napa Valley) has created a real beauty with fruit from one of the oldest vineyards in Knights Valley, a warm and protected enclave on the borders of Napa (although officially a Sonoma AVA, Knights Valley is really an extension of the Napa Valley just north of Calistoga).

Deep purple with a spicy, anise/minty nose; big-framed with jammy, black cherrylike fruit of superb intensity and concentration.

Food match: Prime ribs of beef; soft cheeses like Brie and Camembert

MEDIUM-BODIED REDS

This is a checklist of wines for which tasting notes follow.

Adega Cooperativa de Portalegre, Portalegre VQPRD 1992, Alentejo, Portugal, $6 (p. 208)

Antinori, Chianti Classico Riserva 1990, Tuscany, Italy, $22 (p. 208)

Bodegas y Cavas de Weinert, Carrascal 1988, Mendoza, Argentina, $12 (p. 209)

Brovia, Nebbiolo d'Alba Valmaggione 1990, Piedmont, Italy, $16 (p. 209)

Casal de Tonda, Dão 1990, Dão, Portugal, $8 (p. 210)

Castello di Monte Antico, Monte Antico Rosso 1990, Tuscany, Italy, $7 (p. 211)

Château Charmail, Haut-Médoc 1992, Bordeaux, France, $12 (p. 211)

Château Clos du Marquis 1991, Saint-Julien, Bordeaux, France, $18 (p. 212)

Château Greysac, Médoc 1990, Bordeaux, France, $10 (p. 213)

Château Jonqueyres, Bordeaux Supérieur 1990, Bordeaux, France, $12 (p. 213)

Château Phélan-Ségur 1991, Saint-Estèphe, Bordeaux, France, $13 (p. 214)

Cosimo Taurino, Salice Salentino Riserva 1990, Apulia, Italy, $9 (p. 214)

Cune, Rioja Viña Gran Reserva 1987, Rioja, Spain, $20 (p. 215)

Deux Amis Zinfandel 1993, Sonoma County, California, U.S.A., $14 (p. 216)

Domaine Comte Georges de Vogüé, Chambolle-Musigny 1993, Burgundy, France, $45 (p. 216)

Domaine de Gournier, Merlot Vin de Pays des Cevennes 1993, Languedoc, France, $7 (p. 217)

Domaine de la Pousse d'Or, Bourgogne Rouge 1993, Burgundy, France, $12 (p. 217)

Domaine G. Roumier, Morey-Saint-Denis Clos de la Bussière 1992, Burgundy, France, $28 (p. 218)

Domaine Jean Grivot, Vosne-Romanée 1992, Burgundy, France, $25 (p. 218)

Domaine Sainte-Anne, Côtes du Rhône-Villages 1992, Rhône, France, $11 (p. 219)

Domaine Simon Bize, Savigny-les-Beaune, Les Vergelesses 1993, Burgundy, France, $22 (p. 220)

Domaine Vincent Girardin, Maranges 1er Cru 1993, Burgundy, France, $18 (p. 220)

Edmunds St. John, New World Red 1993, California, U.S.A., $10 (p. 221)

Elyse, Zinfandel Napa Valley Marisoli Vineyard 1992, California, U.S.A., $17 (p. 221)

Georges Duboeuf, Moulin-à-Vent Domaine des Rosiers 1994, Beaujolais, France, $12 (p. 222)

Giacomo Conterno Barbera d'Alba 1993, Piedmont, Italy, $18 (p. 223)

Gilbert Alquier et Fils, AOC Faugères 1991, Languedoc, France, $11 (p. 223)

Grasso, Dolcetto d'Alba 1993, Piedmont, Italy, $13 (p. 224)

Havens, Merlot Carneros, Napa Valley Truchard Vineyard 1992, California, U.S.A., $18 (p. 224)

Jacky Janodet, Moulin-à-Vent 1993, Beaujolais, France, $15 (p. 225)

José Maria da Fonseca, Periquita 1990, Setubal, Portugal, $7 (p. 225)

José Maria da Fonseca, Terra Atlas 1990, Dão, Portugal, $7 (p. 226)

José Sousa, Rosado Fernandes Garrafeira 1990, Alentejo, Portugal, $15 (p. 227)

Manzone, Barbera d'Alba 1991, Piedmont, Italy, $12 (p. 227)

Marqués de Murrieta Gran Reserva 1988, Rioja, Spain, $13.50 (p. 228)

Marquis d'Angerville, Volnay Premier Cru 1992, Burgundy, France, $20 (p. 229)

Mateus, Signature Vinho Tinto 1990, Douro, Portugal, $7.50
(p. 229)

Navarro Correas, Malbec 1991, Mendoza, Argentina, $11
(p. 230)

Onix, Priorat 1992, Catalonia, Spain, $12 (p. 231)

Paul Garaudet, Monthélie-les-Duresses 1992, Burgundy, France,
$20 (p. 231)

Ponzi, Pinot Noir Willamette Valley Reserve 1992, Oregon,
U.S.A., $32 (p. 232)

Quinta de Pancas, Cabernet Sauvignon 1991, Alenquer, Portugal, $9 (p. 232)

La Rioja Alta, Viña Ardanza Reserva 1987, Rioja, Spain, $20
(p. 233)

Rosemount Estate, Shiraz 1993, New South Wales, Australia, $9
(p. 233)

Solis Merlot 1993, Santa Clara, California, U.S.A., $12 (p. 234)

Terrabianca, Chianti Classico Scassino 1993, Tuscany, Italy, $12
(p. 234)

Terra Rosa, Cabernet Sauvignon 1994, California, U.S.A., $12
(p. 235)

La Torre, Rosso di Montalcino 1991, Tuscany, Italy, $13 (p. 236)

Trapiche, Malbec Mendoza Oak Cask Reserve 1990, Mendoza,
Argentina, $8 (p. 237)

Truchard, Merlot Carneros Napa Valley 1991, California,
U.S.A., $22 (p. 238)

La Vieille Ferme, Le Mont Côtes du Ventoux 1992, Vaucluse,
France, $6 (p. 238)

Viña Mayor, Tinto Crianza 1990, Ribera del Duero Catalonia,
　Spain, $8 (p. 239)
Winterbrook, Cabernet Sauvignon 1991, Napa County, Califor-
　nia, U.S.A., $10 (p. 239)

ADEGA COOPERATIVA DE PORTALEGRE, PORTALEGRE VQPRD 1992, ALENTEJO, PORTUGAL, $6

In addition to being a winery, Portalegre is the name of a town
and an IPR (Índicacões de Provenciência Regulamentada, see
page 121) in the Alentejo province of southern Portugal (an area
of up-and-coming wines and also the provider of about half of the
world's wine corks).

Made from the Tinta Amarela grape (also known as the Trincadeira and one of the grapes authorized for Port), this wine is a
beautiful purple/violet with an aroma of violets and lavender. The
soft, broad palate is of cherry and spice.

Food match: Grilled sausages or hamburger

ANTINORI, CHIANTO CLASSICO RISERVA 1990, TUSCANY, ITALY, $22

Antinori is to Tuscan wine what General Motors is to Detroit.
The family tree has roots that extend back over six hundred years
and twenty-six generations of winemakers; the remarkable thing
is that despite this grounding in tradition the house is still dedicated to innovation.

Since Sangiovese is a temperamental grape that responds best
to a warm and dry growing season, it is inclined to be inconsistent. If the weather isn't accommodating the results can be disap-
pointing. Antinori overcomes this by making the *riserva* only
from outstanding vintages.

The nose is dense with ripe black cherry and dusty floral

notes. On the palate it is concentrated and rich, with a smooth mouth-feel and excellent balance.

Food match: Veal chops; bistecca fiorentina, of course

BODEGAS Y CAVAS DE WEINERT, CARRASCAL 1988, MENDOZA, ARGENTINA, $12

I remember very clearly my first taste of Weinert wine. In 1993 a group of us were invited to a Christmas luncheon hosted by the wine critic Robert Parker Jr. He proceeded to serve his unsuspecting guests forty wines over the course of five hours. The name of the game was a blind tasting of wines from only two countries, one of which I knew was to be France. After tasting the likes of Haut-Brion 1959, Hermitage La Chapelle 1961, and some truly great Pomerols, we started to wonder which other country could produce a noble and elegant wine that could hold its own in such regal company. It turned out to be a Weinert Malbec 1977, and I've been a believer ever since.

The Carrascal 1988 is a blend of Malbec, Merlot, and Cabernet Sauvignon from old, low-yielding vines. The result is a very substantial wine with concentrated fruit, a spicy, currant nose, and medium weight. It is smooth and elegant on the palate, somewhat like a middle-aged Bordeaux, possibly a Saint-Émilion. For $12 or thereabouts the Carrascal is great value.

Food match: Roast birds such as duck, guinea hen, squab

BROVIA, NEBBIOLO D'ALBA VALMAGGIONE 1990, PIEDMONT, ITALY, $16

Nebbiolo is the grape of Barolo and Barbaresco, both famous for their power and longevity but the high levels of acid and tannin needed for their ageability do not make them candidates for early drinking. This Nebbiolo, however, is enjoyable in its youth. It's made from 100 percent Nebbiolo that is grown just outside the Barolo and Barbaresco appellations, so it shares some of its more famous neighbors' characteristics: chewy, satisfying, and big hearted.

This Brovia Nebbiolo has an immediately seductive open nose of strawberry jam and smoke. It is round and full on the palate with ripe, sweet-tasting fruit, concentrated and soft-textured with a firm, tannic finish.

Food match: Grilled steak; wild mushroom tart

CASAL DE TONDA, DÃO 1990, DÃO, PORTUGAL, $8

Located in the Dão region near the county of Tondela, this winery was founded by Manuel Ferraz da Costa in 1988. Mr. Ferraz da Costa is passionate about his wines and his region and was determined to use traditional grape varieties rather than go for an

"international" style based on Cabernet Sauvignon, for example. In this he has been very ably abetted by his consultant, João Portugal Ramos, perhaps the best winemaker in Portugal.

When I first tasted this wine I was bowled over by the intensity and complexity of the aroma. Was there a mistake on the price? Surely it should be in the twenty-five-dollar range because it was one of the most compelling and exciting wines I've tasted in a long time. It smells of caraway, black pepper, and cassis with an old-vine character. The palate is full, with dense ripe fruit held together by its strong tannins. And read my lips: "Eight bucks"!

Food match: Mild hard and soft cheeses; roast chicken

CASTELLO DI MONTE ANTICO, MONTE ANTICO ROSSO 1990, TUSCANY, ITALY, $7

For lovers of the Sangiovese grape (the main ingredient of Chianti and Brunello di Montalcino and, after Barbera, the most widely planted variety in Italy), this is a super example and a fantastic value. Monte Antico falls just outside the boundaries of the Brunello di Montalcino DOC and therefore can carry only a proprietory name, but it's made from 100 percent Sangiovese and makes a great stand-in for either Chianti or Brunello. The color is a satisfyingly deep ruby, and there's a ripe blackberry/cassis nose with smooth, rounded fruit and a pleasant, harmonious finish. If anything it lacks a little pizzazz, but what a wine for the money!

Food match: Bistecca fiorentina; veal chop

CHÂTEAU CHARMAIL, HAUT-MÉDOC 1992, BORDEAUX, FRANCE, $12

Charmail is a *cru bourgeois* (see page 85 for more details on this classification) property close to the much better known Château

Sociando-Mallet in the Haut-Médoc next to Saint-Estèphe. The lesser-known appellations of the region are receiving more and more attention because the gap in quality between them and the more expensive classed growths is narrowing. At Charmail there is rigorous selection in both the vineyard and the winery to ensure that only the best lots are chosen for the Château Charmail label, with secondary vats being used for their second label, Château Saint-Seurin.

This wine is made up of about 50 percent Merlot, 30 percent Cabernet Sauvignon, and 20 percent Cabernet Franc. It has a plummy, blackberry nose with notes of cedar and cinnamon. The palate is refreshing, soft, smooth, and forward but at its core there is intensely flavored fruit.

Food match: Lamb chops; root vegetable stews

CHÂTEAU CLOS DU MARQUIS 1991, SAINT-JULIEN, BORDEAUX, FRANCE, $18

Always worth looking for, this second label from Château Léoville-Las-Cases represents a suggestion of what the *grand vin* tastes like for a portion of the price. As usual, the second label of a château is comprised of lots of wine that didn't make the final blend. I've selected this wine to demonstrate how the expertise of a master winemaker can turn out a top-notch wine in what is generally considered a mediocre vintage. This wine is proof that we should not become so obsessed with vintages.

The wine is moderately deep in color with a ruby core. Ripe plummy fruit with nuances of minerals and smoke give this wine an attractive nose. On the palate it is soft and supple, with gentle fruit and modest concentration making it immediately pleasurable.

Food match: Roast duck or pheasant

CHÂTEAU GREYSAC, MÉDOC 1990, BORDEAUX, FRANCE, $10

Those looking for a good, reliable Bordeaux couldn't do much better at this price. A great deal of care goes into the production of Greysac, which makes it a standout *cru bourgeois* (see page 85).

Deep ruby with a nose suggestive of plums and currants and a touch of toasty oak. The soft and generous palate and smooth texture are probably due to the substantial percentage of Merlot (40 percent) to Cabernet Sauvignon (60 percent).

Food match: Broiled sirloin steak; hamburgers

CHÂTEAU JONQUEYRES, BORDEAUX SUPÉRIEUR 1990, BORDEAUX, FRANCE, $12

Entre-Deux-Mers (the region of Bordeaux between the Garonne and Dordogne rivers, from which this wine comes) gives its appellation to white wines only; the reds have to be sold as either Bordeaux or Bordeaux Supérieur. Their enforced anonymity may be tough on the growing number of red-wine producers in the region, but it's great for those of us in search of good-value wine, as much of it can outclass more famous "named" châteaux. And Jean-Michel Arcaute, the owner of Jonqueyres, has made a truly superior red by any standards. To find a Bordeaux with 75 percent Merlot/25 percent Cabernet Sauvignon of this caliber and at this price is a true coup. Here is real "flavor per dollar"!

The wine is deep ruby/purple with a powerful nose that promises a dense, concentrated taste. It does not disappoint with its luscious, supple flavors and soft, ripe tannins. The finish is silky and moderately long.

Food match: Roast lamb or sautéed veal medallions with mushrooms

CHÂTEAU PHÉLAN-SÉGUR 1991,
SAINT-ESTÈPHE, BORDEAUX, FRANCE, $13

Phélan-Ségur is officially classified as a *cru grand bourgeois exceptionnel* (see page 86 for more details on this category) but it has the potential to be ranked as one of the best properties in Saint-Estèphe. Its vineyards border those of Montrose and Calon-Ségur and its relatively new (1985) ownership is committed to making wines of character and breeding.

1991 was a very difficult vintage in Bordeaux. There was a terrible frost in the spring that destroyed many vines in bud, and the fall saw several torrential rainstorms add to the misery. That fact that Phélan-Ségur still produced good wines in 1991 is a testament to the skill of its winemakers and proves you cannot buy wine guided only by vintage charts.

This wine has a moderately deep ruby color and an open, fruity, cedary/spicy nose. The palate is soft, with spiced cherries and plums; the tannins are soft, and the finish is silky. Delicious to drink now.

Food match: Veal or pork chops; roast chicken; grilled salmon with red-wine sauce

COSIMO TAURINO, SALICE SALENTINO
RISERVA 1990, APULIA, ITALY, $9

Apulia is the heel of the Italian boot, and the Salento peninsula is at the tip of the heel. Apulia produces a massive amount of wine (three times as much as the whole of Chile, for example, but less now that wine consumption in Italy, as elsewhere, has dropped) and much of it was used as blending or industrial alcohol. The climate is unrelentingly hot, and many of the wines are highly alcoholic (sometimes as much as 18 percent!) and clumsy, but the Salento, the best wine area of the whole region, benefits from breezes off both the Adriatic and Ionian seas and enjoys desert-like cool nights. This prolongs the growing season and helps keep up good acid levels in the grapes, always a problem in very hot climates. In the hands of producers such as Cosimo Taurino the wines have power but also elegance and grace.

At first whiff one is drawn in and intrigued by this wine. It smells excitingly vibrant, with a penetrating aroma of Kirsch, raspberry, currants, violets, and leather. The flavor is pure, with elegance and balance. A great carafe wine. Delicious!

Food match: Barbecued sausage and steak

CUNE, RIOJA VIÑA REAL GRAN RESERVA 1987, RIOJA, SPAIN, $20

My first visit to Cune (officially CVNE, standing for Compañia Vinicola del Norte de España, founded in 1879 by the Real de Asua brothers, whose family still owns it) was one of the most pleasurable of my trips to Spain. At first the place is a little off-putting, industrially sterile (the sort of place, I thought, where Franco might have come on weekends). But that feeling soon gave way when my hosts, who have a tremendous pride in their vineyards and traditions, and I started tasting and talking about wines. Later, over dinner, all the barriers of culture, age, and language dropped. We were on common ground.

Cune has a stellar reputation for its quality wines and, in addition to the *viña real gran reserva*, also makes a *clarete, crianza, reserva*, and *imperial gran reserva* (as well as a white Rioja and, from another property, the classy Contino).

The *viña real gran reserva* is ripe and seductive. There's concentration and intensity as well as a smoky, meaty quality to it. Absolutely delicious now.

Food match: Grilled lamb chops marinated in olive oil and herbs

DEUX AMIS ZINFANDEL 1993,
SONOMA COUNTY, CALIFORNIA, U.S.A., $14

Zinfandel is a temperamental grape variety. The grape bunch tends to ripen unevenly, which creates a real challenge for the winemaker. Timing is everything, and if he or she chooses to pick late, many of the grapes may be overripe, even shriveled like raisins, creating a sweet, Port-like Zinfandel with a lot of alcohol. On the other hand, if the grapes are picked too soon, the wine will be thin and tart. It is therefore essential to grow the grape variety in a relatively cool but sunny area. Sonoma County has many such vineyard locations.

Deux Amis has struck the right chord in producing a wine that is deeply colored, with a ripe black cherry, brambly aroma with nuances of Kirsch and chocolate. It has luscious ripe, concentrated flavors, bright tones, and lovely balancing acidity to keep it from tasting flabby and jammy.

Food match: Roast duck; cassoulet

DOMAINE COMTE GEORGES DE VOGÜÉ,
CHAMBOLLE-MUSIGNY 1993,
BURGUNDY, FRANCE, $45

This domaine has been in the de Vogüé family since 1450—nineteen unbroken generations! Needless to say it is the standard-bearer for the wines of the village of Chambolle-Musigny as well as being the largest proprietor of *grand cru* Musigny. The wines from Chambolle, highly aromatic, complex, and capable of great longevity, are known for their finesse and power—an iron fist in a velvet glove.

This Chambolle is simply the village wine unadorned with *premier* or *grand cru* status. However, the final blend before bottling contains a percentage of Musigny (usually from young vines or barrels) that just didn't have the right style for the *grand cru*.

The nose is seductive, with roasted, smoky, and ripe black cherry aromas. The palate is fat and rich, with plump, mouth-filling fruit and a wonderful silky texture; the color, a gorgeous ruby—a great Burgundy!

Food match: Roast pheasant or squab, or a mild hard cheese

DOMAINE DE GOURNIER, MERLOT VIN DE PAYS DES CEVENNES 1993, LANGUEDOC, FRANCE, $7

It seems to me that just about any *vin de pays* is worth trying these days. Many producers are experimenting with grape varieties not traditionally grown in their areas, in much the same way Tuscan winemakers did to produce "super-Tuscans." Not all French *vins de pays* may be of "super" caliber, but many of the varietal wines from the south of France give tremendous flavor per dollar for short-term drinking. Most are inexpensive, so there is plenty of incentive to experiment.

Gournier's Merlot is deep ruby with purple highlights and has a ripe-plum-jam nose with hints of chocolate. It is decidedly velvety and luscious with very soft tannins.

Food match: Lamb chops; tuna steak

DOMAINE DE LA POUSSE D'OR, BOURGOGNE ROUGE 1993, BURGUNDY, FRANCE, $12

Pousse d'Or is not only one of the great estates of Volnay but also of the whole of Burgundy. Its history can be traced back to the fifteenth-century dukes of Burgundy and it's still going strong producing wines from Santenay, Pommard, and, of course, Volnay, where its most important vineyards are located. The highest standards are applied by Gerard Potel, the owner, to all their wines, not least the simple (yet not so simple) Bourgogne Rouge. The wine comes from grapes grown in an old vineyard that used to be classified Pommard, and its meaty character is evidence of a higher breeding. There's no doubting that this is real red Burgundy.

The deep color suggests a rich, concentrated wine, and the nose's plummy, smoky aromas prepare the palate for a wine of substance. It tastes soft and full, delivering what it promised.

Food match: Roast chicken, mashed potatoes and mushroom sauce

DOMAINE G. ROUMIER, MOREY-SAINT-DENIS CLOS DE LA BUSSIÈRE 1992, BURGUNDY, FRANCE, $28

Although the wine mentioned here is from a small vineyard in Morey-Saint-Denis owned exclusively by the Roumier family, most of this domaine's production is from the vineyards of Chambolle-Musigny just south of Morey. The wines made by Christophe Roumier are always reliable for full flavor and finesse, but this vineyard seems to turn out wines of great depth of character for its *premier cru* appellation, thereby bringing it up to a level with wines carrying a bigger price tag.

It has a deep ruby color with a ripe berry nose and earthy tones. Full on the palate with a certain meaty texture—a wine of presence and persistence.

Food match: Boeuf bourguignon

DOMAINE JEAN GRIVOT, VOSNE-ROMANÉE 1992, BURGUNDY, FRANCE, $25

This wonderful old estate in the village of Vosne-Romanée is now being managed by the strong-willed and confident Etienne

Grivot. With no fewer than fifteen appellations to vinify (three of which are *grand cru*) between Nuits-Saint-Georges, Vosne-Romanée, Vougeot, Flagey, and Chambolle-Musigny, he has his hands full. This is the village that is home to Domaine de la Romanée-Conti and to the vineyards that many consider to be the best in all of Burgundy.

Grivot's Vosne-Romanée is a perfect example of how seductive Pinot Noir and the wines from Vosne-Romanée can be, a uniquely velvety texture on the palate combined with richness of flavor. It is this seamless expression combined with a smoky, earthy, black cherry aroma that makes this wine irresistible.

Food match: Roasted pheasant with a ragout of mushrooms

DOMAINE SAINTE-ANNE, CÔTES DU RHÔNE-VILLAGES 1992, RHÔNE, FRANCE, $11

Although most of the villages that are allowed to attach their name to the appellation Côtes du Rhône are located on the river's east bank, Domaine Saint-Anne is on the west bank at high altitude near Saint-Gervais. I think it makes some of the best wine in the Rhône Valley.

It's no wonder that this property isn't better known—it's a hike to get to! If you are starting from the east side of the river you have to travel quite a way just to find a bridge, and that's why I was about an hour late on my first visit. M. Stenmeier was very forgiving, however, and spent the rest of the day with me as I tasted through a range of his barrels. At the end of it I knew the journey had been worthwhile, and here was another gem to add to the collection.

Because of its higher elevation the wines of Domaine Sainte-Anne have more finesse and elegance than the big brooding reds from the Vaucluse across the river. But that's not to say they are wimpy wines; there is no lack of concentration and body.

The 1992 has an explosive nose of spice and pepper, with the hefty dose of Syrah very evident. It is well balanced with concentrated fruit coating the palate and leaving a long, pleasing aftertaste. This is a mouthful of delicious wine.

Food match: Beef stew, especially daube provençal

DOMAINE SIMON BIZE, SAVIGNY-LES-BEAUNE, LES VERGELESSES 1993, BURGUNDY, FRANCE, $22

This domaine, now run by Patrick Bize, is one of the most reliable in the village of Savigny. Although Patrick may be a shy type, his wines are far from it. They exude personality and warmth.

The village of Savigny-les-Beaune is located on the northern end of the Côte de Beaune. The *premier cru* vineyard Les Vergelesses tasted here is near the vineyards of Pernand-Vergelesses and Corton and shares some of the characteristics of the bigger-framed wines from the Côtes de Nuits. The vineyard site contributes to the wine's meaty, somewhat rustic character. With a deep color and ripe cherry smoky nose, it is mouth filling and sweet but displays plenty of structure with firm tannins and lively acidity.

Food match: Soft ripened cheese such as Brie or Camembert, sautéed chicken livers with bacon; hamburgers

DOMAINE VINCENT GIRARDIN, MARANGES 1ER CRU 1990, BURGUNDY, FRANCE, $18

Maranges is a collection of three villages at the southernmost end of the Côte de Beaune, about ten miles south of the town of Beaune. I've always remembered the names of these three villages—Cheilly, Dezize, and Sampigny—because for some odd reason they reminded me of the Three Stooges, Moe, Larry, and Curly. Though the association may be zany, the wine is anything but.

This red is 100 percent Pinot Noir and it tastes as good, if not better, than many of its more expensive neighbors to the north. The grapes come from old vines, which contribute intensity and an almost chewy quality. The nose is smoky and ripe with an aroma of raspberry, a great prelude to a rich mouthful of wine with good structure.

Food match: Dark-meat poultry; grilled salmon

EDMUNDS ST. JOHN, NEW WORLD RED 1993, CALIFORNIA, U.S.A., $10

The wines made by Steve Edmunds at Edmunds St. John are among the best examples of Rhône-style wines made in California. This "Rhône Ranger" definitely has the magic touch, producing wines that are fruity yet have a southern warmth as found in the wines of the southern Rhône valley. The blend here is mostly Mourvèdre at 75 percent with the remainder split almost equally between Grenache and Syrah.

The wine is ruby red with a slightly hazy, unfiltered aspect to it. It has a wonderful aroma of black currants, earth, leather, and spice. With sweet fruit, soft texture, and mild tannins, this wine is easy to drink or even quaff.

Food match: Hamburgers; grilled lamb sausages

ELYSE, ZINFANDEL NAPA VALLEY MARISOLI VINEYARD 1992, CALIFORNIA, U.S.A., $17

Elyse was established in 1987 by Nancy and Ray Coursen. It is in the heart of the Napa Valley in the magical Rutherford Bench,

alongside such internationally famous wineries as Beaulieu Vineyards, Inglenook, and Niebaum-Coppola. The Zinfandel from
the Marisoli Vineyard comes from vines planted in 1905, which
accounts for the wine's intensity of flavor and aroma.

The first time I tasted Elyse Zinfandel was at the end of a day-
long marathon of tasting about sixty wines. My palate was tired,
and I really wasn't much interested in tasting any more. However,
a persistent salesman talked me into trying another six, an assort-
ment of Chardonnays, Pinot Noirs, Sauvignon Blancs, and one
Zinfandel, the Elyse. The wine burst through my fatigue like a hot
shower and a change of clothes. My senses perked back up after
just one sniff of its compelling spicy/raspberry/strawberry aroma.
My palate was jump-started by the wine's intensity and liveliness.
Its medium- to full-bodied flavors were as explosive on the finish
as they had been on the entry. What a way to end the day!

Food match: Grilled or broiled lamb chops; steak; cheese; or simply on its own

GEORGES DUBOEUF, MOULIN-À-VENT DOMAINE DES ROSIERS 1994, BEAUJOLAIS, FRANCE, $12

Most people know the Duboeuf label as a guarantee of easy-
drinking Beaujolais that, although good and consistent, rarely has
exceptional character. That is only one level of the Duboeuf line,
however. Another, higher, level carries the name of a single estate
on the label. Duboeuf makes an enormous effort to find the best
small growers in the region and then bottles a finely crafted wine
of individual charm and character.

Moulin-à-Vent is the most serious of the Beaujolais *crus* (see
page 78 for more details), and the Domaine des Rosiers comes
from very old vines which give the wine a great richness and
power that you simply can't get in your everyday quaffing Beaujolais. This wine has a blackcurrant-jam aroma, with smoke and

spice nuances. On the palate it is full, smooth, and richly textured.

Food match: Coq-au-vin; pot-au-feu

GIACOMO CONTERNO BARBERA D'ALBA 1993, PIEDMONT, ITALY, $18

It was a hot night. We had just finished a delicious bottle of a light, zippy German Riesling and we wanted a different wine—this time red but in the same tone. If wine could be translated into music we were certainly playing a staccato passage. The tone was ethereal and high strung yet generous.

This red was perfect. It certainly had a deeper tone than the Riesling, but thanks to the wonderful crispness of the Barbera grape there was still the same tension and lightness that we loved in the white wine. It had the aroma of crushed ripe black cherries and pepper. On the palate it was richly textured, with a broad midpalate feel, yet it finished crisp and light.

Food match: Grilled swordfish; spaghetti and meatballs

GILBERT ALQUIER ET FILS, AOC FAUGÈRES 1991, LANGUEDOC, FRANCE, $11

Gilbert Alquier is one of the most respected winemakers in the Faugères appellation (a district due north of Béziers in the Languedoc) for his very classy Burgundy-style wines. He blends about 45 percent Syrah into his *cuvée,* along with the other classics of Rhône/Midi winemaking, Grenache, Carignan, and Mourvèdre.

The color is a vibrant red/purple and the aroma is beautiful: black cherries, anise, with a slight smokiness. On the palate it is sweet, richly textured, and thoroughly sensuous.

Food match: Omelets with herbs, mushrooms, and smoked duck; soft-ripened cheeses like Saint-Nectaire or Chaumes

GRASSO, DOLCETTO D'ALBA 1993, PIEDMONT, ITALY, $13

I seem to love everything about Dolcetto. I love the name: It means "soft" or "sweet" one (in fact it's usually a dry red wine). I love the aroma of violets, blackberries, and grapes. And most of all I love the taste of crunchy fruit flavors and its round-bodied smoothness. It's really an ideal all-purpose wine, accommodating a wide range of food but also pretty good just on its own. Although some examples are now coming out of California, the classic style is from the Piedmontese hills in the north of Italy.

This one not only has all the above characteristics but also a touch of oak to add complexity and spice.

Food match: Roast chicken; hamburgers

HAVENS, MERLOT CARNEROS NAPA VALLEY TRUCHARD VINEYARD 1992, CALIFORNIA, U.S.A., $18

Michael Havens is a college professor of English turned winemaker who belongs to a talented group of "gypsy" winemakers who do not own their own vineyards or wineries, preferring to rent space in someone else's or to hire themselves out as consultants. Although there are disadvantages to this arrangement, it does allow them to put their stamp on their wines without having to make the very substantial capital investment involved in setting up a winery. Havens was the winemaker at Truchard Winery but now produces under his own label. He makes wine from several varietals but his specialty is Merlot from the Truchard Vineyard.

This one is textbook Merlot of very high quality: deep purple with a seductive plum-jam/cigar-tobacco nose. It is sweet and supple on the palate, with concentrated mouth-coating fruit and superb, ripe tannins.

Food match: Roast goose/turkey; prime ribs of beef

JACKY JANODET, MOULIN-À-VENT 1993, BEAUJOLAIS, FRANCE, $15

One December evening the wine critic Robert Parker Jr. and some friends were dining at Montrachet. It was a holiday celebration, so I decided to open an old but perfectly cellared Moulin-à-Vent as a surprise. And a surprise it was. The vintage was 1929, and no one expected a Beaujolais, albeit the sturdiest of all the Beaujolais *crus*, to age this well. The other *crus* (see page 78), all 100 percent Gamay, have different expressions and structures that give them their individual personalities. This wine was magnificent. It had retained its fresh fruit aromas and flavors but seemed to have more in common with a mature Côte de Beaune than with a Beaujolais. In fact, Robert Parker felt it drank like a wine no more than fifteen years old.

The wines from Janodet are made in the same vein as the '29. Well structured, deep, and concentrated, because the Gamay has soft, light tannins it is also enjoyable in its youth. There's an enticing aroma of violets mingled with cherries and strawberry. On the palate it is lush and full, with roundness and weight. Don't wait seventy years to drink it!

Food match: Shell steak; roasted poultry; soft-ripened cheeses like Camembert and Brie

JOSÉ MARIA DA FONSECA, PERIQUITA 1990, SETUBAL, PORTUGAL, $7

Periquita was established in 1880 by Fonseca in the Setubal Peninsula just south of Lisbon and has become so popular that the grape from which it is made, Castelão Francês, is now known as Periquita.

This is another extraordinary value from Portugal. It's a light ruby/brick red with an exuberant nose of raspberries and spice. On the palate it is soft textured and medium bodied with lively, delicious berry flavors. Not a complex wine but thoroughly satisfying.

Food match: Turkey/chicken sandwiches; cold cuts; vegetable pot-au-feu

JOSÉ MARIA DA FONSECA, TERRA ATLAS 1990, DÃO, PORTUGAL, $7

It wasn't until the late 1980s (and the impact of Portugal's membership in the EEC) that the old protectionist system—whereby cooperatives had an almost exclusive control of wine production, which they sold to *négociants* for maturing and bottling—was opened up to many more independent owners of vineyards determined to improve quality. The Soares brothers, who run the company, have decided to make a break with the traditional woody, hard style of Portuguese wine and capture the fruit and personality of the grapes, and this wine is a great example of a more modern, fresher style.

Their Terra Atlas is made from the Touriga Nacional (one of the main grapes used in making Port), Bastardo, and Tinto Pinheira. The wine is ruby with a full, spicy nose, not unlike something from the Languedoc. There's a similar hint of a roasted landscape heady with wild herbs and aromatic brush. The palate is concentrated and lush, the finish well balanced.

Food match: Grilled lamb sausages; roast pork tenderloin

JOSÉ SOUSA, ROSADO FERNANDES
GARRAFEIRA 1990, ALENTEJO,
PORTUGAL, $15

The winery (owned by J. M. da Fonseca) was founded in 1878 and could well rank as one of the most traditional, not to say downright anachronistic, in the world. The grapes are still crushed by foot and the must fermented in clay amphorae called *talhas* or *potes de barro*. The vineyard is planted with traditional varieties such as Castelão Francês, Trincadeira, Moreto, and Arogonez, all of which are interspersed throughout the vineyard making it impossible to vinify them separately. There are, though, one or two concessions to modernity such as the automatic wine press and the careful hosing of the amphorae to control temperature.

The legal aging requirement for a *garrafeira* is a minimum of two years in cask and one in bottle, but this one is kept in cellar for about five years. It is a deep ruby with black/purple highlights, with an aroma of crushed blackberries displaying real depth and concentration. On the palate it has a richness and succulence that borders on the decadent, but its beautiful balance prevents it from going over the top.

If you are looking for an international style of winemaking, stay away from this one. But if you value personality and class, run, don't walk!

Food match: Herb-crusted leg of lamb; broiled skirt steak

MANZONE, BARBERA D'ALBA 1991,
PIEDMONT, ITALY, $12

It's a little-known fact that the Barbera grape is one of the world's most widely planted, with a particularly large presence in California. In Italy it is second to the Sangiovese. It is at its best around the Piedmontese villages of Alba and Asti and is one of my favorites because of its intensity and early drinkability. With less tannin than Nebbiolo but more than Dolcetto, it is supple yet structured at the same time. The considerable acidity is balanced, especially in ripe vintages, by a lush, jammy fruitiness.

Manzone's has the trademark Barbera "robe" (wine-speak for color): brilliant deep purple with a vibrant cherry rim. It offers a spicy red-fruit nose and cranberry/red-currant flavors with a crisp palate, definition, and good length.

Food match: Dishes with tomato-based sauces, like lasagna and shrimp diavolo

MARQUÉS DE MURRIETA GRAN RESERVA 1988, RIOJA, SPAIN, $13.50

This Rioja house produces traditional full-flavored wines of remarkable value. Unlike many large producers in Rioja, Murrieta's grapes comes from its own seven hundred-plus acres of vineyard. Most producers must purchase grapes to satisfy their needs and thus have less control over the quality of the fruit. Murrieta is a firm believer in lengthy barrel aging, as proved by the Gran Reservas Especial sold under the Castillo Ygay label. These wines used to spend up to forty years in neutral barrels before bottling. Today they are bottled earlier but rarely before ten years. This wine was aged three years in barrel and then three in bottle.

It has a deep ruby color with an aroma of smoke, earth, oak, and minerals. Slightly rustic yet distinctive and seductive, it has sweet ripe fruit, good concentration, real depth of flavor, and a long, nuance-filled finish. An astonishing value for a mature wine with such breeding.

Food match: Lamb is the regional dish in Rioja. Try your favorite lamb recipe with this wine.

MARQUIS D'ANGERVILLE, VOLNAY PREMIER CRU 1992, BURGUNDY, FRANCE, $20

The current marquis, Jacques d'Angerville, is one of the most respected names in Burgundy, and his father was one of those brave souls who blew the lid off many of the questionable practices of the *négociants* who had brought Burgundy into such low repute in the 1920s. Known for the outstanding quality of his Volnay, Jacques d'Angerville also produces small quantities of Meursault and Pommard. What Chambolle-Musigny is to the Côte de Nuits, Angerville's Volnay is to the Côte de Beaune. That is to say they both share a finesse and floral elegance that is a definition of their apellations at their best. His holdings are all *premier cru*, and the wines are bottled and labeled under the name of the particular vineyard. Where his holdings are scattered over small parcels in several vineyards, he blends and labels them "Volnay Premier Cru," his least expensive and in my opinion best-value wines.

The color is a youthful ruby-purple, while the nose has a smoky ripeness that promises a lush, soft texture. And that is just what it delivers, coating the palate with supple, sweet fruit. This is simply delicious wine to drink now, but will also keep for several years.

Food match: Roast chicken; pheasant; grilled swordfish or mahi-mahi

MATEUS, SIGNATURE VINHO TINTO 1990, DOURO, PORTUGAL, $7.50

Mateus is one of the most recognizable wine brands in the world. Who hasn't had at least one Mateus lamp or candleholder in their college dorm? I have fond memories of Saturday evenings spent with my buddies and a squat bottle of that fruity, spritzy rosé which, looking back, was the forerunner of today's coolers. But, hell, it was European, and we felt sophisticated. Now with the Mateus Signature we can revisit our youth without embarrassment because this really is sophisticated wine. It's a dry red made in the same region as Port and from two of the noble grapes used in Port: Touriga Nacional and Tinto Roriz.

The Signature Tinto is a deep garnet color promising a rich, full-bodied wine. The nose is of roasted nuts, coffee, currants, and plums. It is indeed medium to full-bodied and smooth but with a certain pleasing earthiness that reminds us that this is an Old World wine.

Food match: Jugged hare; rich meaty casseroles with beef

NAVARRO CORREAS, MALBEC 1991, MENDOZA, ARGENTINA, $11

Argentina is by far the largest producer and consumer of wine in South America. In fact it's the sixth largest producer in the world (the United States is fifth) and the sixth largest consumer (an average of fifty-two liters per person per year compared to just over seven in the United States—little-known statistics that are a testament to Aragentina's dedication to a wine culture. Many of the country's grapes were brought in by immigrants during the nineteenth century, but among them one stands head and shoulders above the rest: the Malbec. (In the Bordeaux and in Cahors, it is known as the Cot or Auxerrois; in Bordeaux it is blended with Cabernet Sauvignon and Merlot.)

This Malbec comes from Mendoza, the premier wine region of Argentina. It has an attractive aroma of nuts, currants, and menthol and a sweet, ripe flavor with a round, soft palate. The texture is silky and the balance good. Altogether a delicious and approachable wine.

Food match: Sausages; hamburgers; barbecued lamb chops

ONIX, PRIORAT 1992,
CATALONIA, SPAIN, $12

Priorat forms one of the *denominación de origen* in Catalonia, a region in the northeast of Spain bordering on the Mediterranean that is mainly known for Penedès and Cava *(méthode champenoise* sparkling wines).

Without doubt this wine represents one of the remarkable wine values from this part of Spain. Made from Garnacha and Carignan, it is ruby-violet with an aroma of cherry and spice. On the palate it is round and soft, with a silky, medium body that makes it a delicious, unpretentious wine very versatile with food, a characteristic it shares with the lighter styles of Burgundy.

Food match: Grilled swordfish; hard sheep's cheese, like Manchego

PAUL GARAUDET,
MONTHÉLIE-LES-DURESSES 1992,
BURGUNDY, FRANCE, $20

Monthélie is a beautiful little village sitting in a semicircle of distinguished neighbors: Volnay to the north; Auxey-Duresses and Meursault to the south. In fact, until 1937, when Monthélie was awarded its own *appellation contrôlée,* its wine was sold as Volnay. Monthélie's wines tend to be a bit more rustic than Volnay's, although their styles are similar, but because they are much less well known they can't command the higher prices of Volnay.

Garaudet's wines are full of charm and elegance and are decidedly unrustic. The Les-Duresses is from a *premier cru* vineyard at the southern end of the commune, and like all the '92s it is soft and supple. But this one also has real stuffing and concentration, which give it more weight. Plummy, silky, and completely delicious!

Food match: Roast chicken

PONZI, PINOT NOIR WILLAMETTE
VALLEY RESERVE 1992,
OREGON, U.S.A., $32

The cool climate of Oregon's Willamette Valley is similar to Burgundy's, but that doesn't mean that Willamette Pinot Noirs will automatically taste like those of Burgundy—though they can get pretty close when made by a master winemaker such as Dick Ponzi. Ponzi, an engineer by training, was a pioneer Oregon winemaker who moved there in 1969 and established Ponzi Vineyards the next year.

When you have tasted this wine I'm sure you will agree with me that this is the handiwork of one of the world's great winemakers. It is a wine with the complexity and breeding of a Burgundy *grand cru*. The color is deep ruby with dark red, almost black highlights, and a penetrating aroma of black fruit, toasty oak, and spice. The taste is of lush, concentrated fruit beautifully balanced by soft tannins, all rounded off with a long, long finish.

Food match: Grilled salmon; roast chicken, turkey, or pheasant

QUINTA DE PANCAS,
CABERNET SAUVIGNON 1991,
ALENQUER, PORTUGAL, $9

The Alenquer region is just north of Lisbon in the Estremadura. The Quinta de Pancas property is renowned because legend has it that it once belonged to the wife of Christopher Columbus. Had Columbus known of its potential I'm not so sure he would have set sail in search of some foreign land. He might have stayed closer to home to develop what is surely one of the greatest red wine values in the world today.

The blend here is 80 percent Cabernet Sauvignon to 20 percent Periquita, giving a deep ruby hue, a clean, rich nose of cassis and cherry, and medium body and intensity with a light, spicy finish. Your perfect "house wine."

Food match: Grilled chicken; sausages

LA RIOJA ALTA,
VIÑA ARDANZA RESERVA 1987,
RIOJA, SPAIN, $20

One of the wonderful things about Rioja is that in all likelihood it is mature when it reaches the customer. By law a *reserva* must be aged a minimum of three years (one in cask, two in bottle). At La Rioja Alta the Viña Ardanza Reserva goes even further than the appellation demands. Three years are spent in cask before further aging in bottle. It is always astonishing to me to see how many barrels and bottles are kept in the wonderful cellars of these wineries. The cost must be fantastic, yet somehow it seems not to be passed on to the consumer, because these wines still offer tremendous value for money.

This wine has an intense vanilla/smoky/plum fragrance. There is a beautifully smooth, silky texture, good grip, and a long, lingering finish. It's a wine of great finesse.

Food match: Veal scallopini with mushrooms; braised lamb shank

ROSEMOUNT ESTATE, SHIRAZ 1993,
NEW SOUTH WALES, AUSTRALIA, $9

Rosemount was established in 1975 and became the marketing phenomenon of the 1980s and one of the leaders of Australian winemaking. The stated goal is to make immediately accessible, pleasurable wine to be drunk young, and this one certainly reaches it.

The Shiraz grape—the most widely planted in Australia—is

also known there as the Hermitage, and as the Syrah in France (in fact, the grape from which come the great reds of the Rhône Valley). The 1993 is deep purple, almost black, and has a classic black-olive smoky/spicy/nose reminiscent of a superripe Saint-Joseph or Crozes-Hermitage. On the palate it has supple, soft-textured fruit.

Food match: Stuffed shoulder of lamb

SOLIS MERLOT 1993, SANTA CLARA, CALIFORNIA, U.S.A., $12

My advice to Merlot lovers is *caveat emptor*. Although Merlot is quickly gaining ground on other varietals in California, too many producers are taking advantage of this newfound popularity and overproducing wines in order to take advantage of this easy market. The demand is greater than the supply, which also causes prices to be too high in relation to quality, especially if the wine is an overproduced, diluted drink without the trademark lush plummy richness of good Merlot.

The people at Solis have kept an even keel and continue to deliver wines of charm and character. This Merlot is deep in color with ripe plum and cherry aromas. It is soft on the palate, with good definition and concentration, fresh berry flavors, and a pleasant, well-balanced finish.

Food match: Grilled meats and firm-fleshed fish such as swordfish

TERRABIANCA, CHIANTI CLASSICO SCASSINO 1993, TUSCANY, ITALY, $12

Chianti has had its ups and downs. Lazy winemaking that thought a straw-covered flask could camouflage indifferent wine is, hopefully, a thing of the past. Now there seems to be a renewed emphasis on quality, and where once a distinguished winemaker such as Antinori simply walked away from the appellation in disgust, the legislators now seem willing to rewrite the rules to ensure higher standards. The fact is that Chianti is a great all-purpose wine; it's very versatile, neither too heavy nor too light, and has just enough acid and sweetness to make it a perfect match for tomato-based sauces that have a similar acid/sugar balance.

Chianti is divided into seven regions: Classico, Colli Aretini, Colli Senesi, Colli Fiorentini, Colline Pisane, Montalbano, and Ruffina, with Classico generally considered the best. This Classico has a youthful ruby hue, with a telltale brick-orange rim characteristic of wines made predominantly from Sangiovese. Its aroma is a lovely mix of currants, cherry, herbs, and toast. On the palate is has sweet, well-textured fruit with good depth of flavor. A very classy wine.

Food match: Baked chicken; hamburgers; lasagna

TERRA ROSA, CABERNET SAUVIGNON 1994, CALIFORNIA, U.S.A., $12

This wine may be the best value in California Cabernet Sauvignon available anywhere. Made from purchased grapes by Patrick Campbell, who also owns the Laurel Glen winery in Sonoma County, it shows the same dedication to quality as do his banner wines.

In the style of the man himself, this wine has grace and integrity. An open nose of pure, clean Cabernet fruit, with slightly herbal and berry notes, is followed by a refined soft, silky, and well-balanced palate with good concentration, soft tannins, and length.

Food match: Minute steak; veal shank; mild soft and hard cheeses (Camembert, Brie, Morbier, Saint-Nectaire, mild cheddars)

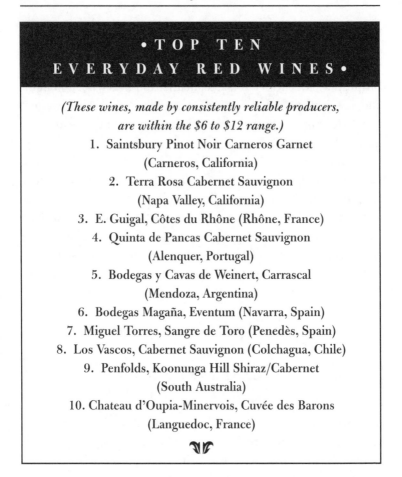

·TOP TEN EVERYDAY RED WINES·

(These wines, made by consistently reliable producers, are within the $6 to $12 range.)

1. Saintsbury Pinot Noir Carneros Garnet
   (Carneros, California)
2. Terra Rosa Cabernet Sauvignon
   (Napa Valley, California)
3. E. Guigal, Côtes du Rhône (Rhône, France)
4. Quinta de Pancas Cabernet Sauvignon
   (Alenquer, Portugal)
5. Bodegas y Cavas de Weinert, Carrascal
   (Mendoza, Argentina)
6. Bodegas Magaña, Eventum (Navarra, Spain)
7. Miguel Torres, Sangre de Toro (Penedès, Spain)
8. Los Vascos, Cabernet Sauvignon (Colchagua, Chile)
9. Penfolds, Koonunga Hill Shiraz/Cabernet
   (South Australia)
10. Chateau d'Oupia-Minervois, Cuvée des Barons
    (Languedoc, France)

LA TORRE, ROSSO DI MONTALCINO 1991, TUSCANY, ITALY, $13

Rosso di Montalcino is the more approachable cousin of the long-aging and somewhat austere (and quite expensive) aristocrat Brunello di Montalcino. Brunellos are tough and unapproachable in youth; by statute they have to be aged for four years before they are released (five for *riservas*), but even then they can always benefit from a few more years' cellaring to round off the hard corners. Rosso, on the other hand, although made from the same clone of Sangiovese as Brunello, has fresher, fruitier flavors that are at their peak just a year after bottling.

Luigi Anania is the young, energetic, and thoroughly entertaining owner and winemaker at La Torre. When I met him I knew what it was I loved about Italians. We got into a hilarious discussion about sausages that ended in rather inebriated attempts to pronounce the word, in English by Luigi and in Italian by me. This wine, like its maker, is full of warmth, exuberance, and vitality. It is also elegant and rich with supple fruit and an earthy, leathery nuance as a reminder of its noble family connections.

Food match: Grilled sausages (sal-SEEch-ay!)

TRAPICHE, MALBEC MENDOZA OAK CASK RESERVE 1990, MENDOZA, ARGENTINA, $8

Argentina is improving so quickly as a winemaking country that its wines can challenge some of the finest *crus* of France. In fact it has a long viticultural history and in terms of quantity is ranked fifth in the world. The most widely planted grape is the Malbec, which is also found in Bordeaux and Cahors, where it is known as the Auxerrois.

The Trapiche winery, owned by Panaflor, is one of the world's biggest volume producers (second only to Gallo) and boasts the world's largest cask, a giant holding about 1.35 million gallons (when it was inaugurated, 220 people enjoyed a sit-down dinner inside!). But it is not only quantity that matters here; there is also a real concern for quality.

This wine is a medium ruby red, with a lovely black cherry and plum aroma. Its smooth ripe fruit flavors are balanced by good acidity enlivened with a touch of spicy oak, all of which gives the wine freshness, balance, and good length on the palate.

Food match: Meatloaf; barbecued pork

TRUCHARD, MERLOT CARNEROS NAPA VALLEY 1991, CALIFORNIA, U.S.A., $22

The Truchards, who purchased their first plot of land in 1973, sold their grapes to other wineries until, in 1988, the very talented winemaker Michael Havens joined them and they began making wine under their own label.

Their hillside vineyards in northern Carneros are rich in clay, an essential component of the great vineyards of Pomerol and Saint-Émilion. The wine is a deep purple-black that seems to coat the glass when swirled, and there is a big aroma of ripe plums, cocoa, and black pepper. On the palate it has wonderful concentration and texture. Altogether an enticing and seductive wine that makes a very acceptable stand-in for a Saint-Émilion, at half the price.

Food match: Roast duck; grilled stuffed vegetables

LA VIEILLE FERME, LE MONT CÔTES DU VENTOUX 1992, VAUCLUSE, FRANCE, $6

La Vieille Ferme is owned by Jean-Pierre Perrin, whose father, Jacques, brought Château de Beaucastel in Châteauneuf-du-Pape to world prominence. Jean-Pierre took a somewhat different route by developing wonderful, inexpensive wines from the Côtes du Ventoux, Côtes du Lubéron, and Côtes-du-Rhône, all located quite close to the family's original business where the Rhône river runs into Provence.

This Côtes du Ventoux is made with traditional Châteauneuf-du-Pape grapes—Grenache, Syrah, Mourvèdre, and Cinsault—and offers up an intense, grapy, and peppery aroma promising a mouthful of ripe fruit. The taste delivers—crunchy, crushed fruit that is soft and round, coating the palate deliciously.

Food match: Roast duck; calves liver; hamburgers

VIÑA MAYOR, TINTO CRIANZA 1990,
RIBERA DEL DUERO, CATALONIA, SPAIN, $8

What I like about this wine, apart from its great-value price, is that it has the taste of a specific location, in this case Catalonia. All too often wines in this price category, although well made, slavishly follow an "international" Cabernet or Chardonnay formula. It doesn't matter whether they come from Chile, California, or Australia—they all taste the same! This *crianza* (see page 114 for more details on Spanish classifications) is made from 100 percent Tempranillo (here in Catalonia called Tinta del País), the great grape of Rioja.

Deep color with ripe fruit; the nose has currant and spice. There's nothing bland about the taste; it's bold and mouth filling, with a fleshy texture and soft, smooth finish. If you want even more body and intensity, try the Viña Mayor Reserva 1989 at about $11.

Food match: Roast beef; cassoulet; roast kidneys

WINTERBROOK,
CABERNET SAUVIGNON 1991,
NAPA COUNTY, CALIFORNIA, U.S.A., $10

There is nothing complex about this Cabernet, but it's about as good a ten-dollar Cabernet as one can get. What makes it special is its purity and clear expression of the essence of the grape. This skillfully made wine is clean and honest, delivering ripe black-fruit aromas with a smooth, well-integrated texture and clarity of flavor.

Food match: Broiled sirloin steak; meat loaf

LIGHT-BODIED REDS

This is a checklist of wines for which tasting notes follow.

Adelsheim Seven Springs Pinot Noir 1993, Oregon, U.S.A., $25 (p. 241)

Au Bon Climat, Pinot Noir Talley Vineyard Rosemary's 1993, Arroyo Grande, California, $28 (p. 242)

Bodegas Campo Viejo, Viña Alcorta Crianza 1989, Rioja, Spain, $9 (p. 242)

Capezzana, Chianti Montalbano 1993, Tuscany, Italy, $7 (p. 243)

Domaine de Vissoux, Beaujolais "Vissoux" 1994, Beaujolais, France, $10 (p. 243)

Domaine Michel Lafarge, Bourgogne Passetoutgrain 1994, Burgundy, France, $9 (p. 244)

Farnese, Montepulciano d'Abruzzo 1993, Abruzzo, Italy, $6 (p. 244)

Henri Marionnet, Gamay de Touraine 1994, Loire, France, $9 (p. 245)

Los Vascos, Cabernet Sauvignon 1992, Colchagua, Chile, $9
(p. 245)

Louis Jadot, Pernand-Vergelesses Clos de la Croix de Pierre
1993, France, $19 (p. 246)

Michele Chiario, Barbera d'Asti 1993, Piedmont, Italy, $9
(p. 246)

Miguel Torres, Sangre de Toro 1991, Penedès, Spain, $7
(p. 247)

Olivet Lane, Pinot Noir Russian River 1992, California, U.S.A.,
$12 (p. 248)

Saintsbury, Pinot Noir Carneros Garnet 1994, Carneros, California, U.S.A., $12 (p. 248)

Tollot-Beaut, Chorey Côtes de Beaune 1993, Burgundy, France,
$16 (p. 249)

Vietti, Barbera d'Alba Bussia 1993, Piedmont, Italy, $13
(p. 250)

ADELSHEIM SEVEN SPRINGS PINOT NOIR 1993, OREGON, U.S.A., $25

This is certainly one of the best Pinot Noirs produced in Oregon,
if not the country. Winemaker and owner David Adelsheim is one
of the pioneers in the Oregon wine industry and is a perpetual
leader and spokesman for his colleagues.

When most American Pinot Noirs tend to be somewhat one-
dimensional, this one offers uncommon depth and complexity. It
has great finesse and the kind of intensity and focus that make it
exciting. You know immediately that you have something special
in your glass.

Food match: Roasted quail or chicken

AU BON CLIMAT, PINOT NOIR TALLEY
VINEYARD ROSEMARY'S 1993,
ARROYO GRANDE, CALIFORNIA, U.S.A., $28

This winery is owned by the dynamic, witty, personable, and incredibly dedicated and knowledgeable winemaker Jim Clendenon. He and his band of buddies practically rule the South Central Coast region. In addition to his individual venture at Au Bon Climat, also known as ABC, he is involved with several other labels such as Vita Nova, Il Podere dell'Olivos, and Hitching Post. He makes many of these other wines with his close friend Bob Lindquist, from Qupé. His real fame is associated with Au Bon Climat, and justly so. Specializing in Chardonnay and Pinot Noir, these are some of the most Burgundian-style wines to be found in California, or anywhere in the United States for that matter.

This wine has a ruby-garnet color and a bright cherry nose, with earth and spice and black-fruit tones. On the palate it is rich and packed with sweet Pinot Noir fruit, with a soft silky texture that makes it incredibly seductive.

Food match: Grilled salmon; roasted vegetables with pasta

BODEGAS CAMPO VIEJO,
VIÑA ALCORTA CRIANZA 1989,
RIOJA, SPAIN, $9

This bodega, created in 1963, now produces five million bottles a year, making it the largest producer in Rioja. They make this wine with a partial whole-grape fermentation—a sort of modification of the carbonic maceration (see page 23) used most commonly in Beaujolais. Unlike Beaujolais, though, here the grapes are not covered by a blanket of carbon dioxide, resulting in a greater extraction of fresh fruit and berry aromas. The wine is then aged in barrel for two years, and a further year in bottle before being released.

Bright cherry red and a floral, peppery nose. On the palate it is soft, light, and gentle with fresh berry flavors that are not unlike those of a Pinot Noir. Very refreshing and versatile.

Food match: Roast chicken; hamburgers; mild chili

CAPEZZANA, CHIANTO MONTALBANO 1993, TUSCANY, ITALY, $7

This is your quintessential quaffing wine: a generic Chianti without the expectations, or price tag, of a Riserva. Montalbano is one of the seven Chianto zones (the others are Classico, Colli Aretini, Colli Fiorentini, Colli Sinese, Colline Pisane, and Ruffina).

A brilliant light red, it has a spicy red-currant nose with earthy tones. It's lively on the palate, soft and forward, with gentle fruit and a crisp finish.

Food match: Pasta 'n' pizza

DOMAINE DE VISSOUX, BEAUJOLAIS "VISSOUX" 1994, BEAUJOLAIS, FRANCE, $10

Jean-Pierre Chermette, proprietor of this small winery, has achieved cultlike status among Beaujolais lovers in France. His wines are found in nearly every chic wine bar and bistro in Paris. Now that they're available in this country, one can understand what all the excitement is about. He makes his wines with limited treatment and manipulation. They are rarely chaptalized and filtered and always have purity and elegance.

This wine has an intense ruby color with brilliant cherry highlights. It has an exuberant nose of small red berries and rose petals. Light on the palate with a moderate level of alcohol (because of no chaptalization), it has refreshing crispness and a juicy seductive finish.

Food match: Sausages; roast chicken; soft-ripened mild cheeses such as Camembert and Brie.

DOMAINE MICHEL LAFARGE, BOURGOGNE PASSETOUTGRAIN 1994, BURGUNDY, FRANCE, $9

Passetoutgrain (meaning literally "any grapes will do" but in effect indicating a blend of not less than one-third Pinot Noir and two-thirds Gamay) is the only appellation in Burgundy that allows blending. Technically, preexisting Pinot Beurot, which was widely planted in Nuits-Saint-Georges, can be blended with Chardonnay, but the Pinot Beurot vines cannot be renewed. White Burgundy has to be either 100 percent Chardonnay or Aligoté (and if Aligoté, the label has to say so); red Burgundy has to be 100 percent Pinot Noir.

Michel Lafarge uses half-and-half Pinot Noir/Gamay, which results in a wine with more body and structure than your run-of-the-mill Passetoutgrain. There's nothing complicated about it. Drink it for innocent pleasure, slightly chilled.

Food match: Pâtés and cheeses

FARNESE, MONTEPULCIANO D'ABRUZZO 1993, ABRUZZO, ITALY, $6

The fact that this grape variety is spelled and pronounced exactly the same as the Tuscan town Montepulciano is the cause of some confusion. There is no other relation, however. And though it is widely planted in the Abruzzi along the Adriatic coast, it is the fifth most widely planted grape variety in Italy after Sangiovese, Barbera, Merlot, and Negroamaro.

A light ruby color with brilliant reflections defines the youthful zesty character of this wine. It has an aroma of dried cherries and herbs. It is light on the palate, with lively cranberry, strawberry flavors and a delicious spicy, fruity finish. Unpretentious and delicious. Serve slightly chilled.

Food match: Cold meat sandwiches; hot dogs; fried chicken

HENRI MARIONNET,
GAMAY DE TOURAINE 1994,
LOIRE, FRANCE, $9

The Loire Valley is the source for so many different types of wines that it sometimes becomes difficult to keep track of them all. But for a light, flavorful, and totally unpretentious drink, look no further than the Sauvignons Blancs and Gamays from the Touraine. This large appellation is home to Vouvray, Montlouis, Chinon, Bourgueil, and Saint-Nicolas-de-Bourgueil. Gamay de Touraine is similar to a Gamay from Beaujolais but a bit lighter and higher in acid, making it an ideal wine to serve slightly chilled as an aperitif or on picnics.

Marionnet is the master of this wine. He manages to extract more body and flavor from it than anyone else. Fruity, redolent of raspberry and crushed strawberries, it is light and succulent.

Food match: Turkey sandwiches; hamburgers; mild-flavored fish such as sole and flounder

LOS VASCOS, CABERNET SAUVIGNON 1992,
COLCHAGUA, CHILE, $9

It's no secret that some terrific wines, especially reds, are coming out of Chile, and it's particularly encouraging to see some very classy producers, such as the Rothschilds of Château Lafite fame, taking an interest there. The Rothschilds own Los Vascos and have invested their financial and technical resources in the creation of one of the very best wineries in Chile. The wine even has a short sojourn in Lafite barrels to give it a bit of swank.

The '92 Cabernet has a bright cherry-red hue and an herbal, earthy, ripe nose. It's soft and light bodied, with light, berrylike fruit; lively, refreshing flavors; and a delicious, honest finish.

Food match: Roast chicken; baked pork chops; pizza

LOUIS JADOT, PERNAND-VERGELESSES CLOS DE LA CROIX DE PIERRE 1993, BURGUNDY, FRANCE, $19

The well-known firm of Louis Jadot produces wines from all over Burgundy, Beaujolais to Chablis. They are a large *négociant*, buying both grapes and juice, but after two recent vineyard purchases their holdings are now more than one hundred acres. With extreme dedication to quality, under the guiding hand of technical director Jacques Lardière, they are one of the leading producers of top Burgundy. And with so many of the best producers in Burgundy having a small production, making it hard to find their wines, this is a reliable name to look for. One of their properties is in the *premier cru* vineyard, En Caradeux. It is entirely owned by Jadot and called Clos de la Croix de Pierre, located in the commune of Pernand-Vergelesses.

This wine has long been a favorite of mine. It has a full, meaty, even slightly rustic side to it. With plenty of blackberry sweet fruit on the palate, it has a round, supple but well-structured mouth-feel with good concentration and length.

Food match: Roast chicken and mashed potatoes; grilled tuna steak

MICHELE CHIARIO, BARBERA D'ASTI 1993, PIEDMONT, ITALY, $9

It is surprising to learn that Barbera is one of the world's most widely planted grape varieties and in California constitutes 12 percent of the state's red wine production. However, it is from Italy's Piedmont region that probably the best Barbera in the world comes. The relatively cool climate gives a long enough growing season for the grapes to fully ripen (Barbera lends itself to early drinking, but its characteristically high acid levels need to be balanced by rich, ripe fruit.). Barbera d'Asti is one of the two Piedmontese areas (the other is Barbera d'Alba) that must contain 100 percent Barbera to qualify for the appellation.

Purple with a brilliant cherry rim, this wine has a peppery aroma of violets and raspberries that leaps out of the glass. There is a lovely, bright sour-cherry fruit with good concentration and body that gives a silky texture. The finish is crisp and delicious.

Food match: Tomato-based dishes such as spaghetti marinara; lasagna; pizza

MIGUEL TORRES, SANGRE DE TORO 1991, PENEDÈS, SPAIN, $7

Although the Torres family have owned a bodega in the Penedès since 1870, it wasn't until the 1960s, when the prodigal son, Miguel, returned from his enological studies in France, that the business really took off on the international level. He was the first to introduce foreign grapes into the vineyard (most notably Cabernet Sauvignon) and modern technology into the winery. Others followed, but few are as well-equipped as Torres.

This is good wine, a traditional blend of local Garnacha (65 percent) and Cariñena (35 percent). It's wonderfully expressive with dried herbs, ripe black fruit, anise, and even arid soil notes on the nose. The palate is sweet, soft, and fruity with a delightfully round texture.

Food match: Barbecued meat and shish-kebabs; mild, soft cheeses

OLIVET LANE, PINOT NOIR
RUSSIAN RIVER 1992,
CALIFORNIA, U.S.A., $12

The Russian River AVA is a Region 1 on the heat-summation scale (see page 135), making it ideal for Chardonnay and Pinot Noir. Olivet Lane, owned by the Pellegrini family, not only produces great Pinot Noir itself but also provides fruit for the some of the region's other best winemakers. Look to the Pellegrinis, though, for real value for money.

Bright cherry color and a nose of violets and red berries. There's a ripe, almost sweet crushed-fruit taste. Supple and crunchy, it's an unpretentious wine that's simply, and immediately, delicious.

Food match: Poached chicken; mild cheeses (Camembert, Brie, Chaumes, Vacherin)

SAINTSBURY, PINOT NOIR
CARNEROS GARNET 1994,
CARNEROS, CALIFORNIA, U.S.A., $12

The Saintsbury winery is in Carneros, an AVA (see page 137) sandwiched between the Napa and Sonoma valleys. But Carneros's very special climate sets it apart from its two neighbors. It is cool like Burgundy (here in Carneros the cooling is done by maritime breezes), and like Burgundy is a region in which Chardonnay and Pinot Noir flourish. Saintsbury is a locomotive force in maintaining the region's premier reputation for Pinot Noirs; they are not necessarily Burgundian in style but do have their own pure and honest expression.

Saintsbury's Garnet is their basic *cuvée*, with the Reserve being more concentrated as well as more expensive (about $25). I've always found the Garnet to be one of the best Pinot Noir values in the country, and the 1994 doesn't disappoint. It has bright cherry aromas, with sweet berrylike richness on the palate and a great purity of flavor. The finish is lively and refreshing. All in all a very happy wine!

Food match: Roast chicken; broiled salmon

TOLLOT-BEAUT,
CHOREY CÔTES DE BEAUNE 1993,
BURGUNDY, FRANCE, $16

My love affair with Pinot Noir began with a bottle of Corton Bressandes from Tollot-Beaut. It's a totally reliable domaine, located in the commune of Chorey-lès-Beaune. The winemaking is very traditional here, and the wines have a purity of fruit and a core of flavor that embody the essence of Pinot Noir. Chorey-lès-Beaune is part of the Côte de Beaune-Villages appellation, and since the

grapes for this wine come from the commune of Chorey, the domaine can use the name on its label.

The wine has a pure, clean, ripe-cherry, smoky nose with a touch of vanilla from the oak barrels in which it was aged. It is soft and juicy, with a flavor of crushed cherries and strawberries. Luscious and seductive, this is a great Burgundy value.

Food match: Roast chicken; soft-ripened cheese like Camembert

VIETTI, BARBERA D'ALBA BUSSIA 1993, PIEDMONT, ITALY, $13

Barbera suffers from an ugly duckling complex. It's one of the most widely planted grapes in Italy, but perhaps because of this, it's underappreciated and undervalued, commanding only about half the price of Nebbiolo. Given its low price and youthful drinkability, this is perfect wine for those who want mouth-filling fruit, crisp, lively flavors, and a dry finish.

I love the color of this wine—a brilliant cherry that seems to glow in the glass. There is a floral, red-currant, and berry aroma, while the palate is rounded, sweet with cranberry and strawberry, and a delicious, lively finish. A joyful, zippy wine, perfect for picnics.

Food match: Chicken; grilled firm-fleshed fish such as bass, salmon, mahi-mahi; mild semi-soft cheeses like Morbier

FULL-BODIED WHITES

This is a checklist of wines for which tasting notes follow.

Au Bon Climat, Chardonnay Santa Maria 1993, Santa Maria
Valley, California, U.S.A., $22 (p. 253)

Domaine des Comtes Lafon, Meursault 1993, Burgundy, France,
$45 (p. 253)

Domaine Louis Carillon et Fils, Puligny-Montrachet 1993,
Burgundy, France, $30 (p. 254)

Domaine Louis Latour, Corton-Charlemagne 1992, Burgundy,
France, $65 (p. 255)

Hanzell Vineyards, Sonoma Chardonnay 1992, Sonoma, California, U.S.A., $30 (p. 255)

Kistler, Chardonnay Sonoma Mountain McCrea Vineyard 1992,
Sonoma, California, U.S.A., $30 (p. 256)

Lindemans, Chardonnay Bin 65 1994, Coonawarra, Australia,
$7 (p. 257)

Lindemans, Padthaway Chardonnay 1993, South Australia, $14 (p. 257)

Marcassin, Gauer Ranch Chardonnay 1992, Sonoma, California, U.S.A., $35 (p. 258)

Michel Juillot, Mercurey Blanc 1992, Burgundy, France, $19 (p. 259)

Michel Niellon, Chassagne-Montrachet 1993, Burgundy, France, $28 (p. 260)

Newton Vineyard, Chardonnay Napa Valley Unfiltered 1992, Napa, California, U.S.A., $25 (p. 261)

Olivier Leflaive, Rully 1er Cru 1992, Burgundy, France, $17 (p. 262)

Orlando, Jacob's Creek Chardonnay 1993, Barossa, Australia, $7 (p. 262)

Peter Michael Winery, Chardonnay Cuvée Indigène 1992, Sonoma, California, U.S.A., $32 (p. 263)

Ravenswood, Chardonnay Sonoma Valley Vintner's Blend 1993, Sonoma, California, U.S.A., $13 (p. 263)

Santa Rita, Chardonnay Reserva 1993, Maule, Chile, $8 (p. 264)

Schoffit, Gewürztraminer "Harth-Cuvée Caroline" 1993, Alsace, France, $19 (p. 265)

Talley Vineyards, Chardonnay Arroyo Grande Valley 1993, California, U.S.A., $16 (p. 265)

Trimbach, Tokay Pinot Gris Réserve Personelle 1990, Alsace, France, $22 (p. 266)

Wolf Blass, Chardonnay Barrel Fermented 1994, Barossa Valley, Australia, $9.50 (p. 267)

Wynns, Chardonnay 1992, Coonawarra, Australia, $10 (p. 267)

AU BON CLIMAT, CHARDONNAY SANTA MARIA 1993, SANTA MARIA VALLEY, CALIFORNIA, U.S.A., $22

Jim Clendenon is the uncompromising, dedicated, and super-knowledgeable owner of Au Bon Climat. Au Bon Climat specializes in Chardonnay and Pinot Noir that are as Burgundian in their complexity as anything you can find in America (his knowledge of Burgundy is about as good as any American's, and probably better than most Burgundians'!). Clendenon's winemaking philosophy is to respect the vineyard and the grape and to create as unmanipulated a wine as possible. They are rarely filtered and may appear a bit hazy, but on flavor they're as clear as you can get.

This Chardonnay is no exception. It is a light straw color and has a toasty, ripe apple/pear and mineral nose, with tropical fruit and lemon notes. There's richly textured mouth-feel and zippy acidity on the finish.

Food match: Grilled shrimp with mango salsa; crab cakes; baked chicken

DOMAINE DES COMTES LAFON, MEURSAULT 1993, BURGUNDY, FRANCE, $45

It wasn't too long ago that one could find Burgundian vignerons who not only had never tasted the wine of their neighbors (let alone Oregon Pinot Noir, heaven forbid!) but were quite proud of their insularity. Today a new breed is blowing away the cobwebs. There's much more emphasis on communication and sharing ideas, and an openness to experimentation; Dominique Lafon is leading from the front. Lafon is the present manager and winemaker at the family's domaine, which dates back to the early 1900s. After extensive travel (including a stint making wine in California), he finally came home to the domaine, where he remains in firm control. Although he is traditional in his wine-making and true to the domaine style, he is one of the most artic-ulate and knowledgeable winemakers in Burgundy and is passionate about making the best wine he can every year. The key to good Burgundy is not its vintage or appellation but its pro-ducer. And a Lafon Meursault is a virtual guarantee of quality.

This wine has a full-blown floral, nutty, and mineral nose. It's round and supple, with lemony flavors, a medium concentration, and a deliciously long, well-focused finish.

Food match: Firm, white-fleshed fish such as turbot or cod

DOMAINE LOUIS CARILLON ET FILS, PULIGNY-MONTRACHET 1993, BURGUNDY, FRANCE, $30

There are plenty of fine Chardonnays in the world, but there's nothing like a really good Burgundy. Domaine Carillon can trace its origins in Puligny back to 1520, and with the young François Carillon in charge, its future seems assured. Of the three premier Burgundy white-wine villages (Chassagne-Montrachet, Meur-sault, and Puligny-Montrachet), Puligny has the greatest cachet (it can boast the *grand crus* Le Montrachet, Bâtard-Montrachet, and Chevalier-Montrachet; over a dozen *premier cru* vineyards, as well as eighteen *village* vineyards) even though, amazingly, it has few top-quality domaines. The wines from Carillon are underrated and consequently offer super value.

This Puligny is a *village* wine (see page 61) and will not have the concentration and intensity of a *grand* or *premier cru;* nor does it carry their price tag. The nose is spicy and toasty, with a hint of smoke and ripe fruit. On the palate it's quite rich and well structured, with a broad mouth-feel and a firm, long finish. Drink it young.

Food match: Sautéed sole or cod with a lemon sauce

DOMAINE LOUIS LATOUR,
CORTON-CHARLEMAGNE 1992,
BURGUNDY, FRANCE, $65

In today's market it is almost impossible to find *grand cru* white Burgundy of this caliber at this price and from one of the most respected houses in the Burgundy. *Grand crus* have the greatest concentration and are the most expressive of their *terroir* and grape (Chardonnay). Corton-Charlemagne is the largest of the *grand cru* vineyards, and legend has it that it was owned by Charlemagne, the Holy Roman Emperor, who acquired it in 775 and planted it with red-wine grapes. As Charlemagne aged, the story goes, and his beard turned white, his wife, Liutgarde, objected to the stains on his beard caused by red wine and insisted that the vineyard be replanted with white grapes. An expensive alternative to a tube of Grecian 2000!

The color is light gold/straw, with a green tint reflecting its youth. The nose is toasty and smoky, with white peachlike aromas. It tastes wonderfully rich and intense, with great concentration and power. This is a wine of tremendous structure and although delicious to drink now will provide enjoyment for ten to fifteen years.

Food match: Lobster; halibut; turbot with butter sauce

HANZELL VINEYARDS,
SONOMA CHARDONNAY 1992,
SONOMA, CALIFORNIA, U.S.A., $30

A taste of Hanzell is a taste of history. The winery was founded in 1952 by J. D. Zellerbach. He had a passion for Burgundy, and it was he who pioneered Chardonnay and Pinot Noir in the Sonoma Valley. He was the first in California to use stainless-steel fermentation tanks, today a staple of any modern winery, and to use small French barrels for aging the wine. Zellerbach died in

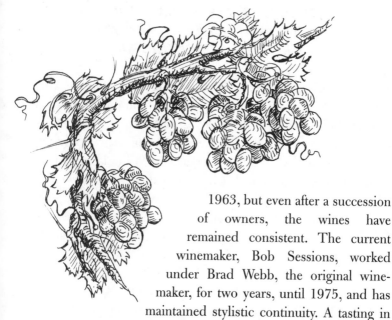

1963, but even after a succession of owners, the wines have remained consistent. The current winemaker, Bob Sessions, worked under Brad Webb, the original winemaker, for two years, until 1975, and has maintained stylistic continuity. A tasting in 1994 of Hanzell Chardonnays going back to 1973 proved to me that Californian Chardonnays can age. These were richly concentrated yet still fresh and elegant.

This Chardonnay is a deep gold/straw, with a nose of ripe pear, pineapple, citrus, and butter. On the palate it is rich and full, with lush, round fruit, great balance, and a long finish. This is not a French wannabe but a great Californian Chardonnay, proud of its own personality.

Food match: Lobster with drawn butter

KISTLER, CHARDONNAY SONOMA MOUNTAIN McCREA VINEYARD 1992, SONOMA, CALIFORNIA, U.S.A., $30

The Kistler winery was founded in 1979 by Steve Kistler and Mark Bixler and produces some of the best Chardonnay to be found in America today. It sells quickly, but grab it when you can, because they are benchmark wines. Of all their Chardonnays (there are seven *cuvées,* with grapes from various sources, such as the Vine Hill Road Vineyard, Dutton Ranch, and Durrell Vineyard), I always find the most complex and perhaps the most Burgundian to be the McCrea Vineyard *cuvée.*

The mineral, hazelnut nose has notes of toasty oak and vanillin. On the palate, there's a beautiful balance and round, honeyed pear flavors. The finish is smooth and long.

Food match: Crab cakes; sautéed firm-fleshed fish, such as scrod

LINDEMANS, CHARDONNAY BIN 65 1994, COONAWARRA, AUSTRALIA, $7

Although the Lindemans winery is in the Coonawarra area of South Australia, most of the fruit for this delicious Bin 65 comes from the celebrated Padthaway district, about fifty miles farther north. This wine could be considered the baby cousin of the Lindemans Padthaway Chardonnay discussed below; it's more restrained and less complex than the Padthaway. Nonetheless it has a wonderful nose of ripe melon, butter, and honey, while the palate is full and smooth, with silky, luscious fruit.

Food match: Delicate-flavored fish, such as sole and trout; cold cuts; poultry

LINDEMANS, PADTHAWAY CHARDONNAY 1993, SOUTH AUSTRALIA, $14

Padthaway is a region in South Australia just north of Coonawarra. Where Coonawarra is famous for its reds, Padthaway, with its cooler climate, has emerged as a white-wine area producing elegant Chardonnay. Australian Chardonnays are often heavily alcoholic, with low acidity, but this Lindemans version, by comparison, certainly has a lighter touch.

Having said that, though, this is certainly a big mouthful of wine, and not one for confirmed Chablis drinkers! With an oaky, buttery, pineapple aroma, it has sweet, viscous fruit on the palate, with a nuance of citrus lending some refreshing acidity. Almost edible!

Food match: Roast chicken or turkey; pork with a fruit-based sauce

MARCASSIN, GAUER RANCH CHARDONNAY 1992, SONOMA, CALIFORNIA, U.S.A., $35

This is a difficult wine to find, made in limited quantities, and it's not cheap. So why is it in a book that is focused mainly on good-value wines? Because it is one of the best Chardonnays made in California in 1992, or in any year for that matter. When you consider that we are talking about a wine that ranks right up there with great white Burgundies, the price begins to look bargain-basement.

Helen Turley, the winemaker at Marcassin, who previously worked at Simi, B. R. Cohn, and Peter Michael Winery, is one of the best in the business. She makes this wine in a French style. It's fermented in new Limousin oak with 100 percent natural yeasts, and undergoes a full malolactic fermentation (see page 26), then remains on its lees, with an occasional stir, to give it extra richness.

New oak has to be handled with care if it isn't going to dominate the taste of the wine, and the problem with too many American wineries is that the quality of the fruit cannot compete with the aggressive flavoring of the oak. This wine has a smoky, mineral quality on the nose that is fabulously seductive. On the palate it is rich and forceful yet impeccably balanced, so that no one component overpowers another. The finish is gorgeously long, resonant, and completely satisfying. With apologies to Erica Jong, this is the zipless sip of Californian Chardonnays.

Food match: Firm-fleshed fish such as monkfish or halibut, broiled or baked; roasted guinea hen; roasted cornish hen

MICHEL JUILLOT, MERCUREY BLANC 1992, BURGUNDY, FRANCE, $19

Mercurey, along with Givry, Montagny, Rully, and Bouzeron, is one of the villages of the Côte Chalonnaise that are entitled to use the village name on the label. All of them produce red and white wine, except for Montagny and Bouzeron, which make white only. The reds are made exclusively from Pinot Noir and the whites from Chardonnay and Aligoté (which must proclaim itself as Aligoté on the label).

The Côte Chalonnaise is at the southern tip of the Côte de Beaune, and the wines are similar in style to their northern neighbors, if a bit lighter and a touch more rustic. But for full expression of Pinot Noir and Chardonnay, not to mention the humbler Aligoté, there are few areas of the world that can compete dollar for dollar.

This wine is certainly one of the best examples of a great Chalonnaise white. In fact, it could easily stand in for a top-notch Chassagne-Montrachet or Meursault. The full, ripe nose is scented with toasty, vanillin-flavored oak, while on the palate there is concentrated fruit, smooth-textured mouth-feel, and a good length. A bargain at the price.

Food match: Steamed lobster; baked swordfish; cold poached salmon

• TOP TEN WHITES FOR GRAND OCCASIONS •

(These wines, made by consistently reliable producers, are within the $25 to $65 range.)

1. Michel Niellon, Chassagne-Montrachet Les Vergers (Burgundy, France)

2. Marcassin, Chardonnay Lorenzo Vineyard (Sonoma, California)

3. Kistler, Chardonnay, McCrea Vineyard (Sonoma, California)

4. Trimbach, Riesling Clos St. Hune (Alsace, France)

5. Zind-Humbrecht, Tokay Pinot Gris Clos Windsbuhl (Alsace, France)

6. F. X. Pichler, Riesling Smaragd (Wachau, Austria)

7. Jean-François Coche-Dury, Meursault-Perrières (Burgundy, France)

8. Laville-Haut-Brion (Graves, France)

9. Louis Latour, Corton Charlemagne (Burgundy, France)

10. Jean-Marie Raveneau, Chablis Valmur (Burgundy, France)

MICHEL NIELLON, CHASSAGNE-MONTRACHET 1993, BURGUNDY, FRANCE, $28

Chassagne-Montrachet is the home of some of the greatest Chardonnay produced in the world. Along with Puligny-Montrachet and Meursault, this is the part of Burgundy where the best whites are made.

The proprietor of this domaine, Michel Niellon, is one of the most understated, gentle, and honest men I have ever met. And as is often the case, his wines express his personality with the same kind of purity of flavor and honesty.

The 1993 has a mineral green-apple nose. On the palate it is lively, with crisp acidity, layers of rich fruit flavors, medium concentration, and a pleasant clean long finish. This wine is a find every year.

Food match: Sautéed scallops; steamed crab or lobster; lemon chicken

NEWTON VINEYARD, CHARDONNAY NAPA VALLEY UNFILTERED 1992, NAPA, CALIFORNIA, U.S.A., $25

So why has "unfiltered" become the buzz word these days? Filtration is a common practice during winemaking, either when the wine is bottled or at an earlier stage. Some filters remove largish particles such as dead yeast cells, while others can be fine enough to screen out bacteria that might cause spoilage or further unwanted fermentation. So why run these risks by not filtering the wine? Many studies have shown that unfiltered wine has more aroma, body, and complexity. A winemaker striving to make a premium *cuvée* is willing to take these risks because when it works it pays off big.

This wine is unfiltered proof! It has a slight haziness characteristic of unfiltered wine, but the nose is clean and forceful with a flood of aromas, with toasty oak, fruit, and mineral nuances dominating. On the palate it is rich and powerful, with mouth-filling fruit and a long, intense finish. I don't think it's any surprise that in a recent professional blind tasting this wine was mistaken for a top *premier cru* white Burgundy.

Food match: Poule-au-pot (chicken poached with vegetables)

OLIVIER LEFLAIVE, RULLY 1ER CRU 1992, BURGUNDY, FRANCE, $17

Olivier Leflaive is the nephew of the late Vincent Leflaive, who directed Domaine Leflaive in Puligny-Montrachet. White Burgundies carrying either Leflaive name are of undeniably high quality. In fact, in recent years the wines from Olivier have been recognized in some circles as being almost as good, although in a different style, as those of Domaine Leflaive.

Rully is one of the five villages of the Côte Chalonnaise that are allowed to use the village name on the label (the others are Givry, Montagny, Mercurey, and Bouzeron). The style of these Chalonnaise whites is similar to those farther north in the Côte de Beaune, but they are perhaps a bit more forward and softer in their youth.

This wine comes from a *premier cru* vineyard and has a ripe, toasty, concentrated nose, with pear and melon nuances. It is quite full and powerful on the palate, with firm structure and an almond-pit, mineral finish.

Food match: Baked shrimp; white-fleshed fish such as bass, turbot, cod, flounder, baked or broiled

ORLANDO, JACOB'S CREEK CHARDONNAY 1993, BAROSSA, AUSTRALIA, $7

Orlando Wines is a massive winery producing about three million cases a year from over 260 acres of its own vineyards as well as bought-in grapes. It was founded in 1847 by Johann Gramps, a member of one of the original twenty-eight families from Silesia, Germany, who established the Barossa Valley in South Australia as a winemaking area. Now it's the most important region in the country.

This wine is a blend from the Barossa and the cooler area of

Padthaway, farther to the south. It's well balanced, with ripe melon, mango, and pear aromas, refreshing acidity, and nice texture. On the palate it has a lovely peachy smoothness.

Food match: Barbecued shrimp or chicken

PETER MICHAEL WINERY, CHARDONNAY CUVÉE INDIGÈNE 1992, SONOMA, CALIFORNIA, U.S.A., $32

The Peter Michael Winery is located in the Knights Valley AVA of Sonoma. The wines here are outstanding and among the best examples of Chardonnay produced in the United States. Cuvée Indigène refers to the wild yeasts used to start the fermentation (the preference of many French winemakers). Most American Chardonnays use cultured yeasts in order to ensure a more controlled and faster fermentation. Using wild yeats can be risky and may result in a stalled fermentation, but the advantage is a wine of greater complexities of taste and aroma.

The nose is clean and toasty; the taste rich and full-bodied, with superb balance and focus. This is a wine of great intensity, elegance, and length, with a formidable concentration that avoids going over the top into heaviness.

Food match: Roasted swordfish with a citrus sauce

RAVENSWOOD, CHARDONNAY SONOMA VALLEY VINTNER'S BLEND 1993, SONOMA, CALIFORNIA, U.S.A., $13

Joel Peterson, the owner and winemaker at Ravenswood, would figure very high on my list of the wine world's greats. He worked with Joseph Swan in the early 1970s and made his first wine at Ravenswood in 1976. Ravenswood does not own vineyards and buys in grapes from sources they find of superior quality (usually they are "dry farmed," i.e., not artificially irrigated, and have old, low-yielding vines that give a more intense flavor to the wine). Once he's found the right vineyard, Peterson intervenes as little as possible with the vinification. For example, he allows fermentation to start with wild yeasts rather than inoculating with commercial strains, and he bottles without filtration.

Although the winery is known for Zinfandel, it also produces Merlot, Cabernet Sauvignon, and a Meritage (a blend, in this case, of one third each Cabernet Sauvignon, Merlot, and Cabernet Franc) called Pickberry. While most of Ravenswood wines carry a vineyard designation, the "Vintner's Blend" is a mix of sources that make for a more approachable wine, to be drunk young. As with all Peterson's wines, though, the hallmark here is impeccable balance.

This Chardonnay has a citrus, toasty aroma; a mineral quality and firmness give it drive and tension yet it retains great balance.

Food match: Shrimp with lemon dressing; white-fleshed fish such as cod and flounder; fried chicken

SANTA RITA, CHARDONNAY RESERVA 1993, MAULE, CHILE, $8

Vine growing has a long history in Chile. The sixteenth-century Spanish conquistador Cortés gave an order that 1,000 vines were to be planted for every 100 Indians killed (luckily not a rule of thumb still used in viticulture). The European influence remained strong with the arrival of French, primarily Bordelais, rootstock in the late eighteenth century. Phylloxera never invaded Chile, whose vines still flourish on ungrafted rootstock.

Santa Rita is Chile's second largest bodega (the giant Concha y Toro is first) and, due to its modern facilities, has always been a high achiever. Their Chardonnay Reserva certainly delivers a big taste bang for the buck. Its nose is oaky and nutty, with a whopping dollop of butter. The palate is ripe and full, with moderate concentration and a big oaky finish. A wine for those who really do believe that bigger is better!

Food match: Grilled fish with orange butter

SCHOFFIT, GEWÜRZTRAMINER "HARTH-CUVÉE CAROLINE" 1993, ALSACE, FRANCE, $19

The wine gushes personality, which presupposes you like the personality! At least it takes a stand.

Gewürztraminer is one of the "noble" grape varieties of Alsace that can manifest itself as a fairly light dry wine or a full-bodied, honied sweet wine affected by botrytis. In general, this grape variety is low in acid, rather high in alcohol, and rich in flavor.

Schoffit has mastered it wonderfully here with a wine nuanced with aromas of roses, lychee, and spice. It has a mouth-filling presence without being heavy or overbearing. Powerful and long, it is a show-stopping performance!

Food match: Broiled lobster or foie gras

TALLEY VINEYARDS, CHARDONNAY ARROYO GRANDE VALLEY 1993, CALIFORNIA, U.S.A., $16

The Arroyo Grande Valley of California's South Central Coast region, nestled between the Edna Valley to the north and Santa Barbara County to the south, benefits from a long growing season, thanks to its cool climate. This gives the wine greater aroma and complexity, with less tannin and alcohol.

Talley provides fruit to some of the best winemakers in the region, but the finest fruit seems to be reserved for the Talley family's own wine. This Chardonnay has a great aroma of pineapple, tropical and citrus fruits, intermingled with toasty oak nuances. There is a rich-textured mouth-feel, concentrated and intense flavor with good balancing acidity.

Food match: Baked monkfish; broiled swordfish; roast chicken

TRIMBACH, TOKAY PINOT GRIS RÉSERVE PERSONELLE 1990, ALSACE, FRANCE, $22

In Alsace, Tokay is the old name for the Pinot Gris (a mutation of Pinot Noir). It's not to be confused with the Tokay of Hungary, which is a dessert wine made from the Furmint and Hárslevelü grapes. (Some legends have it that Pinot Gris was brought to Alsace by one Baron Lazare de Schwendi in 1568 on his return from soldiering in Hungary. Others contend that this is mere myth.) Nor is it to be confused with Tocai from the Friuli-Venezia region of northern Italy. Nor with the sweet Tokay-Muscadelle of Australia. Anyway, in an attempt to make everything clear, the European Economic Community lawmakers have now ruled that the word Tokay can be used on a label of Alsace wine only in conjunction with Pinot Gris. What is sure is that the grape is capable of producing some of the spiciest, smokiest wine of Alsace, and it's a shame that consumers tend to shy away from Alsace wines because they come in bottles of similar shape to German wines that are automatically, if wrongheadedly, assumed to be sweet. In Germany (where its called the Ruländer) and in Italy (Pinot Grigio), the style is lighter, whereas the Alsatian treatment is quite full-bodied and rich, with a certain satisfying, mouth-filling oiliness, something that should appeal to Chardonnay lovers.

This wine has a forward, rich, almost *sauvage* nose (literally "wild," a winespeak term that's meant to suggest a very full, almost aggressive aroma). It is multilayered on the palate, with full earthy and mineral flavors. This is a high-energy, intense wine that does acrobatics on the tongue and delivers a great encore performance with a long, lingering finish.

Food match: Roast pork; veal tenderloin; soft, flavorful cheeses such as Vacherin, Munster

WOLF BLASS,
CHARDONNAY BARREL FERMENTED 1994,
BAROSSA VALLEY, AUSTRALIA, $9.50

Wolf Blass may have been described as a "pint-sized, bow-tied salesman," but he has probably done more to teach Australians (he's a German by birth) the finer points of winemaking (particularly red) and blending than practically anyone else. He works in the Barossa Valley, Australia's most important wine area, which is responsible for about half the country's total wine production, but it was his training in Champagne that taught him to blend wine that is ready to drink the day it is bottled.

This Chardonnay is a yellow/gold, with a ripe melon, peach, and tropical fruit aroma accented by the vanillin which has been contributed by the new oak barrels in which it is fermented. It's full and opulent, just bursting with juicy fruit flavors. Great value for those who like a full-blown style of Chardonnay.

Food match: Cold poached salmon

WYNNS, CHARDONNAY 1992,
COONAWARRA, AUSTRALIA, $10

Australian wine aficionados get very excited about the very special *terra rossa* that runs like a ten-mile long, one-mile-wide carpet through this cool area of South Australia (on the Winkler scale, it's about equivalent to Champagne or Burgundy). Wynns (one of the oldest wineries in South Australia and now part of the giant Penfolds) offers some great values apart from this Chardonnay. Look out for their Hermitage (made from Shiraz, which is the Rhône's Syrah grape by another name), Cabernet Hermitage, Cabinet Sauvignon, and the outstanding John Riddock Cabernet Sauvignon.

This Chardonnay struck me with its purity and balance. While many Australian Chardonnays may be a bit low on acidity and too high on alcohol, this one is full-flavored, with oaky, peachy accents, yet is still quite elegant, with good intensity and length.

Food match: Sautéed sweetbreads; sautéed pork; broiled red snapper

MEDIUM-BODIED WHITES

This is a checklist of wines for which tasting notes follow.

A. & P. de Villaine, Aligoté de Bouzeron 1992, Burgundy, France, $12 (p. 271)

Albert Mann, Pinot Blanc Auxerrois Vieilles Vignes 1993, Alsace, France, $13 (p. 272)

Bachelier, Petit Chablis 1993, Burgundy, France, $13 (p. 272)

Carmenet, Old Vines Colombard Saviez Vineyard 1992, Sonoma, California, U.S.A., $10 (p. 273)

Casa Lapostolle, Sauvignon Blanc 1994, Colchagua, Chile, $7.50 (p. 274)

Chalk Hill, Sauvignon Blanc Chalk Hill 1992, Sonoma, California, U.S.A., $12 (p. 275)

Château de Baun, Russian River Chardonnay 1993, California, U.S.A., $12 (p. 276)

Columbia, Chardonnay Columbia Valley Woodburne Cuvée
  1993, Washington State, U.S.A., $11 (p. 276)

Domaine Auvigue, Pouilly Fuissé Solutré 1993, Burgundy,
  France, $14 (p. 277)

Domaine Beaumard Savennières Clos Saint Yves 1993, Loire,
  France, $18 (p. 277)

Domaine Philippe Foreau, Vouvray Sec Clos Naudin 1993,
  Loire, France, $15 (p. 278)

Domaine René Bourgeon, Givry Clos de la Brûlée 1992, Burgundy, France, $15 (p. 278)

Domaine Weinbach, Riesling Alsace Cuvée Théo 1992, Alsace,
  France, $20 (p. 279)

Domaine Zind-Humbrecht, Pinot d'Alsace 1992, Alsace, France,
  $14 (p. 280)

Estancia Estates, Chardonnay Monterey County 1993, California, U.S.A., $12 (p. 280)

Françoise and Denis Clair, Saint-Aubin 1er Cru Les Murgers des
  Dents de Chien 1992, Burgundy, France, $22 (p. 281)

Georges Duboeuf, Viognier Vin de Pays de l'Ardèche 1994,
  Rhône, France, $9 (p. 281)

Granja Fillaboa, S.A., Fillaboa Albariño 1994, Rias Baixas,
  Spain, $14 (p. 282)

Hugel el Fils, Gentil Hugel 1993, Alsace, France, $10 (p. 282)

Josmeyer, Alsace Pinot Auxerrois "H" Vieilles Vignes 1989,
  Alsace, France, $22 (p. 283)

Louis Jadot, Saint-Aubin 1993, Burgundy, France, $16 (p. 284)

Louis Michel et Fils, Chablis Montée de Tonnerre 1992, Burgundy, France, $18 (p. 285)

Muré, Pinot Blanc Côte de Rouffach 1992, Alsace, France, $10 (p. 285)

Normans, Family Reserve Chardonnay 1993, Southern Vales, Australia, $10 (p. 286)

Olivier Leflaive, Bourgogne Chardonnay 1993, Burgundy, France, $10 (p. 287)

Ponzi, Pinot Gris 1994, Oregon, U.S.A., $16 (p. 287)

Qupé, Marsanne Los Olivos Vineyard 1993, California, U.S.A., $12 (p. 288)

Redbank, South Eastern Australia Chardonnay 1992, Australia, $10 (p. 289)

René et Vincent Dauvissat, Chablis Vaillons 1er Cru 1992, Burgundy, France, $30 (p. 289)

J. Rochioli, Sauvignon Blanc 1994, Russian River Valley, California, U.S.A., $12 (p. 290)

Verget, Saint-Aubin 1er Cru 1993, Burgundy, France, $16 (p. 291)

J. J. Vincent, Saint-Véran 1992, Burgundy, France, $9 (p. 291)

Zaca Mesa, Chardonnay Santa Barbara County 1993, California, U.S.A., $11 (p. 292)

A. & P. DE VILLAINE, ALIGOTÉ DE BOUZERON 1992, BURGUNDY, FRANCE, $12

The Aligoté grape is found not only in the Côte Chalonnaise (where this wine comes from) but throughout the Côte d'Or. It used to form part of the blend (with Chardonnay and Pinot Blanc) of white Burgundy, but the appellation laws have tightened up, and now white Burgundy has to be 100 percent Chardonnay or, if made from Aligoté, advertise itself as Bourgogne Aligoté. Given the popularity of Chardonnay, Aligoté has a bit of a struggle to maintain itself in the Burgundy (growers get twice as much for Chardonnay), but good producers still grow it. One of those outstanding growers is Aubert de Villaine, who was instrumental in getting Aligoté de Bouzeron its own appellation (M. de Villaine is also the co-owner of Domaine de la Romanée-Conti in Vosne-Romanée).

Although Aligoté has some similarity with Chardonnay, it lacks the finesse, body, and aging potential. Nevertheless, in the hands of a producer such as de Villaine, it can be delicious and good value.

Food match: Cold shellfish (such as oysters, clams, shrimp)

ALBERT MANN, PINOT BLANC AUXERROIS VIEILLES VIGNES 1993, ALSACE, FRANCE, $13

The debate goes on. Is Auxerrois a separate grape variety or a part of the Pinot family? In Alsace it is often blended with Pinot Blanc and labeled simply as Pinot Blanc or Pinot d'Alsace. Auxerrois is fatter and spicier than Pinot Blanc and comes across like a lighter Pinot Gris.

This version is made from the fruit of sixty-year-old vines and is correspondingly rich, with a characteristically buttery/honeyed aroma cut through with hints of orange blossom and apricot. It is spicy and intense, with great concentration and a long finish. A delicious alternative to Chardonnay.

Food match: Baked halibut or hake with drawn butter sauce

BACHELIER, PETIT CHABLIS 1993, BURGUNDY, FRANCE, $13

Petit Chablis is at the bottom of the totem pole in the hierarchy of the classification of the Chablis vineyard. Usually considered better and just about always more expensive are Chablis, Chablis *premier cru,* and Chablis *grand cru.* As always, the key to good value is to look for a "lesser" wine from an excellent producer. Just as the super second growths in Bordeaux are often as good as the firsts, the lower-classified wines in Burgundy and elsewhere taste as good as the category above when put in the hands of a master winemaker.

This Chablis is classic in style, with a mineral, flinty, and almond-like nose. On the palate it is zesty and charged with precise concentrated flavors. Pure, clean, and stony, this wine leaves a refreshing and tingling aftertaste.

Food match: Bring on the platter of shellfish!

CARMENET, OLD VINES COLOMBARD SAVIEZ VINEYARD 1992, SONOMA, CALIFORNIA, U.S.A, $10

Up on the south-facing slopes of Mount Veeder, above the Sonoma Valley, Carmenet (owned by the Chalone group) is best known for its Cabernet Sauvignon. The wine I've chosen here, though, gives an exciting new twist to an old jug-wine grape, the Colombard (in fact, Colombard is the most widely planted grape in California). The secret here is to limit the yield of Carmenet's venerable vines and so extract the highest-quality juice and to vinify it much like Chardonnay. The barrel fermentation gives a toasty nose infused with apples and flowers. The palate is round and well textured with layers of flavor, and the good concentra-

tion and length all help to elevate this otherwise ignoble grape into much more exalted company.

Food match: Baked chicken wings; turkey medallions

•TOP TEN THANKSGIVING WINES•

*(These wines, made by consistently reliable producers,
are within the $12 to $35 range.)*

1. Bonny Doon, Le Sophiste,
(Santa Cruz Mountains, California)

2. Au Bon Climat, Chardonnay (Santa Barbara, California)

3. Domaine Marcel Deiss, Tokay-Pinot Gris (Alsace, France)

4. Domaine Louis Carillon, Puligny-Montrachet Les Combettes
(Burgundy, France)

5. Ravenswood Zinfandel Dickerson Vineyard
(Napa Valley, California)

6. Domaine Drouhin Pinot Noir (Dundee, Oregon)

7. Edmunds St. John, Syrah "Grand Heritage" (California)

8. Étude Cabernet Sauvignon (Napa Valley, California)

9. Domaine Simon Bize, Savigny-les-Beaune Les Vergelesses
(Burgundy, France)

10. Georges Duboeuf, Morgon Jean Descombes
(Beaujolais, France)

CASA LAPOSTOLLE, SAUVIGNON BLANC 1994, COLCHAGUA, CHILE, $7.50

Welcome to the revolution! Here's a wine that embodies it. Casa Lapostolle is owned by the Marnier-Lapostolle family (the owners of Grand Marnier), who hired one of the most sought-after consultants in Bordeaux, Michel Roland, to oversee the Casa Lapostolle enterprise. In the old days, Chilean wineries were equipped with the most outdated machinery and made crude red or flabby white. Now that there's serious international money and expertise going into the Chilean wine industry, it's becoming commonplace to see temperature-controlled fermentation tanks, pneumatic presses, oak barrels, and small hordes of enologists.

This wine is a child of the revolution. It has an explosive nose of pure, clean fruit suggestive of ripe pineapple, peaches, and flint. It's rich and mouth-filling, with a crisp, refreshing finish.

Food match: Baked snapper with a splash of lemon; fried chicken

CHALK HILL, SAUVIGNON BLANC CHALK HILL 1992, SONOMA, CALIFORNIA, U.S.A., $12

This is a great example of a winery turned around by a brilliant winemaker. Although the wines at Chalk Hill have always been decent, no one would say they were exciting. All that changed with the arrival of winemaker David Ramey, who had spent two years at Château Pétrus in Pomerol, four years at Simi, and five years at Matanzas Creek.

Sauvignon Blanc has many faces. It is greatly influenced by soil and climate, and the hand of the winemaker plays an important part as well. Ramey's decision to ferment and age the wine in oak, as is done in Bordeaux, makes for a round, soft style (compared, say, to the practice of fermenting and aging in stainless steel used in Sancerre and Pouilly Fumé, which emphasizes the fruit and can sometimes be quite grassy—"cat's pee" to those who don't care for it!).

Thanks to its oak, this wine has a gently toasty, vanilla nose with hints of pine, tangerine, and melon. The texture is soft; the finish fine, well focused, and crisp.

Food match: Mild-flavored fish such as sole, flounder, trout; cold poached chicken with a tarragon dressing

CHÂTEAU DE BAUN, RUSSIAN RIVER CHARDONNAY 1993, CALIFORNIA, U.S.A., $12

Here is a good example of the terrific lush style of Chardonnay coming from the Russian River Valley of Sonoma County. Pacific breezes make it one of the coolest areas of grape growing in California (a Region 1 on the Winkler and Amerine scale; see page 134). Although the area shares with Burgundy a climate cool enough for the finest Chardonnay and Pinot Noir, this is definitely not a Burgundian Chardonnay. It's uncompromisingly Californian, with a big, buttery tropical-fruit nose, a taste of ripe apple and melon, rounded off with a wallop of butter and oak on the finish.

Food match: Sautéed prawns, crayfish, soft-shell crabs

COLUMBIA, CHARDONNAY COLUMBIA VALLEY WOODBURNE CUVÉE 1993, WASHINGTON STATE, U.S.A., $11

If California is the godfather of North American wine, then Washington State, as the second largest producer in the country and the loss leader in terms of quality, is definitely the godson.

If you love the true expression of Chardonnay without the heavy flavors of oak or alcohol substituting for taste, then this is your wine. Made by David Lake, it has pure and focused flavor, with just a hint of oak, and is one of the best-value Chardonnays in not only North America but the world.

Food match: Mild fish such as sole, scrod, flounder, and shellfish, especially with a lemon butter or white sauce

DOMAINE AUVIGUE,
POUILLY FUISSÉ SOLUTRÉ 1993,
BURGUNDY, FRANCE, $14

Pouilly Fuissé is enormously popular in the United States. At the restaurant, it's probably one of the most requested—even before the diner has looked at our wine list! There are probably two main reasons: it's made from Chardonnay, and it's mid-priced.

Fuissé can come from four communes: Vergisson, Solutré, Fuissé, and Chaintré, with Solutré being the most robust. Auvigue is one of the best, and this one delivers a generous, ripe nose with a touch of tasty oak. It's round in the mouth, with good concentration, intensity, and balance.

Food match: Sautéed shrimp with white wine and shallots

DOMAINE BEAUMARD, SAVENNIÈRES
CLOS SAINT YVES 1993,
LOIRE, FRANCE, $18

Savennières, located in the Anjou, is one of the lesser-known appellations in the Loire Valley, which is too bad because it produces some of the most exciting wine in the region. The grape of choice here is the Chenin Blanc, and the wines are dry (a little sweet is made, but it's only the rump of what was once a much larger production). Although Chenin Blanc is also the grape of Vouvray, the style there is very different from Savennières. Where Vouvray has a silky smoothness (Rabelais called it "taffeta"), Savennières has a sleek frame but tremendous energy and drive.

The Beaumard has an appley, mineral, and smoky nose. It is rich and mouth-filling, with great intensity. A vein of racy acidity keeps the rich fruit on track and well focused. A truly noble wine.

Food match: Steamed lobster; baked crabs; sautéed soft-shell crabs—all with a squeeze of lemon!

DOMAINE PHILIPPE FOREAU,
VOUVRAY SEC CLOS NAUDIN 1993,
LOIRE, FRANCE, $15

Vouvray is the largest white-wine appellation in the Touraine region of the Loire. Its vineyards, on the north bank of that beautiful river, are planted on flint, clay, and limestone-rich soil known locally as *tuffe.* Rabelais, the sixteenth-century author of the rollickingly bawdy *Gargantua and Pantagruel,* came from nearby Tours and wrote of his native wine: "Upon my soul, this is a wine like taffeta." A good description of these wines from the noble Chenin Blanc grape. Although Chenin Blanc (also called Pineau de la Loire locally) makes wonderfully dry wines, it can also be used for delicious demi-secs ideal for aperitifs and to accompany charcuterie, as well as luscious, honeyed sweet wines *(moelleux)* and semi *(pétillant)* and fully sparkling versions.

This dry Vouvray has an enticing aroma of flowers, flint, and quince. It is intense and focused, with well-delineated flavors accented with mineral and citrus. When a wine is this expressive and alive, I sometimes wonder why we're so fixated on Chardonnay.

Food match: Baked trout; steamed lobster with lemon butter

DOMAINE RENÉ BOURGEON,
GIVRY CLOS DE LA BRÛLÉE 1992,
BURGUNDY, FRANCE, $15

Another superbargain from the Chalonnais. René Bourgeon's estate has had roots in the village of Givry since 1530. After World War II, René had to reconstruct the vineyards because the fields were abandoned while his father was held prisoner by the Germans for more than five years. Now he grows Pinot Noir, Chardonnay, and a small amount of Aligoté on his ten-hectare (twenty-four-acre) estate. Although the reds are handled by traditional vinification, René Bourgeon gives his whites a different treatment. Unlike the standard processing, where white wine grapes are crushed immediately and the juice is separated from the skins and stalks, here they are destalked and put into vats, where they are allowed to macerate for up to twenty hours before crushing and fermenting (*macération pelliculaire*—maceration on the skins), which helps develop aroma and give an exta richness to the finished wine.

The nose on this wine, with its floral/honey/hazelnut nuances, is more complex than most from this appellation. On the palate it has a round, creamy texture, with good body and a pleasant soft finish.

Food match: Poached halibut or sautéed scrod

DOMAINE WEINBACH, RIESLING ALSACE CUVÉE THÉO 1992, ALSACE, FRANCE, $20

Madame Colette Faller is a force of nature in the Alsace. As the owner of Domaine Weinbach (established in 1898 on the site of a Capuchin monastery), she is charming and indefatigable in the promotion of her wines. I remember a visit there that was meant to be a quick thirty-minute tour of the winery and a tasting of the current vintage. This turned into an hour and half's tasting of current and past vintages and a not-so-small slice of Kugelhopf.

Riesling Cuvée Théo is a gorgeous wine and would be proud to stand alongside a more expensive Californian or Burgundian Chardonnay. It has brilliant clarity, with light-gold reflections. The aroma is of ripe summer fruit and flowers, with a hint of mint and orange peel. On the palate it is round, luscious, and quite intense, but beautifully balanced by an acidity found in young Riesling.

Food match: I drank it with swordfish steak with a lime-basil dressing, and it was superb!

DOMAINE ZIND-HUMBRECHT,
PINOT D'ALSACE 1992,
ALSACE, FRANCE, $14

This is another superb wine from one of the greatest estates in
Alsace. Olivier Humbrecht (the young proprietor of the domaine
and the only Frenchman to pass the ferociously stiff exams to
become a Master of Wine) calls it Pinot d'Alsace because it's a
mix of three Pinots: Blanc, Auxerrois, and Gris, but it also has—
and this is entirely the result of Humbrecht's inquisitive and
innovative mind—25 percent Chardonnay, a varietal that until
now was practically unheard of in the Alsace.

Like most of the '92 vintage, this wine is ripe and forward, with
a lovely floral, grapy nose. The taste is generous and round, with
a mouth-filling spiciness that reveals the influence of the Pinot
Gris and Auxerrois. The Chardonnay gives a classy gloss usually
associated with much more expensive wines.

Food match: Baked halibut, grouper; roast chicken

ESTANCIA ESTATES, CHARDONNAY
MONTEREY COUNTY 1993,
CALIFORNIA, U.S.A., $12

Estancia Estates is owned by Franciscan Estates Selections, a
group that includes top properties in Chile and California, including Franciscan Oakville Estate and Mount Veeder Winery in
the Napa Valley. The group believes that the Alexander Valley is
better suited to Bordeaux varietals, while cool Monterey is better
for Chardonnay; so they have two estates, one for white, the other
for red. This kind of commitment to *terroir* and quality pays off.

This Chardonnay is straw gold in color, with a ripe, peachy nose
and a touch of oak. Soft and round, it is plush with juicy fruit.

Food match: Grilled fish with a citrus or fruit salsa

FRANÇOISE AND DENIS CLAIR, SAINT-AUBIN 1ER CRU LES MURGERS DES DENTS DE CHIEN 1992, BURGUNDY, FRANCE, $22

The Saint-Aubin appellation (just behind Puligny- and Chassagne-Montrachet) can usually be relied on for good-value reds and whites, but this particular wine has something extra to offer. It is made from grapes from the Murgers des Dents de Chien vineyard, on the western slope of Mont Rachet, directly behind the great *grand cru* Le Montrachet and Chevalier-Montrachet vineyards. It shares its eastern boundary with the very fine *premier cru* vineyard of Puligny-Montrachet Champ Gain, so it's not surprising that Les Murgers has some of the characteristics of its illustrious neighbors.

I love the very clean, pure scent of stones and minerals, intermingled with floral notes. On the palate it has plenty of intensity and a well-knit firmness that suggests aging potential. There are layers of flavors and good length to the finish.

Food match: Baked tilapia or scrod with leeks

GEORGES DUBOEUF, VIOGNIER VIN DE PAYS DE L'ARDÈCHE 1994, RHÔNE, FRANCE, $9

Although Duboeuf is irrevocably linked to the wines of the Beaujolais and Maconnais, he has a keen marketer's eye and saw the enormous potential of the Rhône Valley and the Pays d'Oc. There is now a bevy of fine wines bearing his name from these regions.

The Ardèche is a *département* on the west side of the Rhône and a hotbed of varietals of superior quality. This Viognier (the noble grape of Condrieu) is terrific, with a clean, peachy, melony nose and lush, concentrated fruit with exotic fruit nuances and good acidity that holds it all together. Most good Viognier costs twice as much.

Food match: Poached lobster; pastas with cream-based sauces; crab cakes

GRANJA FILLABOA, S.A.,
FILLABOA ALBARIÑO 1994,
RIAS BAIXAS, SPAIN, $14

The Albariño grape is found in the vineyards along the Atlantic coast in the northwest corner of Spain in the region of Galicia. It is also grown in the Vinho Verde region of Portugal. This unusual and delicious grape, which may have originated in Germany, produces some of the best white wines in Spain and is a perfect accompaniment to the sparkling fresh seafood preparations in the local restaurants. It combines the floral aromatics of Riesling with the textural and aromatic qualities of Viognier—two of the world's most exciting grape varieties.

This wine, one of the best examples, has a pure and penetrating aroma of tropical fruit and grapefruit. Beautifully constructed, it has focused, intense, and concentrated fruit on the palate, with impeccable balance. All of its components are delicately stacked to create a harmonious, vibrant wine.

Food match: Fresh grilled marinated shrimp, seafood salads

HUGEL ET FILS,
GENTIL HUGEL 1993,
ALSACE, FRANCE, $10

Although Alsace was one of the first wine regions to market its wines by varietal, it also has a little-known tradition of blending grapes. Today these wines are called Edelzwicker and are, for the most part, innocuous blends from overproducing vineyards, destined for the carafes of the local *vinstubes*. However, tradition has it that in the nineteenth century there were some very fine blends produced by top estates that went under the generic heading "Gentil" (literally "well-bred"). It's particularly fitting that the ancient firm of Hugel (established 1639) should revive the tradition. Their blend is 60 percent noble grape varieties (Gewürztraminer, Riesling, Pinot Gris, and Muscat), with Sylvaner making up the difference. The Gewürztraminer and Pinot Gris give it body and alcohol, while the Riesling and Muscat contribute aromatics and acid structure. The Sylvaner makes it affordable!

The wine is superb, with a forward, mineral/rose-petal/lychee nose. It is quite rich on the palate, with smooth, spicy, melony fruit and moderate intensity.

Food match: Steamed crayfish; mild cheeses such as Gouda, Port Salut, Havarti

JOSMEYER, ALSACE PINOT AUXERROIS "H" VIEILLES VIGNES 1989, ALSACE, FRANCE, $22

The Josmeyer family domaine, established in 1854 and one of the best in Alsace, is in Wintzenheim, in the heart of the Haut-Rhin, where the best of Alsace wine is made. The Josmeyers grow all of the noble grapes—Riesling, Pinot Gris, Gewürztraminer, and Muscat (the only grapes permitted in the *grand cru* appellation)—as well as so-called lesser grapes: Pinot Blanc, Auxerrois, and Sylvaner. The number of *grand cru* sites in Alsace has grown from twenty-five in 1983 to fifty-one today, and Josmeyer grows the Auxerrois of this wine in *grand cru* vineyards, where it takes on a definitely noble quality.

Auxerrois, also called Pinot Auxerrois, is different from Pinot Blanc, although it is often blended with Pinot Blanc and is part of the Pinot family. The "H" in this wine's name refers to the *grand cru* Hengst Vineyard, while the *vieilles vignes* give it concentration and complexity.

On the evidence of this wine, I would certainly argue that Auxerrois is not a "lesser" varietal. The ripe pear and mineral nose is backed up by a real intensity and concentration on the palate. The wine is fatter in style than Pinot Blanc and has the spiciness and force often found in Pinot Gris. A long and complex finish makes this an extremely stylish wine.

Food match: Roast chicken or quail; monkfish in tarragon cream sauce

LOUIS JADOT,
SAINT-AUBIN 1993,
BURGUNDY, FRANCE, $16

Saint-Aubin is a sleepy little Burgundian village off the main wine route, behind the more illustrious villages of Chassagne-Montrachet and Puligny-Montrachet. The vineyards of the Saint-Aubin appellation reach right up to the western slopes of the *grand cru* vineyards of Puligny and Chassagne. Although Saint-Aubin has a less desirable exposure than its prestigious neighbors and lacks their complexity, a really good Saint-Aubin does share some of the same breeding and class, at half the price of a good *village* Chassagne and Puligny and a quarter the price of one of the *grands cru.*

Jacques Lardière, technical director and winemaker for Jadot, has successfully made a wine that outclasses many white Burgundies at twice the price. This one has a delicious aroma of honeysuckle and apples, with a generous palate of ripe, rich fruit and layers of flavor all beautifully balanced.

Food match: Baked swordfish steaks; mild soft-ripened cheeses like Chaumes, St.-Nectaire, St. André

LOUIS MICHEL ET FILS,
CHABLIS MONTÉE DE TONNERRE 1992,
BURGUNDY, FRANCE, $18

Although the town and vineyards of Chablis are about 125 miles from the heart of the Burgundy, the whites wines made in Chablis are definitely Burgundian. Forget the cheap white jug wine sold as "Mountain Chablis" or some such fanciful and completely misleading name. Real Chablis, like all great white Burgundy, has its own personality, which is rooted in its unique *terroir* (an elusive word that describes a wine's "genetic makeup": a combination of soil, climate, exposure, and viticultural tradition that imparts its "somewhereness," its genius of place).

There are two schools of thought concerning the production of Chablis: the wooden-barrel and the stainless-steel-vat advocates. Although barrel fermentation can add complexity and nuance, some feel it masks the true expression of the *terroir*. Louis Michel is a stainless-steel man, and his wines are wonderfully pure and expressive.

This wine is a *premier cru,* with a stony, mineral nose accented by a hint of oranges. The palate is well defined and focused, with intense, ripe flavors and a long, lingering finish.

Food match: Sautéed crayfish; sautéed shrimp; oysters on the half shell

MURÉ, PINOT BLANC
CÔTE DE ROUFFACH 1992,
ALSACE, FRANCE, $10

Pinot Blanc (which the wine press has pushed hard as a great alternative to Chardonnay) is the rising star of Alsace. There are similarities, and with Chardonnay the most popular white wine grape in the world, it is not surprising that the wine producers of

Alsace saw an opportunity to capture a potentially huge market by offering delicious, rich wines at great prices.

This very classy Pinot Blanc comes from the hillside appellation of Côte de Rouffach on the slopes of the Vosges, near the village of Rouffach. The nose has characteristic floral, ripe pear, and apple nuances, with a smoky hint as though the wine had been aged in oak casks (unlikely, as very few producers use this technique in Alsace). The taste is round and succulent, quite concentrated, harmonious, with a creamy texture and moderately long finish.

Food match: Sautéed catfish or flounder fillets

NORMANS, FAMILY RESERVE CHARDONNAY 1993, SOUTHERN VALES, AUSTRALIA, $10

South Australia (the capital is Adelaide) is the home of some of Australia's most prolific and famous wine districts: Adelaide Hills, Barossa Valley, and Coonawarra. Viticulture in Southern Vales can be traced back to Thomas Hardy in 1857, and even further to John Reynell in 1838. The Thomas Hardy wine company is not only still around; it's the third largest producer in Australia (although the region as a whole is more noted for boutique wineries).

Normans is considered a moderate-size operation with a reputation for turning out high-quality, reasonably priced wines. This one has a brilliant, straw/light-gold color, with ripe pear and butter aromas. It tastes full and round, with crisp lemon/lime tones and a clean finish.

Food match: Cold poached chicken; baked white-fleshed fish such as turbot or halibut with lemon butter

OLIVIER LEFLAIVE, BOURGOGNE CHARDONNAY 1993, BURGUNDY, FRANCE, $10

Olivier Leflaive is a *négociant* as well as a grower and is also co-manager of the famed (if not deified) Domaine Leflaive in Puligny-Montrachet. His reputation is immense and a guarantee of quality even when, as in this case, he is only buying the grapes for this generic 100 percent Chardonnay Burgundy.

The aroma of this wine hints at toasted brioche and ripe pears. On the palate there is a full juicy, sweetish mouth-feel with medium weight and a moderately long finish. It is a bargain wine and a ringer for a white Burgundy with much fancier breeding—and the price tag to go with it!

Food match: Deep-fried batter-dipped sole or catfish; chicken salad

PONZI, PINOT GRIS 1994, OREGON, U.S.A., $16

The Ponzis founded the Ponzi vineyards in Oregon in 1970 and were pioneers in creating the state's standing as a producer of world-class wines. The Ponzis' fame is based on their Pinot Noir; of their white varietals, the Pinot Gris is the most exciting. Its style falls somewhere between Italy (where the grape is known as the Pinot Grigio and produces light, spritzy, crisp wines) and the Alsace (where it is called Tokay, producing richer, slightly "oily," full-bodied wines reminiscent of great white Burgundy). The Ponzi version is probably closer to the style of Alsace in its weight and concentration.

Food match: Grilled fresh sardines, mushroom omelet; fried chicken

QUPÉ, MARSANNE LOS OLIVOS VINEYARD 1993, CALIFORNIA, U.S.A., $12

Qupé, in the Santa Maria Valley AVA of California's South Central Coast region, was founded by owner/winemaker Bob Lindquist in 1982 and has been in the forefront of experimenting with classic Rhône grapes such as Syrah, Mourvèdre, Viognier, and Marsanne. Lindquist is one of the original "Rhône Rangers," along with Randall Grahm of Bonny Doon and Steve Edmunds of Edmunds St. John.

Marsanne is an important grape of the northern Rhône, found particularly in the powerful white Hermitage and Saint-Joseph. If not treated carefully, it can produce heavy, highly alcoholic, undistinguished wine, but in the coolness of the Santa Maria Valley it seems to do very well indeed.

This 1993 is light gold, with an enticing aroma of flowers and

tropical fruit, even orange blossom. The flavors are round and soft, with a medium body and good balance, so you are not sledgehammered by excessive alcohol. The finish is gentle and honeyed.

Food match: Steamed lobster with drawn butter

REDBANK, SOUTH EASTERN AUSTRALIA CHARDONNAY 1992, AUSTRALIA, $10

In the 1970s, when Australia was making its mark as a wine-producing nation, it turned out Chardonnays with the boozy punch and oaky swagger to rival its Californian counterparts at the time. You can still get these blockbusters from Australia (and California, for that matter), but a lot has changed in both places. There's been a swing away from this crude style toward more finesse and elegance, typified by this Redbank Chardonnay.

The wine has crispness and balance, along with plenty of ripe tropical fruit that hasn't been blitzed with oak, so there is a freshness and harmony here. It is medium-bodied and smooth, with a clean, refreshing finish.

Food match: Linguine with shellfish in a light cream sauce; cold cuts

RENÉ ET VINCENT DAUVISSAT, CHABLIS VAILLONS 1ER CRU 1992, BURGUNDY, FRANCE, $30

The quality of wine produced at this family estate is powerful fuel for the argument to use barrels in the Chablis winemaking process. Oak was often used as a method for storing and selling Chablis. But it wasn't considered the traditional method of vinification, nor were new barrels employed as a flavoring element in the wine. Today, however, there are two camps, favoring wood or stainless steel. One is not better than the other. They are just two different styles. The oak-aged are influenced by the wood flavors, while the stainless-steel-aged are pure expressions of grape and *terroir*. Your choice. Dauvissat wines are barrel fermented and aged in cask for ten months; 20 to 40 percent new wood is used for the *grand crus*.

This wine has the green/gold twinkle of a young Chablis. It is aromatic, with the telltale *pierre à fusil* flinty nose, and pear and vanilla nuances. It is rich and penetrating, with focus, structure, and concentration. The wine has great balance and length. Powerful without being heavy. This is great Chardonnay!

Food match: Warm oysters; stone-crab claws with drawn butter; steamed lobster

J. ROCHIOLI, SAUVIGNON BLANC 1994, RUSSIAN RIVER VALLEY, CALIFORNIA, U.S.A., $12

The grape variety Sauvignon Blanc is a bit of a chameleon. Sometimes it is light and flinty, as it often is in the Loire Valley at Sancerre; sometimes it is rich, smooth, and complex, as demonstrated by the barrel-fermented examples in the Graves, where it is likely to be blended with Sémillon. It is a grape that responds to its *terroir* and treatment, allowing it to express itself in these different fashions. It rarely improves with age and is often at its best when fresh and young.

This one is from the cool Russian River Valley in California, where old vines help to contribute to this wine's intense flavor. It has a truly explosive nose of ripe melons and fig. On the palate it reveals rich, juicy flavors, with smooth texture and lively acidity keeping it all in balance.

Food match: Sautéed skate with fresh lemon; baked scallops

VERGET, SAINT-AUBIN 1ER CRU 1993, BURGUNDY, FRANCE, $16

Verget is a newish (1990) *négociant* in Burgundy, established by Jean-Marie Guffens (who first came to the Mâconnais and established his own domaine in 1980). Because Guffens wants to be able to control the whole vinification, he looks to buy grapes only from the best vineyard sites and the oldest vines, where other *négociants* are content to buy juice or even ready-made wine. His wines are barrel fermented and aged in about 50 percent new wood, which gives them a nice oakiness that is counterbalanced by the great fruit concentration in his wines.

This Saint-Aubin is another example of how good a lesser appellation can be in the hands of a master winemaker. Located just behind the villages of Chassagne-Monrachet and Puligny-Montrachet, this is better wine, at about half the price, than many produced by its illustrious neighbors. It's ripe and grapey (reminiscent of freshly crushed grapes and apples). Very classy on the palate: creamy, smooth, and fat.

Food match: Baked swordfish; pumpkin ravioli with a walnut cream sauce

J. J. VINCENT, SAINT-VÉRAN 1992, BURGUNDY, FRANCE, $9

Think of Saint-Véran as the younger brother of Pouilly-Fuissé but the big brother of Mâcon-Villages. It doesn't have quite the glamour (or the price tag) of the former, but it has a bit more prestige than the latter. Before it was graced with its own appellation in 1971, Saint-Véran was sold as "Beaujolais Blanc."

Jean-Jacques Vincent is one of the master *négociants* of the Mâconnais and the producer of the famous Château Fuissé, from which comes a *cuvée vieilles vignes* (old-growth vines) that can rival the best of the Côte de Beaune in class and longevity.

This Saint-Véran has a typical mineral, stony nose, with a touch of butter. It is soft, with a moderate intensity, which makes it perfect for drinking now, and the finish has a bitter-almond nuance which, for me, is the signature of a good Mâconnais white.

Food match: Steamed mussels; sautéed shrimp

ZACA MESA, CHARDONNAY
SANTA BARBARA COUNTY 1993,
CALIFORNIA, U.S.A., $11

Zaca Mesa is one of the largest producers in the Santa Ynez Valley AVA of the South Central Coast (one of my favorite areas for delicious Chardonnay with tropical-fruit flavors and well-balanced acidity). The winery was founded in 1972 and has been home to some of California's most famous winemakers, great names such as Jim Clendenon of Au Bon Climat, Bob Lindquist of Qupé, and Adam Tolmach of Ojai. The current winemaker is Daniel Gehrs, formerly of Congress Springs, where he became the most awarded winemaker in the country.

Barrel fermenting gives this wine a nuance of tasty oak, with layers of pineappley, orange fruit on the nose. On the palate it has a crunchy, juicy texture with good balance. It's not particularly complex. Just particularly good.

Food match: Grilled shrimp with a citrus salsa; turkey sandwiches

LIGHT-BODIED WHITES

This is a checklist of wines for which tasting notes follow.

Alois Lageder, Pinot Bianco 1993, Alto Adige, Italy, $10 (p. 295)

Caliterra, Chardonnay 1994, Curicò, Chile, $6 (p. 296)

Can Feixas, Blanc Seleccio 1993, Penedès, Spain, $9 (p. 296)

Casal Garciá, Vinho Verde Non Vintage, Vinho Verde, Portugal, $6 (p. 297)

Château Bonnet, Entre-Deux-Mers 1993, Bordeaux, France, $8 (p. 298)

Chateau Ste. Michelle Riesling 1994, Columbia Valley, Washington State, U.S.A., $6 (p. 299)

Daniel Gehrs, Muscadet 1992, Monterey, California, U.S.A., $9 (p. 300)

Deinhard, Pinot Blanc QbA 1992, Pfalz, Germany, $6 (p. 300)

Domaine Bregeon, Muscadet sur lie 1994, Muscadet, France, $9
(p. 301)

Domaine de Bagnols, Cassis Blanc 1993, Provence, France, $12
(p. 302)

Domaine de Fontanelles, Sauvignon Blanc 1994, Languedoc,
France, $7.50 (p. 302)

Domaine Marcel Deiss, Riesling Bergheim 1992, Alsace, France,
$14 (p. 303)

Domaine Moreau, Chablis 1992, Burgundy, France, $12
(p. 304)

Domaine Provenquière, Chardonnay Vin de Pays d'Oc 1993,
Languedoc, France, $8 (p. 304)

Domaine Zind-Humbrecht, Riesling Alsace Turkheim 1992,
Alsace, France, $15 (p. 305)

Fattoria Sovestro, Vernaccia di San Gimignano 1992, Tuscany,
Italy, $10 (p. 305)

Flora Springs, Napa Valley Sauvignon Blanc Floréal 1992, Napa,
California, U.S.A., $10 (p. 306)

Fortant de France, Chardonnay Vin de Pays d'Oc 1993, Languedoc, France, $5 (p. 306)

Fratelli Bisci, Verdicchio di Matelica, Le Marche, Italy, $11
(p. 307)

Georges Duboeuf, Chardonnay Vin de Pays d'Oc 1993, Languedoc, France, $8 (p. 307)

Gunderloch, Reisling Jean Baptiste 1994, Rheinhessen, Germany, $13 (p. 308)

Hogue Cellars, Fumé Blanc Columbia Valley 1993, Washington
State, U.S.A., $8 (p. 308)

Lenz, Gewürztraminer 1993, Long Island, New York, U.S.A., $9 (p. 309)

Millbrook, Chardonnay 1992, Hudson Valley, New York, U.S.A., $8 (p. 309)

Mondavi, Fumé Blanc 1994, Napa, California, U.S.A., $10 (p. 310)

Pierre Morey, Bourgogne Blanc Chardonnay 1992, Burgundy, France, $16 (p. 310)

Schloss Lieser, Estate Riesling Medium Dry 1993, Mosel, Germany, $7 (p. 311)

Selbach-Oster, Zeltinger Himmelreich Riesling Kabinett 1993, Mosel, Germany, $12 (p. 312)

Soalheiro, Alvarinho 1992, Vinho Verde, Portugal, $13 (p. 312)

Voss, Sauvignon Blanc Napa Valley 1993, Napa, California, U.S.A., $9 (p. 313)

ALOIS LAGEDER, PINOT BIANCO 1993, ALTO ADIGE, ITALY, $10

The Alto Adige was part of the Austro-Hungarian Empire until after World War I and is even now sometimes referred to as the Sudtirol. German is still the official second language, and there's a marked Germanic slant to the area's winemaking. Not only is the Alto Adige Italy's most northerly viticultural region; it is also the home of her finest white wines (although, surprisingly, the region produces more red than white). Due to its Alpine climate, the growing season is long, perfect for light, aromatic, flavorful whites such as Pinot Bianco, Pinot Grigio, Gewürztraminer, and Sauvignon Blanc.

The family of Alois Lageder has been making wine in the region for 150 years and today is known as being not only technologically innovative but also environmentally sensitive to the needs of its vineyards.

This Pinot Bianco has a freshly crushed white-grape-and-apple nose. It's soft, light, and very refreshing, with a round, clean, and fruity palate.

Food match: Grilled squid with lemon; sautéed shrimp

CALITERRA, CHARDONNAY 1994, CURICÒ, CHILE, $6

Although I usually look to South America for red wine values, this winery consistently puts out one of the best Chardonnays at the price. It's never a blockbuster but is always light, pure, and clean-tasting. The winery is in a subregion, Curicò, of the Maule district, at the southern end of the Central Valley. Because the area is cooled by breezes off the Pacific, the white grapes benefit from a longer growing season and are able to develop aromas and acidity.

The 1994 has a clean, pear, mineral-scented nose, with soft Chardonnay fruit. It's light-bodied and crisp, not unlike a Mâcon from Burgundy.

Food match: Cold shellfish such as shrimp, crayfish; pan-fried filet of sole

CAN FEIXAS, BLANCO SELECCIO 1993, PENEDÈS, SPAIN, $9

Although 80 percent of the grapes grown in the Penedès go into the production of Cava, the sparkling wine of Spain made by traditional methods (see page 114 for more on Cava), there are many other varieties under cultivation. In fact, the whole region has become known for its innovative wines, thanks in large part to the work of Miguel Torres, who studied his winemaking in France.

This wine is a blend of Parellada, Macabeo, and Chardonnay, grown at high altitude to give elegance and crispness. It has a clean, stony, citrusy nose, with a crisp, fresh, and quite intense taste that has the lingering finish reminiscent of a good Chablis.

This may be a slightly difficult wine to pronounce, but it is different, exciting, and, above all, absolutely delicious.

Food match: Raw oysters; poached salmon

CASAL GARCIÁ, VINHO VERDE NON VINTAGE, VINHO VERDE, PORTUGAL, $6

The dry white wines of Portugal are little known in this country, which is a great shame because they can be some of the best values around. This one comes from one of the country's largest producers, the Guedes family at the Aveleda estate.

Vinho Verde comes from the Douro, in northwest Portugal. It is a region of ample rainfall and therefore high humidity, so in order to reduce the risk of rot, the vines are trained on a unique trellising system that can elevate them as high as a medium-size cherry tree: perhaps twelve feet from the ground, compared to the more conventional five to six feet.

Although everything in this region seems green, the wines are mainly red (although not much exported). Vinho Verde is really a description less of color and more of taste. They have a freshness and crispness that is best appreciated young. Most of them are made from a variety of grapes (as is this one) and tend to have low alcohol levels of around 9 percent. They are crackling fresh, with the added spritz of a touch of carbon dioxide. The single-varietal Alvarinhos tend to be more alcoholic (around 12 percent), richer, and more complex.

I think this is one of the most delicious light white wines I have tasted in a long time. There is a citrus nose with a nuance of red currants. There is lively spritz and a crispness that is nicely rounded off by a very gentle dose of added sugar (not unlike a

German Kabinett). At about 8.5 percent alcohol, this is a wine to gulp rather than sip.

Food match: Fruit salad; tomato and mozzarella sandwiches

CHÂTEAU BONNET, ENTRE-DEUX-MERS 1993, BORDEAUX, FRANCE, $8

Although Entre-Deux-Mers translates as "between two seas," it is in fact between two rivers: the Garonne and the Dordogne. This is the region that produces the largest volume of wine in the Bor-

deaux (and until relatively recently, when winemakers literally and figuratively cleaned up their act, too much of it was nasty). It has traditionally been a white-wine region (only white wines can carry the appellation "Entre-Deux-Mers," while reds have to be sold simply as "Bordeaux" or "Bordeaux Supérieur") but in recent years there has been an increased demand for the red wine of the area, and more vineyards have been planted to Cabernet Sauvignon and Merlot. The white-wine grapes of the region are Sauvignon Blanc, Sémillon, and Muscadelle.

Château Bonnet is owned by André Lurton, who also owns Château Louvière in Graves and Clos Fourtet in Saint-Émilion. This wine is made from 50 percent Sémillon, which contributes to its richness, 30 percent Sauvignon Blanc, and 20 percent Muscadelle. Combined, they give the wine a slightly herbal, citrus, and clean sea-air nose. It is fresh and lively on the palate, with good intensity and a tingling lemon-zest finish.

Food match: Sautéed trout with citrus and lemon

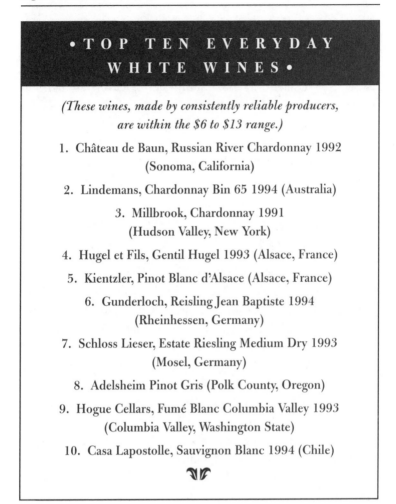

• TOP TEN EVERYDAY WHITE WINES •

(These wines, made by consistently reliable producers, are within the $6 to $13 range.)

1. Château de Baun, Russian River Chardonnay 1992 (Sonoma, California)

2. Lindemans, Chardonnay Bin 65 1994 (Australia)

3. Millbrook, Chardonnay 1991 (Hudson Valley, New York)

4. Hugel et Fils, Gentil Hugel 1993 (Alsace, France)

5. Kientzler, Pinot Blanc d'Alsace (Alsace, France)

6. Gunderloch, Reisling Jean Baptiste 1994 (Rheinhessen, Germany)

7. Schloss Lieser, Estate Riesling Medium Dry 1993 (Mosel, Germany)

8. Adelsheim Pinot Gris (Polk County, Oregon)

9. Hogue Cellars, Fumé Blanc Columbia Valley 1993 (Columbia Valley, Washington State)

10. Casa Lapostolle, Sauvignon Blanc 1994 (Chile)

CHATEAU STE. MICHELLE RIESLING 1994, COLUMBIA VALLEY, WASHINGTON STATE, U.S.A., $6

Riesling, sometimes called Johannisberg Riesling in the United States, is a particularly successful grape variety in Washington State. In fact, it was partly responsible for the recognition the state is getting for its superior wines.

The style of wine tasted here is closer to that of a German Kabinett than to Riesling found in Alsace or Austria. It has a fresh floral, white peach, and citrus aroma. In this case the wine tastes the same as it smells. These mouth-watering flavors are light on the palate, with low alcohol, a hint of sweetness, and, as a result of well-charged acidity, a clean, refreshing dry finish.

Food match: Softshell crabs splashed with freshly squeezed lemon, or seafood salad

DANIEL GEHRS, MUSCADET 1992, MONTEREY, CALIFORNIA, U.S.A., $9

Muscadet in California? Well, the iconoclastic Daniel Gehrs is the only American winemaker specializing exclusively in Loire-style wines (in fact, his back label proudly proclaims "Loire-California Wines"). He's also a vocal advocate of the ABC movement ("Anything But Chardonnay").

French Muscadet (the wine is named after the varietal) is made at the western end of the Loire, near the coastal city of Nantes, while Daniel Gehrs makes his from Monterey County grapes. I'm normally suspicious of American wines that jump on the coattails of famous foreign appellations (e.g., Mountain Chablis, Hearty Burgundy, Champagne), but this one really does taste like the genuine stuff. It has that faintly musky, stony aroma, with ripe, clean juice, supple flavors, and a straightforward, almost salty, finish.

Food match: Wheel on the oysters!

DEINHARD, PINOT BLANC QBA 1992, PFALZ, GERMANY, $6

Pinot Blanc (which appears to have originated in Alsace, where it is also known as Clevener or Klevener) makes a great alternative to Chardonnay. It has a similar texture but is slightly less aggressive on the palate, which makes it a bit more versatile with food.

Deinhard, established in 1794, is not only one of the largest estate owners and *négociants* in Germany but also one of the most innovative. It was the first to simplify its labels by stating the varietal without confusing the customer with vineyard designations and ripeness levels. Since the 1989 vintage, they have also been making exclusively drier-style wines, without stating on the label whether they were *trocken* (dry) or *halbtrocken* (semi-dry).

This wine has a clean, peachy, citrus aroma and is light and soothing on the palate, with refreshing acidity. A great "house white."

Food match: Salmon ravioli with herb butter; steamed vegetables

DOMAINE BREGEON, MUSCADET SUR LIE 1994, MUSCADET, FRANCE, $9

Muscadet is the name of the region. The grape variety is also called Muscadet, although the ampelogical term is Melon de Bourgogne, whose origins are thought to be Burgundian (as suggested by the name). *Sur lie* literally means "on the dead yeast cells," what is left of the yeast bacteria after fermentation. Leaving these cells in the wine protects it from oxidation and continues to nourish it with proteins, thereby adding extra body and richness to the finished wine. A small amount of carbon dioxide is left in the wine, providing a slight spritz and contributing to its zesty, lively character.

This undervalued wine is a classic example of the appellation. Its stony mineral aroma makes it easy to imagine waves crashing on a sandy beach. The palate is light- to medium-bodied, with fresh, crisp, and ripe fruit flavors.

Food match: Oysters by the dozen!

DOMAINE DE BAGNOLS, CASSIS BLANC 1993, PROVENCE, FRANCE, $12

Cassis is a small appellation next to Marseilles on the Mediterranean, and of the seven appellations of Provence (Bandol, Coteaux d'Aix-en-Provence, Bellet, Côtes de Provence, Pallette, and Coteaux d'Aix-en-Provence-Les-Baux are the others), it is the only one to produce more white than red or rosé, which is unusual, given the region's warm climate. The primary grape of Cassis, the Ugni Blanc, is often blended with Granache Blanc, Sauvignon Blanc, and Marsanne, as is the case with this wine.

There's a pretty golden straw color and a warm aroma of peaches, orange blossom, and honey. It is light yet has good texture and, like the Mediterranean sea breezes, a slightly salty tang.

Food match: Fish stews; grilled red snapper

DOMAINE DE FONTANELLES, SAUVIGNON BLANC 1994, LANGUEDOC, FRANCE, $7.50

A stunning Sauvignon Blanc from the Languedoc? This must be a mistake! It must be from Bordeaux. Graves maybe. Or maybe it's New World. Yes, it could be from California or Australia. True, many of the varietal wines coming from the Languedoc taste modern and technical, but they also taste damn good. And as I've stated so many times before, it's hard to find more flavor for your dollar than with the wines from the Languedoc-Roussillon.

This domaine hired Australian consultants to help them with their Sauvignon Blanc production. In fact, when referring to this wine they simply call it "l'Australienne." With Sauvignon Blanc, the Australians tend to emphasize perfume, richness, and freshness. They allow extended skin contact with the juice—somewhat dangerous, because of the risk of oxidation. But when it is performed well, the finished wine tends to have more texture and richness than traditionally vinified white wines.

Fontanelles is pale gold-green in color. It has a penetrating nose of fresh flowers, citrus, peach, and pineapple. This lovely aroma is followed by a smooth-textured wine with terrific intensity, moderate body and complexity, good refreshing acidity, so often lacking in hot climates, and a tingling finish.

Food match: Grilled fish; grilled chicken; mild cheeses

DOMAINE MARCEL DEISS, RIESLING BERGHEIM 1992, ALSACE, FRANCE, $14

The dynamic, incredibly talented, eccentric Jean-Michel Deiss heads this family estate of twenty hectares and produces some of the most intense wine in Alsace. He is a believer in and strong promoter of the concept of *terroir* and how the finished wine is indelibly imprinted with the influence of a site's soil composition, exposure, microclimate, and the correct grape variety. The other school of thought says the personality of the wine is made by the winemaker and will not be much different if the grapes come from different sources. One taste of Jean-Michel's Rieslings from the same vintage but different vineyard sites answers the questions emphatically.

The house style is one of incredible balance. These wines aren't heavy but have profound finesse and intensity.

This Riesling is made from grapes grown in the commune of Bergheim, where the Deisses reside. It has the most wonderfully seductive aroma of ripe peaches, citrus fruits, and honeysuckle. On the palate it provides a mouthful of delicious concentrated fruit with an ethereal touch and a long, zesty finish.

Food match: Sautéed halibut or other delicate, flaky white-fleshed fish with fresh herb sauce

DOMAINE MOREAU, CHABLIS 1992, BURGUNDY, FRANCE, $12

This is your basic Chablis. Not *grand cru,* not *premier cru,* but good and honestly made. Although this wine comes from vineyards on the perimeter of the best sites, its integrity elevates it way above the second-class status you would normally expect from its location. There is nothing complicated or reserved about this wine; it's honest and pure and unpretentious, admirable qualities both in wine and in people!

Here is a textbook Chablis with racy mineral aroma and steely nervousness on the palate that give it great focus and intensity. The beauty of Moreau's Chablis, however, is that the steel core is wrapped in a coat of fleshy fruit.

Food match: Oysters on the half-shell. What else!

DOMAINE PROVENQUIÈRE, CHARDONNAY VIN DE PAYS D'OC 1993, LANGUEDOC, FRANCE, $8

Another winner from the hotbed of *vin de pays,* where winemakers are making more and more use of those old warhorse "fighting varietals" Chardonnay, Merlot, and Cabernet Sauvignon. The problem with many regions making Chardonnay is that they are trying to produce Burgundy wannabes instead of letting the grape express itself in its native climate and geography. Domaine Provenquière doesn't make that mistake. This is a delicious, pure, and unpretentious Chardonnay that is perfectly happy being what it is, rather than trying to be a Burgundy or Santa Barbara. As you might expect from a hot climate, there is plenty of straightforward fruit, but it is well balanced by its acidity. Light and clean-tasting, it has a slight hint of apple and a crisp finish.

Food Match: Cold cuts; chicken sandwiches; fried fish sandwiches

DOMAINE ZIND-HUMBRECHT,
RIESLING ALSACE TURKHEIM 1992,
ALSACE, FRANCE, $15

In Alsace, Zind-Humbrecht is the equivalent of Romanée-Conti in Burgundy, Vega Sicilia in Spain, or Angelo Gaja in Italy: the best! Here is a domaine that operates with a rigorous attention to detail and an almost evangelical devotion to producing the best wine it can, year in, year out. For example, where the appellation law allows a seventy-hectoliter-per-hectare yield, Olivier Humbrecht believes the maximum should be thirty-five hectoliters per hectare; anything more, he feels, dilutes the juice. It's hardly surprising, then, that his wines are among the most concentrated and expressive in all Alsace.

This Riesling is made from the fruit of the young vines of the *grand cru* vineyard. It is pale-straw yellow, with a pure, ripe pear/quince nose and mineral and citrus overtones. On the palate it is rich and firm, with good concentration, and its breeding shows through in the long, well-focused finish.

Food match: Lobster with drawn butter; sautéed scallops

FATTORIA SOVESTRO,
VERNACCIA DI SAN GIMIGNANO 1992,
TUSCANY, ITALY, $10

Although the area centered on the Tuscan town of San Gimignano was Italy's first *denominazione di origine controllata,* it does not mean that all the wines under its banner are good. Far from it. The massive tourist attraction that the many-towered medieval hill town has become caused many producers to take liberties with quality. As a consequence, the notorious overproduction and dilution of taste put the skids under the whole appellation. But thanks to several small and reputable winemakers, such as the Baroncini at Sovestro, there is still some wonderful Vernaccia to be had.

The nose of this wine is an explosion of ripe pear and melon, while the taste is of freshly crushed fruit. There's great balance and relatively low alcohol (11.5 percent).

Food match: Melon and prosciutto; fettucine with butter and herbs

FLORA SPRINGS, NAPA VALLEY SAUVIGNON BLANC FLORÉAL 1992, NAPA, CALIFORNIA, U.S.A., $10

Floréal is the second label of awarding-winning Flora Springs. Their premium wine is made from exclusively estate-grown grapes, whereas Floréal comes from a mix of estate-grown and purchased fruit.

This wine has a terrific, open, forward nose of tropical fruit and lime. It is soft on the palate, with a smooth richness that comes from aging the wine on the lees of the premium Flora Springs Sauvignon Blanc. The finish is crisp and stimulating.

Food match: Smoked salmon or trout; ceviche salad; fried chicken

FORTANT DE FRANCE, CHARDONNAY VIN DE PAYS D'OC 1993, LANGUEDOC, FRANCE, $5

Fortant de France, founded in 1982 by Robert Skalli, is the largest producer of varietals in France, working with grapes grown on seventeen thousand acres in the Languedoc-Roussillon. This wine is a perfect example of straightforward Chardonnay. It's not complicated or complex but has a very clean appley, anise nose and pure well-balanced fruit.

Food match: Turkey sandwiches; sautéed cod or catfish

FRATELLI BISCI,
VERDICCHIO DI MATELICA,
LE MARCHE, ITALY, $11

The Verdicchio, although not the most widely planted grape of Le Marche (a region of central Italy, on the Adriatic coast), is easily the most famous. It used to have the dubious distinction of an amphora-shaped bottle that put it on the same level as the straw-covered Chianti flask—i.e., tacky packaging to hide tacky wine. Producers of Verdicchio have now mostly ditched the hokey bottle and improved the wine.

Fratelli Bisci have probably done more than anyone to improve the quality of Verdicchio. They have extracted aromas and flavors from a grape that most people thought simply didn't have the right stuff. It is the quintessential fish wine, with a floral, honeysuckle, peachy nose and an ample and textured palate with a lovely fresh lemony finish.

Food match: Sea bass with a white-wine sauce, pasta with shellfish

GEORGES DUBOEUF,
CHARDONNAY VIN DE PAYS D'OC 1993,
LANGUEDOC, FRANCE, $8

This is a formidable combination: Chardonnay; Georges Duboeuf; Vin de Pays d'Oc. Chardonnay is the world's most popular white. Georges Duboeuf is the leader in producing good-quality inexpensive wines. And although he is better known for his Beaujolais, in recent years he has been applying his skills as a *négociant* to other parts of France. Either he looks for good-quality growers and buys and blends their grapes for a consistent *cuvée,* or he will buy the entire output of an exceptional grower and bottle the wine under the name of the domaine. The third part of the equation is the region, one of the most exciting for good-value wines in all of France.

This Chardonnay is clean and fruit, with an apple nose, fresh-tasting and round-textured on the palate. All of which adds up to a light-bodied, well-balanced, and thoroughly unpretentious wine. In a region that can easily produce highly alcoholic, clumsy wines, it is interesting to note that this one is only around 12 percent.

Food match: Roast chicken; rice pilaf

GUNDERLOCH, RIESLING JEAN BAPTISTE 1994, RHEINHESSEN, GERMANY, $13

While the wines of the Mosel are floral, with the flavor of autumn apples and pears, the wines of the Rhine are fuller and plumper, with the summer tastes and aromas of peach and apricot. The Gunderloch estate, owned by Fritz and Agnes Hasselbach, produces wines of great personality, due partly to the iron ore that reddens the soil and gives the wines power and richness.

The nose is floral, smoky, tangily scented. The palate is crisp, with broad, earthy, stony flavors of great depth. Beautifully balanced by an acidity that leaves a long, lingering aftertaste.

Food Match: Sautéed brook trout with brown butter, or can be enjoyed on its own

HOGUE CELLARS, FUMÉ BLANC COLUMBIA VALLEY 1993, WASHINGTON STATE, U.S.A., $8

This is consistently one of my favorite Sauvignon Blancs, although I must say that varietal is not my white wine of choice. It can sometimes have a musky, herbal nose that I find too intense, even downright rank (particularly characteristic of Sauvignon Blancs from the hotter areas of California and Australia). I like it best in the Loire's Sancerre and Pouilly Fumé. Washington State's cool climate is also sympathetic to the grape.

Hogue Cellars' Fumé Blanc is lovely, with a vibrant, floral nose intermingled with a slightly grassy, flinty note. It is dry and moderately rich, with good texture and intensity. Very refreshing.

Food match: Poached salmon with tarragon mayonnaise; clams on the half shell

LENZ, GEWÜRZTRAMINER 1993, LONG ISLAND, NEW YORK, U.S.A., $9

The young Long Island wine industry is struggling for recognition. But I sometimes wonder if it isn't fighting for a share of an already overcrowded market when in fact its real strength is in Sauvignon Blanc and Gewürztraminer for the whites and Cabernet Franc for the reds: varietals that do best in cool-climate regions.

Gewürztraminer often makes low-acid wine with an alcohol wallop that can make it too blowsy and heavy. But this one is varietally aromatic, with rose-petal, lychee, and pear aromas. It has a good core of fruit, which is light and well balanced, with a bracing acidity that leaves a clean aftertaste.

Food match: Your next clambake; roast cornish hen; Chinese food

MILLBROOK, CHARDONNAY 1992, HUDSON VALLEY, NEW YORK, U.S.A., $8

When John Dyson, the owner of Millbrook, is not being deputy mayor of New York, he is a very talented winemaker. He founded his winery in 1981 in this miniature paradise in the Hudson Valley, about an hour and a half's drive from New York City. There he grows Chardonnay, Gamay Noir, Pinot Noir, Cabernet Franc, Cabernet Sauvignon, Merlot, and Italian varietals such as Nebbiolo, Sangiovese, and Tocai Friulano (hard to find but worth the effort, because it's absolutely scrumptious).

This Chardonnay defines how elegant and discreet this grape can be when handled with care. Instead of trying to produce great big oaky and alcoholic blockbusters, the people at Millbrook understand their soil and climate. Hudson Valley wines tend to be more understated, gentle, and subtle—allowing the grape to express its natural qualities without being masked by oak or excessive alcohol.

Food match: Rice salad; cold pasta salad; chicken noodle soup

MONDAVI, FUMÉ BLANC 1994, NAPA, CALIFORNIA, U.S.A., $10

Robert Mondavi is the father of modern Sauvignon Blanc. When, in 1967, he decided to ferment it at cool temperatures, mature it in French barrels, and call it Fumé Blanc (borrowed from Pouilly Fumé), he not only revived a style but also created an industry. Before 1967 there had been 232 acres planted to Sauvignon Blanc in the Napa Valley; today there are over 13,000 acres and rising.

Here is a fresh-cut grass, herbal, and melon aroma sweetened by a hint of vanilla from the oak barrels. With good presence on the palate, it is light- to medium-bodied, lively with a long finish.

Food match: Chicken with tarragon; linguine with smoked scallops

PIERRE MOREY, BOURGOGNE BLANC CHARDONNAY 1992, BURGUNDY, FRANCE, $16

The dominance of Chardonnay as a brand-leader varietal has meant that its name appears more frequently on the labels of

French wines from Burgundy. Just bear in mind that Bourgogne Blanc must, by law, be made from Chardonnay unless it says Bourgogne Aligoté, in which case it is made from Aligoté.

Pierre Morey is a master winemaker and longtime resident of Meursault, although he does not own any of his own vineyards there. He has been employed as a *mettayeur* (winemaker) for some of the most famous vineyards in Burgundy (until recently at the Domaine des Comtes Lafon). The energetic M. Morey is presently employed as chief winemaker at Domaine Leflaive in Puligny-Montrachet, in addition to running his own domaine (Pierre Morey) and a *négociant* business (Morey Blanc).

It wouldn't surprise me if the grapes used for this wine were taken from young Meursault vines or barrels that Pierre Morey did not feel were quite good enough for his prestige *cuvées*. There's a Meursault nose with hints of honey and nuts, and on the palate it is soft and juicy. This wine has breeding and balance, and a nice smooth finish.

Food match: Sea bass, turbot, or scrod with beurre blanc

SCHLOSS LIESER,
ESTATE RIESLING MEDIUM DRY 1993,
MOSEL, GERMANY, $7

Importer Rudi Weist of Cellars International/ILNA Selections has been engaged in a courageous effort to make German wines more accessible to an American market that traditionally has always been a bit wary. The marketing program is called "Estate Riesling," and it aims, among other things, to make the labels of its German wines as easy to read as American wines. Gone is all the heavily gothic-type verbiage that puts off so many American customers. Now the winery and grape type are predominant. But this is not just about labeling. With this program, the grapes may be blended from more than one site in order to achieve consistency from vintage to vintage. These are hand-harvested estate-grown Rieslings, and Rudi has persuaded some of the most famous estates in Germany to participate in the program, so that now one can find some of the greatest Rieslings from revered vineyards for under $10.

The Schloss Lieser Estate Riesling 1993 is an excellent example of the program. Not only is the label easy to read and understand, but the wine is also a fine Mosel with floral, mineral, and citrus elements on the nose. On the palate it is stony and well focused, with good grip and balance. It is only 10 percent alcohol, light and beautifully refreshing.

Food match: Mildly spicy food, such as Indonesian satays or Thai dishes

SELBACH-OSTER, ZELTINGER HIMMELREICH RIESLING KABINETT 1993, MOSEL, GERMANY, $12

The slate slopes rise to seven hundred feet above the river Mosel, and the steeper they are, the better the wine. The portion of the Himmelreich vineyard owned by Johannes Selbach in the commune of Zeltingen is almost sheer and faces south. This is one of my favorite Mosel wines, embodying everything I love about them.

The aroma is citrusy, with mineral and green-apple tones. On the palate it has explosive, crunchy fruit, with slate and lemon-zest accents that give the wine an incredible zippy focus and drive. A mouth-watering wine that I find absolutely irresistible.

Food match: Pasta with light cream and cheese sauces; pork chops and apple sauce

SOALHEIRO, ALVARINHO 1992, VINHO VERDE, PORTUGAL, $13

This Alvarinho is an incredible Vinho Verde and not at all like the easygoing, light, and slightly spritzy versions found for five or six dollars. I love those wines also, but they are for casual drinking and picnics. This is a more serious wine, which would not disgrace the wine list of any fine restaurant or a special occasion at home.

The Alvarinho grape (called the Albariño in Spain's northern province of Galicia) is found in the northernmost part of Portugal, where it makes a unique varietal Vinho Verde that, because it is low-yielding, produces a higher alcohol level and more body than most Vinho Verdes.

The color is light gold, and the nose is redolent of ripe peaches, melon, and lemon zest. The texture is smooth and luscious but balanced by crisp acidity, while the finish is long and refreshing.

Food match: Grilled snapper; fried calamari with lemon

VOSS, SAUVIGNON BLANC
NAPA VALLEY 1993,
NAPA, CALIFORNIA, U.S.A., $9

Voss is owned by Robert Hill Smith, who also owns the Yalumba winery in southern Australia's hilly Pewsey Vale. His winemaker works at both Yalumba and Voss, which gives him a unique opportunity to make two vintages a year, one in the southern hemisphere and one in the northern. Given these transcontinental connections, it's not surprising that they produce Sauvignon Blanc in a manner the French call *à l'australienne.* That is to say, the grapes are crushed and vinified at very low temperature (about thirty-five degrees Fahrenheit), after a few hours' skin contact in order to enhance the aroma and retain freshness.

The nose on this wine made me think immediately of tangerines and pineapples: a real fruit salad. It has good focus on the palate, with moderate concentration and a pleasant, clean, refreshing finish.

Food match: Chicken salad with oranges or mango; sushi; cold seafood salad

ROSÉS

This is a checklist of wines for which tasting notes follow.

Bodegas Vinicola de Navarra, Las Campañas 1994, Navarra, Spain, $6 (p. 315)

Château de Jau, Clos de Paulliles 1993, Roussillon, France, $9 (p. 315)

Commanderie de Peyrassol, Coteaux d'Aix-en-Provence 1993, Provence, France, $12 (p. 316)

Domaine de Triennes, Gris de Triennes 1994, Provence, France, $7 (p. 317)

Étude, Rosé of Pinot Noir 1993, California, U.S.A., $12 (p. 317)

J. Phelps, Vin de Mistral Grenache Rosé 1994, California, U.S.A., $9 (p. 318)

Juliàn Chivite, Gran Fuedo Rosado 1993, Navarra, Spain, $7 (p. 318)

McDowell, Grenache Rosé McDowell Valley Les Vieux Cépages 1992, Mendocino, California, U.S.A., $8 (p. 319)

BODEGAS VINICOLA
DE NAVARRA, LAS CAMPAÑAS 1994,
NAVARRA, SPAIN, $6

Navarra is probably one of the best regions in the world for rosé. Its soil, climate, and grape varieties are ideal. The Garnacha (Grenache in France) is the predominant grape, and as in France, where arguably the best rosé is Tavel made from Grenache, it produces the best rosé in Spain.

This wine is a remarkable value. The color is quite pale, with red reflections. The nose is spicy and fruity. It's slightly *pétillant,* with a lovely fruity but dry light-to-medium-bodied palate.

Food match: Cold cuts; fish soup; saffron-flavored and mildly spicy dishes

CHÂTEAU DE JAU,
CLOS DE PAULLILES 1993,
ROUSSILLON, FRANCE, $9

The winery (owned by the family who brought us Ja Ja de Jau, a brand of inexpensive red and white) is in the Roussillon, not far from the Spanish border, a region that's not afraid of rosé! The locals drink it with seafood, charcuterie, grilled meats, spicy fish soup, and as an aperitif. It is so versatile because it is a red wine made like a white. It has body that will stand up to richer dishes but, served chilled, is just fine with seafood.

The nose on this wine jumps out of the glass with crushed plum and strawberry aromas; and on the palate it is mouth-wateringly rich and spicy. This is the vinous equivalent to potato chips—I bet you can't drink just one glass!

Food match: See above!

• TOP TEN ROSÉS •

*(These wines, made by consistently reliable producers,
are within the $7 to $15 range.)*

1. Juliàn Chivite, Gran Fuedo Rosado 1993
(Navarra, Spain)

2. Sierra Cantabria Rosé (Rioja, Spain)

3. Domaine de Triennes Gris de Triennes 1994
(Provence, France)

4. Commanderie de Peyrassol, Coteaux d'Aix-en-Provence
Rosé 1993 (Provence, France)

5. Castello Di Ama Chianto Rosso (Tuscany, Italy)

6. Château d'Aqueria, Tavel (Rhône, France)

7. Château de Tigné, Rosé d'Anjou (Loire, France)

8. Domaine de Bagnols (Cassis, France)

9. Saintsbury Vin Gris (Carneros, California)

10. Bonny Doon, Vin Gris de Cigare (Santa Cruz, California)

COMMANDERIE DE PEYRASSOL, COTEAUX D'AIX-EN-PROVENCE ROSÉ 1993, PROVENCE, FRANCE, $12

The large appellation of Coteaux d'Aix-en-Provence is in the hill country behind Marseilles and east of the river Rhône. The landscape is rugged and hot, the hills are dotted with wild herbs and umbrella pines. The people there live outdoors in the summer and like their wine and food to have a certain spicy zestiness.

I love rosé and this one in particular. I'm refreshed just by looking at its beautiful salmon color. The nose is peppery/raspberry, while the palate, although cooling, has a richness and texture.

Food match: Brandade de morue (baccalao); tomato-based dishes, hard cheeses; roast vegetable aioli

DOMAINE DE TRIENNES, GRIS DE TRIENNES 1994, PROVENCE, FRANCE, $7

What better pedigree can a wine have than Aubert de Villaine of Domaine de la Romanée-Conti and Jacques Seysses of Domaine Dujac, both great Burgundy estates? In 1989 they bought an existing winery in the Var department of Provence and started making wine with the local grapes, Syrah, Mourvèdre, and Cinsault, as well as Cabernet Sauvignon and Merlot. The results reflect the enormous skill of these two world-class winemakers.

Gris de Triennes is a *gris de gris,* or in other words, a rosé. *Gris de gris* may be slightly paler than most rosés because it has a shorter maceration period in which to pick up color from the grapeskins. This one is a typical blush but has an exuberant nose of cherries and pepper. Thoroughly refreshing, with a slightly spicy finish, this is a perfect summer thirst quencher.

Food match: Turkey sandwiches; steamed clams with a drop of Durkees

ÉTUDE, ROSÉ OF PINOT NOIR 1993, CALIFORNIA, U.S.A., $12

In the words of Étude's owner and winemaker, Tony Soter, "This wine is the result of me trying to make a better red wine." One way to make a better red wine is to draw off some of the juice after crushing the grapes to increase the ratio of stems, skins, and pulp to the juice (a method called *saignée,* or "bleeding," in France). The result is a more structured and concentrated wine. Since the grape's pigment is concentrated in the skin, the amount of time the juice macerates with the skin determines the wine's depth of color.

This wine from Carneros has a superb salmon/tangerine hue and a floral nose, with small red-berry aromas typical of Pinot Noir. It's dry but has a ripe red raspberry, juicy quality that makes it refreshing. It's quite rich and full-bodied enough to work with many types of food.

Food match: Grilled spiced shrimp; honey-glazed baked chicken; pasta with grilled vegetables and tapenade

J. PHELPS, VIN DE MISTRAL GRENACHE ROSÉ 1994, CALIFORNIA, U.S.A., $9

Famous Napa Valley producer Joseph Phelps fell in love with the wines of the south of France during a vacation (he now owns a house in Provence). He was one of the first to make Syrah in California and in 1989 started the Vin de Mistral label.

This rosé reflects the warmth of Provence transplanted to the Napa Valley. With a blush red/orange robe, it looks like a sunset in a glass. It has an explosive aroma of crushed strawberries and spiced red currants. Fruity and rich on the palate, this wine must be what they had in mind when they created the cooler.

Food match: Hot dogs; hamburgers; vegetable fritters; grilled squid with curry oil

JULIÀN CHIVITE, GRAN FUEDO ROSADO 1993, NAVARRE, SPAIN, $7

Why does rosé suffer from an inferiority complex? I guess because there's so much lousy rosé around. Much "Rosé d'Anjou" is nothing more than candy water, and "white" Zinfandel doesn't even have the chutzpah to call itself rosé. Nobody with any sophistication would drink rosé, would they? Surely that's strictly for the pink-syrup sippers. Well, if you think that, you haven't been drinking the right rosés.

Although not all white Zinfandels are cloying and heavy-handed, the place to look for good dry rosés is on the French and Spanish Mediterranean. Mediterranean cuisine, with its lusty flavors of garlic, herbs, and tomato, can often overwhelm a fine white or red, and it's certainly more likely than not that diners in the south of France or in Spain will choose a dry, slightly fruity, spicy rosé to accompany their grilled fish, or their creamy bourride, or their brandade, heady with garlic and salt cod. As Mediterranean food is now so popular in our kitchens, perhaps it's time we had a closer look at these European rosés, so brilliantly suited to a more casual but full-flavored cuisine.

The wonderful salmon/cherry color of Chivite's rosado is almost enough on its own to quench a thirst. This, together with the vibrant raspberry nose and bright fruitiness with a hint of spice on the palate, will refresh even the most jaded taste buds. Yet for all its prettiness, there's a real wine here, with enough body to carry the flavor and provide a good satisfying mouthful.

Food match: Grilled fresh anchovies; Greek salad; tuna Niçoise

McDOWELL, GRENACHE ROSÉ McDOWELL VALLEY LES VIEUX CÉPAGES 1992, MENDOCINO COUNTY, CALIFORNIA, U.S.A., $8

McDowell established McDowell Valley in Mendocino County as an AVA (see page 137) and was the first and only winery with that appellation. They are also dedicated to producing wines from grape varieties commonly found in the Rhône Valley of France, making them one of the original Rhône Rangers.

This is a textbook dry rosé in the style of the aromatic wines of Provence. It has a beautiful pale-salmon hue and an expressive nose that would smell of sunshine if such a thing were possible in a wine. The lively, rich berry notes and dry mouth-feel make it a wonderful accompaniment to many kinds of food.

Food match: Try with grilled red snapper drizzled with olive oil; melon and prosciutto; pizza

SPARKLING WINES
AND
CHAMPAGNE

This is a checklist of wines for which tasting notes follow.

Segura Viudas, Cava Aria Estate Brut, Penedès, Spain, $10
   (p. 328)

Veuve Clicquot Ponsardin, Champagne, France, $32 (p. 329)

ALSACE WILLM, CRÉMANT D'ALSACE, ALSACE, FRANCE, $14

The production of Crémant d'Alsace is subject to the same regulations as Champagne. And the permitted grape varieties are
Pinot Blanc, Pinot Noir, Pinot Gris, and the related Auxerrois.
Most Crémant d'Alsace are a bit higher in acid than Champagne,
since the base wine is rarely allowed to go through its malolactic
fermentation, which transforms the tart malic acid to the softer
lactic acid. This makes for a light, crisp style of sparkling wine.

   This one from Willm is consistently one of the best examples.
It is made entirely from Pinot Blanc, and it has a pale-straw color
with a very lively "mousse." It has a slightly biscuity nose with
apple and pear notes and a fresh, clean citrusy palate. Good
intensity and body.

Food match: Quiche; onion tart; can also be enjoyed as an aperitif

ARGYLE, BRUT 1989, WILLAMETTE VALLEY, OREGON, U.S.A., $15

The wine industry in Oregon is fairly recent. It is only since the late
'60s that the industry has taken hold, and growth continues at a
good clip. The early pioneers experimented with Pinot Noir, sus-
pecting that the cool climate might be just right for this capricious
grape variety. As grapes grown in cool climates with longer growing
seasons appear to develop greater complexity, Oregon just might
prove to be the promised land in this country for Pinot Noir. But
Argyle seems to have opened the door to another type of wine.
Champagne is made with Pinot Noir and Chardonnay, also in a

cool climate region of France. And if others can produce sparkling wines of equal quality to Argyle, then Oregon may emerge as a leader in producing world-class sparkling wine as well.

This wine is made from 60 percent Pinot Noir and 40 percent Chardonnay. It is light-straw-colored, with a fine bubble. It smells of freshly toasted bread and pears with good body and texture, and a crisp refreshing finish.

Food match: Cheese fritters or puffs; macaroni and cheese

BATISTE PERTOIS CRAMANT BRUT BLANC DE BLANCS N.V., CHAMPAGNE, FRANCE, $30

This is another small privately owned Champagne house that doesn't get the recognition it deserves. It doesn't belong to the Syndicat de Grandes Marques de Champagne (see page 167), but membership to this exclusive club is not a guarantee of quality, and many houses not included, such as this one, are truly superior. It makes Champagne the old-fashioned way. The base wine is vinified and aged in oak, a practice employed by Krug, and it is bottled unfiltered. The *grand cru* village of Cramant in the Côte des Blancs is authorized only to produce Chardonnay, which in turn is the only permitted grape in Blanc de Blancs Champagne.

It is light-straw-colored, with a mildly yeasty, perfumed, appley nose with a hint of spice. It is elegant and light, with terrific intensity of flavor. Its lively citrusy finish is everything I look for in a Blanc de Blancs, leaving the palate stimulated and refreshed.

Food match: Caviar; fried oysters; lobster omelet

BOUVET, SAUMUR BRUT SAPHIR 1990, LOIRE, FRANCE, $14

The name for sparkling Saumur is Saumur d'Origine. It is made by the *méthode champenoise* and uses mostly Chenin Blanc, with up to 20 percent each of Sauvignon Blanc and Chardonnay permitted. This appellation is the largest producer of Champagne-style wine outside Champagne itself.

The house of Bouvet is the shortened name for Bouvet-Ladubay, one of the leading sparkling Saumur houses, founded in 1851 by the Champagne firm of Taittinger. This association with one of the top Champagne producers goes a long way to explain its very high level of quality.

The wine has a clean, flowery, and quince/pear nose, expressing the high percentage of Chenin Blanc. It is fresh-tasting, with light lemony flavors, a creamy palate, and lively zesty acidity for a tingling, appetite-stimulating finish. A remarkable value.

Food match: Vegetable curries; satays; mildly spicy Chinese food; cold fried chicken

DOMAINE CARNEROS BY TAITTINGER, CALIFORNIA, U.S.A., $18

In a tribute to the potential of California sparkling wine, the *grand marque* Champagne house Taittinger purchased land and planted Chardonnay and Pinot Noir in the cool Carneros district in 1982 and 1983. Unlike most Champagne houses, they own their own vineyards and consequently have far greater control over the quality of the grapes used for the wine than do houses that must purchase grapes.

In the Taittinger tradition, the style of the wine emphasizes elegance. It is made predominantly from Chardonnay, yet the Pinot Noir contributes richness and perfume. It is persistent and well defined on the palate, with a fine bead and toasty nuances. Displaying richness and depth of flavor, it is a wine of great finesse and length.

Food match: Oysters; sushi; tempura; linguine with vodka sauce

J. C. THEVENET, BLANC DE BLANCS DE CHARDONNAY, BURGUNDY, FRANCE, $15

This fine producer in the Mâconnais turns out flavorful white wines with the Macon Pierreclos and Saint Véran appellations, produced from the Chardonnay grape. In addition to these still wines, he produces this Champagne look-alike, also from 100 percent Chardonnay. Anytime "Blanc de Blancs" appears on a label of French sparkling wine, it is made from Chardonnay only.

After searching my wine cellar for a pre-mealtime drink, I came across this wine and a bottle of Pol Roger Champagne. Confronted with the dilemma of having to choose between the real thing and a Champagne alternative, I usually go for the real thing. But knowing this was an aperitif only, on a warm spring night, and the chances of finishing the bottle were slim at best, I opted for the Blanc de Blancs. I was glad I did. It has a yeasty floral nose with a slightly almondy accent. It is light and refreshing, with a crisp lemony palate and a creamy mouth-feel. It has less finesse than Champagne as a result of shorter aging on the lees, yet it is delicious and reasonably priced, leaving one satisfied and guilt-free if one has not finished the bottle.

Food match: Great aperitif; also good with cheese puffs, seafood crêpes, crab salad

JACQUESSON, CHAMPAGNE BRUT N.V., CHAMPAGNE, FRANCE, $19

This relatively little-known Champagne house is not a Grande Marque (see page 167), but in quality it can and does compete with some of the larger houses. Sixty percent of its grapes are supplied by its own vineyards, and the overall rating of the grapes averages 96 percent. Jacquesson presses 75 percent of the grapes at its cellars, while most Champagne houses buy already pressed grape must. After the Champagne is made, it ages in bottle with the lees, or dead yeast cells, for a period of time. This aging period gives added richness and complexity to the finished wine. The longer the period of aging, the better. Where many Champagne houses age for several months, Jacquesson ages its Brut N.V. for two to two-and-a-half years. Likewise, while most Champagne has a small amount of sugar syrup *(dosage)* added to the Champagne after disgorging, to sweeten the final product and hide flaws, Jacquesson adds less than most. A *dosage* of ten to twelve grams per liter is not unusual; Jacquesson adds only seven. All of these measures stand as proof of their dedication to producing very high-quality Champagne.

The Brut N.V. has a yeasty, fresh-baked-bread nose. It is very fresh and clean on the palate, with lots of fruit and a crispness that belies its low *dosage.*

Food match: Terrific with scallops with butter, tarragon white wine sauce; gravlax

PLOYER-JACQUEMART, BRUT N.V., CHAMPAGNE, FRANCE, $26

It seems that maybe the best buys in Champagne are from the little-known privately owned houses that practice traditional

methods. They don't have public-relations guesthouses and big marketing budgets, so none of that gets reflected in the sticker price. The problem is that it is more difficult to find these wines, because of small production and limited distribution.

Ployer-Jacquemart, founded in 1930, is a family operation dedicated to the age-old techniques of handcrafted Champagne. The grapes are rated 98–99 percent (see *Échelle des Crus,*

• T O P   T E N   S P A R K L E R S •

(These champagnes and sparkling wines, made by consistently reliable producers, are within the $15 to $110 range.)

1. Roederer Estate, Anderson Valley Brut
(Anderson Valley, California)

2. J. C. Thevenet, Blanc de Blancs de Chardonnay
(Burgundy, France)

3. Perrier-Jouët, Grand Brut (Champagne, France)

4. Guy Larmandier, Brut Premier Cru N.V.
(Champagne, France)

5. Jacquesson, Champagne Brut N.V. (Champagne, France)

6. Veuve Clicquot Ponsardin (Champagne, France)

7. Drappier, "Les Demoiselles" Rosé Brut N.V.
(Champagne, France)

8. Moët et Chandon Dom Perignon (Champagne, France)

9. Bollinger, Grande Année (Champagne, France)

10. Krug, Grande Cuvée (Champagne, France)

p. 164); the blend is about 50 percent Pinot Noir and 50 percent Chardonnay.

The wine has a wonderfully lively *mousse,* with a toasty, citrus, rich aroma. Quite complex and intense. It is very dry, suggesting a low *dosage.* Powerful and well balanced, with a long, spicy finish.

Food match: Filet of sole with lemon butter; moules marinières

ROEDERER ESTATE,
ANDERSON VALLEY BRUT,
CALIFORNIA, U.S.A., $17

This Californian sparkling-wine house is owned and operated by Champagne Louis Roederer, and the key to its success is linked to the same philosophy that makes this French house one of the leading brands in Champagne. They believe in owning the vineyards that produce the grapes and the use of oak barrels for aging the reserve wines. Vineyard ownership gives them greater control over the quality of the grapes, and the oak aging is what gives the wine a unique full-bodied style. The cool Anderson Valley seems to be ideal for the Chardonnay and Pinot Noir used in the Roederer blend. The final *cuvée* is approximately 30 percent Pinot Noir and 70 percent Chardonnay. The wine is made by the *méthode champenoise* and has become one of the top examples of American sparkling wine.

This wine, with its radiant straw color, has an attractive mildly yeasty and winy aroma. Its fine stream of bubbles and creamy texture reveal some properly aged reserve wine in the blend. It has substantial weight and texture and flavor.

Food match: Chicken pot pie; veal scallopini; crab cakes

SEGURA VIUDAS,
CAVA ARIA ESTATE BRUT,
PENEDÈS, SPAIN, $10

Segura Viudas was taken over by Freixenet, arguably the best-known Cava house, in 1984. Now Freixenet's top-of-the-line sparkling wine, it triumphed as the preferred wine of the ten tasters in a blind tasting of sparkling wines other than Champagne for a prestigious wine publication.

Cava, the Spanish word for "cellar," is the name adopted for the *méthode champenoise* sparkling wines produced primarily in

Catalunia. Although the most common grape varieties for Cava are Macabeo, Parellada, and Xarel-lo, more and more of the Cava houses are employing Chardonnay and blending it with black grapes *à la champenoise.*

This Cava has an exciting, even complex, aroma of flowers, stones, and minerals and a good clean attack on the palate, with uncommon intensity for such an inexpensive sparkling wine. It is pure and vibrant, with a creamy texture, refreshing crisp acidity, and good length.

Food match: Fried smelts with a squeeze of lemon; linguine and clam sauce; quiche

VEUVE CLICQUOT PONSARDIN, CHAMPAGNE, FRANCE, $32

Veuve means "widow," and as the story goes, Mademoiselle Ponsardin married Monsieur Clicquot, who shortly thereafter died and left the widow to carry on the affairs of the company. At a time when feminism was not as accepted as it is today, the success of the company is a testament to the Veuve's perseverance. Much as Dom Perignon is credited with creating Champagne as we know it today, Veuve Clicquot is responsible for discovering the *remuage* process, which removes the dead yeast cells from the bottle after the secondary fermentation, resulting in a clarified wine. As the product of one of the best *grande marque* houses, the Clicquot style is always refined and full-flavored.

The Brut N.V. is about 50 percent Pinot Noir, 30 percent Chardonnay, and 20 percent Pinot Meunier. Light-straw gold in color, it has a toasty nose with ripe fruit character. This medium-to-full-bodied Champagne has real presence on the palate, quite rich and textured.

Food match: Lobster or light poultry; guinea hen or chicken with Champagne sauce; sautéed sweetbreads; rabbit stew

APPENDIX I

A Tasting Vocabulary

Aggressive. Harshly tannic or too acidic.

Apple. The bouquet of young white wines such as Vinho Verde, Riesling, and Chardonnay. The richer caramelized aroma of baked apples is often associated with Riesling.

Apricot. Associated with botrytised grapes (i.e., those that have been affected by "noble rot," which dehydrates them and concentrates the juice and sugars) and from white Rhônes such as Condrieu.

Attack. The first impact of the wine on your palate. Flabby, soft wines do not have enough acid to make an impression. It does not necessarily have to be a big-flavored impact, but it should have a kind of flavorful energy.

Austere. Wine that may need to air, or warm slightly in the mouth, for the fruit flavor, held down by the tannins, to be released.

Balance. Achieved when fruit, alcohol, tannin (for reds), and acid work together harmoniously. Sometimes wines can be unbalanced when young, a fault rectified by aging.

Banana. Associated with young wines fermented by carbonic maceration.

Barnyard. A ripe, earthy accent; sometimes used in describing the gaminess of red Burgundies.

Big. Referring to a satisfying, often strongly alcoholic, wine that quickly fills the nasal cavities with its volatile esters. Red Rhônes, Californian Cabernets, Barolo, come to mind.

Bite. The good acidic attack of well-made white wine.

Body. Enough fruit and acid in balance to fill the palate with solid flavor.

Bottle stink. A musty smell of newly opened, usually aged, wines, which will disappear after a little airing in the glass. It may be the result of excessive sulphur or a bacterial problem.

Bouquet. The perfume of an aged wine (as against aroma, the fruitier, less complex smell of a young wine).

Butter. A slightly creamy richness found in mature Chardonnay and Champagne.

Cassis. French for black currant. Often used in connection with Cabernet and Pinot Noir and referring to a rich, ripe luscious fruitiness.

Cedar. The scent of cigar boxes that is associated with Cabernet Sauvignon aged in oak.

Cherry. A trademark accent of some Beaujolais *crus* and Pinot Noir.

Chewy. Referring to a lovely full flavor with plenty of fruit and enough acid and tannins to create body. Such a wine you will want to keep in your mouth, to let it warm and release its flavors.

Chocolate. Often invoked when talking about fine old full-bodied reds.

Closed. When the fruit is still locked in by tannin. Will need some bottle age to soften and open up. A couple of hours in a decanter can also do the trick.

Cooked. A stewed-fruit flavor resulting from fermentation at too high a temperature, or poorly stored wine.

Corked. Used of a wine spoiled by the musty-tasting infection of its cork (see page 42).

Crisp. Fresh, lively young white wine.

Fat. Mouth-filling, with nice soft-textured fruit. A high level of glycerin (see "Legs") will make a wine taste fat.

Finish. The length of time it takes for flavors and aromas to fade once the wine has been swallowed. A "long" finish is a sign of quality.

Flabby. Little acidity, so no definition of the fruit flavor. Very boring to drink.

Flinty. Used in connection with dry whites such as Pouilly Fumé and Sancerre, with their slightly stringent acidity.

Goût de terroir. A term used in France to sum up the absolutely characteristic group of flavors and aromas of wine made from a particular site with its attendant microclimate—i.e., the wine's unique fingerprint of flavor.

Hazelnut. Like toasted almonds, a word associated with mature Chardonnay.

Herbaceous. The newly cut grassiness of young Sauvignon Blanc.

Honey. Used to describe the richness more than the sweetness of mature white Burgundy, Vouvray, and Sémillon.

Jammy. Aromas and flavors associated with wine made from exceptionally ripe and overripe grapes.

Kerosene. As unlikely as it sounds, this is a word used approvingly to describe the characteristic flavor accent of aged Riesling.

Legs. The glycerin trails that run down the inside of the glass after wine has been swirled. Glycerin is a natural by-product of the fermentation of sugar into alcohol and gives wine a full and satisfying character (which unscrupulous winemakers can fake by simply adding glycerin, sometimes with fatal results, as in the great Austrian "antifreeze" scandal of 1985).

Lemon. The dominant accent of some Sauvignon Blanc, Riesling, Chenin Blanc, Spanish, and Gascon whites made in modern wineries.

Length. See "Finish."

Licorice. A not unpleasant slight bitterness at the end of the taste of some white wine.

Lychee. The exotic fruit aroma common in Gewürztraminer.

Maderized. A fault in red wine when it becomes oxidized (perhaps due to an ill-fitting cork) and takes on a sticky, unpleasant burned-toffee flavor. (The term derives from the *rancio,* or controlled oxidation, of Madeira.)

Meaty. Like "chewy" and "big," something that is very satisfying and full-bodied.

Menthol. Or mint. Sometimes evident in younger Cabernets.

Mouth-feel. Used to describe the texture of a wine on the palate. Light wines have an airy mouth-feel while full-bodied wines have a thicker mouth-feel.

Nose. The smell of a wine. See "Bouquet." A "big nose" does not refer to Cyrano de Bergerac. It means that the bouquet fills the nasal cavities (unromantic-sounding but as great a treat as the flavor).

Nutty. Hazelnut flavor, used for Chardonnay, Champagne, Sherry.

Oaky. The slight vanilla/cedary accent of wine that has been aged in oak barrels.

Oxidized. Spoiled by overexposure to air if a red wine is brown, or a white a dull yellow orange.

Pepper. Sometimes used to describe the aroma of Grenache and Syrah from the Rhône.

Pétillant. Slightly sparkling or spritzy.

Plum. Used to describe the aromas of Rioja, red Burgundy, and Merlot.

Raspberry. Syrah, Gamay, Zinfandel and Pinot Noir. Used to describe bright fruit tones.

Smoky. Associated, not surprisingly, with Pouilly Fumé, but also with Alsace Tokay-Pinot Gris, as well as full-bodied reds.

Spicy. Most famously, Gewürztraminer (*Gewürz* means "spicy"), as well as many Rhônes.

Spritz. The term for the bubbles in sparkling wine. Spritz can be harsh, as in cheap sparkling wine (the sort that is so hard and fierce it makes your eyes water!), or gentle, as in *crémant* (a term originally applied to half-sparkling Champagne but now used as an appellation for high-quality wine made by traditional methods in Alsace, the Loire, Bourgogne, Bordeaux, and Limoux).

Structure. The balance between the main elements that go into a wine, such as acid, sugar content, and tannins.

Tannin. A preserving extract from the grape stem and seeds that is an essential agent if the wine is to age successfully. Tannin is naturally astringent but mellows out during the aging process. Young red wines will often have a mouth-puckering harshness due to tannin.

Toast. Toast is the very slightly roasted/charred flavor accent that is imparted to wine by an oak barrel (the staves that become the sides of the barrel are roasted over a fire, small or large, depending on the degree of "toastiness" desired)—one of the most debated areas of wine connoisseurship. French oak, Bulgarian oak, American oak . . . all fuel for aficionados.

Vanilla. Vanillin is one of the extracts of oak. The newer the oak barrel or vat in which the wine is matured, the more pronounced will be the vanilla accent.

Violets. Red Burgundy, as well as Chianti, can have an intense violent scent.

Yeast. Champagne, Muscadet *sur lie* . . . white wines that are left on their yeast sediment (lees) will often have that new-baked-bread aroma and taste.

APPENDIX II

The Daniel Johnnes Cellar Selections

This is not an investment guide. I believe a wine cellar should be a source of enjoyment, of wines to be drunk sooner rather than later. Putting a cellar together can save you money because you are buying in quantity and should get a discount. Ten percent is standard, and I have assumed that in my final calculations, and have included a seven percent sales tax. I'm assuming, and hoping, that you drink wine regularly and by having a stock of wines will be enabled to orchestrate your meals with greater wine options. Remember, when buying a wine you haven't tasted before, buy only one bottle and taste it before committing to larger quantities. I have taken three cost points: a cellar for $500, $1,000 and another for $5,000. With these, though, I have chosen a range of good-value wines that will fit different occasions and will accompany foods of varying flavor intensity. I have organized them under the following categories:

Casual
Sparkling
Aperitifs

Light food
Medium-flavor food
Full-flavor food
Sweet wines
Special occasions

THE $500 CELLAR

Casual

White

3 bottles, Georges Duboeuf, Viognier Vins de Pay de l'Ardèche 1994, Rhône, France, $9	$27
3 bottles, Casa Lapostolle, Sauvignon Blanc 1994, Chile, $6	$18
3 bottles, Juliàn Chivite, Gran Fuedo Rosado (rosé), Navarra, Spain, $7	$21

Red

3 bottles, Henri Marionnet, Gamay de Touraine 1995, Loire, $9	$27

Sparkling

White

3 bottles, Bouvet, Saumur Brut Saphir N.V., Loire, $9	$27
1 bottle, Jacquesson Champagne Brut N.V., France, $18	$18

Aperitif

White

1 bottle, Emilio Lustau, Fino Reserva "Jarana"
    Sherry, Spain, $10 $10

Light food

White

3 bottles, Hugel et Fils, Gentil Hugel 1994, Alsace, $10 $30
3 bottles, Domaine de la Pepière
    Muscadet Côtes de Grand Lieu 1994, Loire, $9 $27
2 bottles, Domaine Provenquière
    Vin de Pays d'Oc Chardonnay 1994, France, $8 $16

Red

3 bottles, Antinori, Santa Cristina
    Sangiovese Toscano 1993, Italy, $9 $27
2 bottles, Oak Knoll, Pinot Noir 1994, Oregon, $13 $26

Medium-flavor food

White

3 bottles, Verget, Mâcon-Villages 1994,
    Burgundy, $9 $27
2 bottles, Havens, Sauvignon Blanc 1994,
    California, $12 $24
3 bottles, Los Vascos, Colchagua Cabernet
    Sauvignon 1993, Chile, $7 $21
3 bottles, Daniel Rion, Bourgogne Rouge 1994,
    Burgundy, $14 $42

Full-flavor food

White

3 bottles, Wyndhams, Oak Cask Chardonnay 1994,
   Australia, $9 $27

Red

3 bottles, Catena, Cabernet Sauvignon 1993,
   Argentina, $12 $36
3 bottles, Bodega Nekeas, Vega Sindoa 1994,
   Spain, $9 $27

Sweet wines

Emilio Lustau, Pedro Ximénez Reserva San Emilio,
   Spain, $14 $14

Special occasions

Red

1 bottle, Château Prieuré-Lichine 1990,
   Bordeaux, $28 $28

THE $1,000 CELLAR

Casual

White

3 bottles, Herbert Mesmer, Riesling Halbtrocken 1994,
   Germany, $8 (liter) $24
3 bottles, Henri Marionnet,
   Sauvignon de Touraine 1994, Loire, $9 $27
3 bottles, Soalheiro Alvarinho, Vinho Verde 1994,
   Portugal, $8 $24

3 bottles, Adelsheim, Pinot Gris 1994, Oregon, $12 $36

3 bottles, Columbia, Chardonnay
    Woodburne Cuvée 1994, Washington, $10 $30

Red

3 bottles, Las Campañas, Rosado (rosé) 1994,
    Spain, $6 $18

3 bottles, Georges Duboeuf, Beaujolais-Villages
    1995, France, $6 $18

3 bottles, Miguel Torres, Sangre de Torro 1994,
    Spain, $7 $21

3 bottles, Santa Rita, Reserva Cabernet
    Sauvignon 1990, Chile, $6 $18

Sparkling

White

4 bottles, Willm, Crémant d'Alsace,
    France, $14 $56

2 bottles, Jacquesson, Champagne Brut N.V.,
    France, $18 $36

Aperitif

White

1 bottle, Hidalgo, "La Gitana" Manzanilla Sherry,
    Spain, $10 $10

Light food

White

3 bottles, Günderloch, Riesling Kabinett
    Halbtrocken 1994, Germany, $13 $39

3 bottles, Château Bonnet, Entre-Deux-Mers 1994,
    Bordeaux, $7 $21

3 bottles, Domaine de la Maladière, Chablis 1994,
  Burgundy, $15 $45

Red

3 bottles, Domaine Raffault, Chinon 1993, Loire, $12 $36
3 bottles, Alma, Navarra 1994, Spain, $6 $18
3 bottles, Saintsbury, Garnet Pinot Noir 1994,
  California, $12 $36

Medium-flavor food

White

3 bottles, Lindemans, Chardonnay Bin 65 1994,
  Australia, $9 $27
3 bottles, Schleret, Pinot Blanc 1994, Alsace, $12 $36
3 bottles, Domaine J. G. Thevenet, Mâcon
  Pierreclos, Burgundy, $14 $42

Red

3 bottles, Navarro, Correas, Malbec 1992, Chile, $11 $33
3 bottles, Casal de Tonda, Dão 1994, Portugal, $7 $21
3 bottles, Isola e Olena, Chianti Classico 1993,
  Tuscany, $12 $36
2 bottles, Marquis d'Angerville, Volnay 1er Cru 1993,
  Burgundy, $20 $40

Full-flavor food

White

2 bottles, A. Mann, Tokay Pinot Gris 1994,
  Alsace, $19 $38
2 bottles, Normans, Family Reserve Chardonnay 1994,
  Australia, $12 $24

Red

2 bottles, Ravenswood, Sonoma Zinfandel 1993,
California, $19 — $38

3 bottles, Guelbenzu, Tinto Navarra 1994, Spain, $9 — $27

3 bottles, Alain Graillot, Saint-Joseph 1994,
Rhône, $16 — $48

Sweet wines

White

2 bottles, Yalumba, Clocktower Port,
Australia, $10 — $20

1 bottle Domaine Coyeux, Muscat de
Beaumes-de-Venise, Rhône, $20 — $20

Special occasions

White

2 bottles, Louis Latour, Meursault 1994,
Burgundy, $20 — $40

Red

2 bottles, Château Marbuzet, Saint-Estèphe 1990,
Bordeaux, $24 — $48

THE $5,000 CELLAR

Casual

White

6 bottles, Selbach-Oster, Zeltinger Sonnenuhr
Riesling Kabinett 1994, Mosel, $12 — $72

6 bottles, Domaine Bregeon, Muscadet sur lie 1994,
Loire, $8 — $48

6 bottles, Caliterra, Chardonnay 1995, Chile, $6 $36

6 bottles, Hogue Cellars, Fumé Blanc 1995,
Washington State, $8 $48

6 bottles, Gini, Soave Classico, Veneto 1994, Italy, $12 $72

Red

6 bottles, Vietti, Barbera d'Alba 1993,
Piedmont, Italy, $15 $90

6 bottles, Oak Knoll, Pinot Noir 1994, Oregon, $13 $78

6 bottles, Marqués de Caçeres, Rioja Crianza,
Spain, $8 $48

Sparkling

White

6 bottles, Michel Frères, Crémant de Bourgogne 1990,
Burgundy, $12 $72

4 bottles, Bouvet, Saumur Brut Saphir,
Loire, $15 $60

4 bottles, Iron Horse, Sonoma Green Valley Brut 1990,
California, $22 $88

4 bottles, Veuve Clicquot Ponsardin, Champagne
Brut N.V., France, $29 $116

2 bottles, Moët et Chandon, Dom Pérignon
Champagne 1988, France, $75 $150

Aperitifs

White

2 bottles, Lustau, "Jarana" Fino Sherry,
Spain, $12 $24

2 bottles, Saint-Raphael, white Vermouth,
France, $12 $24

1 bottle, A. de Fussigny, Pineau des Charentes,
France, $18 $18

Light food

White

6 bottles, Archambault, Sancerre Clos de la
Perrière 1994, Loire, $15 — $90

6 bottles, Carment, Sonoma Old Vines
Colombard 1994, California, $10 — $60

6 bottles, F. E. Trimbach, Pinot Blanc 1994, Alsace, $9 — $54

6 bottles, Martin Codax, Rias Baixas Albariño 1994,
Spain, $12 — $72

6 bottles, Alois Lageder, Pinot Grigio 1994,
Alto Adige, Italy, $11 — $66

Red

6 bottles, Tollot-Beaut, Chorey Côte de Beaune 1993,
Burgundy, $15 — $90

6 bottles, Michele Chiario, Barbera d'Asti 1993,
Piedmont, Italy, $7 — $42

6 bottles, Bodegas Campo Viejo, Viña Alcota Rioja
Crianza 1993, Rioja, Spain, $9 — $54

6 bottles, Columbia, Merlot, Washington
State 1993, $12 — $72

Medium-flavor food

White

6 bottles, Zind-Humbrecht, Riesling Brand 1993,
Alsace, $30 — $180

6 bottles, Louis Michel, Chablis Vaillons 1994,
Burgundy, $24 — $144

6 bottles, Château Carbonnieux 1993,
Bordeaux, $16 — $96

6 bottles, Orlando, Jacob's Creek Chardonnay 1993,
Australia, $8 — $48

Red

6 bottles, Col d'Orcia, Rosso di Montalcino 1993,
Tuscany, $10 ..... $60

6 bottles, Ponzi, Pinot Noir Reserve 1994,
Oregon, $30 ..... $180

6 bottles, Quinta da Aveleda, Charamba 1992,
Douro, Portugal, $7 ..... $42

6 bottles, Elyse, Morisoli Zinfandel 1993, Sonoma,
California, $18 ..... $108

6 bottles, Rosemount, Balmoral Syrah 1993,
Australia, $12 ..... $72

6 bottles, Louis Jadot, Beaune 1er Cru 1993,
Burgundy, $24 ..... $144

Full-flavor food

White

6 bottles, Phelps, Napa Vin de Mistral Viognier 1994,
California, $26 ..... $156

12 bottles, Rothbury Estate, Hunter Valley
Chardonnay 1994, Australia, $9 ..... $108

6 bottles, Josmeyer, Auxerrois "H," 1993,
Alsace, $22 ..... $132

6 bottles, Frank Prager, Riesling Steinriegl Smaragd
1993 (dry), Austria, $32 ..... $192

Red

6 bottles, Étude, Napa Cabernet Sauvignon 1992,
California, $30 ..... $180

6 bottles, Andrew Will, Merlot 1992, Washington
State, $26 ..... $156

6 bottles, Château Prieuré-Lichine 1990,
Bordeaux, $24 ..... $144

12 bottles, Penfolds, Shiraz Bin 389 1992,
Australia, $16 ..... $192

6 bottles, Jaboulet, Crozes-Hermitage "Thalabert"
  1994, Rhône, $18 $108

Sweet wines

White

4 bottles, Château Lafaurie Peyraguey 1990,
  Sauternes, $18 (half-bottle) $72
4 bottles, Bonny Doon, Muscat Canelli,
  California, $20 $80

Red

2 bottles, Blandys, 10-Year-Old Malmsey,
  Madeira, $30 $60
4 bottles, Grahams, Vintage Port 1977, $60 $240

Special occasions

White

4 bottles, Michel Niellon, Chassagne-Montrachet
  "Les Vergers" 1993, Burgundy, $35 $140
4 bottles, F. X. Pichler, Riesling Smaragd (dry)
  1994, Austria, $32 $128

Red

4 bottles, Domaine Roumier, Morey-Saint-Denis
  "Clos de la Bussière" 1993, Burgundy, $35 $140
3 bottles, Château Pichon-Baron-Longueville 1990,
  Bordeaux, $50 $150

Cellar prices are based on 10 percent discount and 7 percent tax.

STORAGE CONDITIONS

Most of us do not have the luxury of a belowground cellar, where the temperature maintains itself at a year-round fifty-five degrees Fahrenheit—which is perfect as the serving temperature for most white wines and the maturing temperature for reds. As long as the temperature does not reach above sixty-eight degrees Fahrenheit, a gradual fluctuation is all right. We will probably have to make do with nooks and crannies: under the stairs; in a disused fireplace; in the garage. Try to keep your bottles horizontal, so

that there is wine contact with the cork. This keeps the cork moist and prevents it from shrinking, which would allow air to enter or wine to seep out. Try to keep the temperature cool, because the higher it is, the quicker the wine will mature. Do not store wine in direct sunlight; the darker the space, the better. A bowl of water or a wet sponge will keep up the humidity and help prevent the cork from drying out (too much humidity, however, and your labels will slide off or turn to mush). Try to prevent drafts, as they cause the temperature to fluctuate and create miniclimates within your wine store. Avoid storing the wine in an area that has vibrations.

CELLARING

There are three good reasons for storing wine (and I'm talking here about enough space in which to keep 100 bottles and up).

1. To take advantage of deals on everyday wine when buying a case or two at a time.

2. To buy wines that have a good chance to age, and by buying them when they are younger and cheaper. The whole business of aging is a vexed one, and there is no guarantee that wine will age in a predictable way or at a predictable rate. There are guidelines that have been established over long experience, but the modern obsession with aging means that wines are too often allowed to go over the hill. A wine has many different phases in its development and can be enjoyed with equal, though different, pleasure at various stages of its life: fruity and luscious when younger; complex and resonant when older (Beaujolais crus such as Morgon and Moulin-à-Vent come to mind, as do Loire reds such as Chinon and Bourgueil). It depends on the vintage and the producer. A first-growth Médoc from a strong, tannic vintage is unpleasant to drink too young. Burgundies tend to be less hardy than Bordeaux because they do not have the tannic structure that promotes aging, and it is a wise precaution to taste the Burgundy at much more regular intervals (say, every two years) than you would the Bordeaux, to keep track of its progress.

Do white wines need aging? Most of them do not. They should be drunk young, while their fruit is still colorful. But there are whites that will improve with age. Big Burgundies such as a Montrachet or a Meursault can easily take five to ten years, but do not push your luck with lesser white Burgundies, which are at their best between two and five years old. Good examples of Alsace can age surprisingly well, particularly the late-picked sélection de grains nobles and vendange tardive, but this goes for most dessert wines: Sauternes, Barsac, and German Trockenbeerenauslese, for example.

3. To have a nice selection available for different occassions and types of food.

APPENDIX III

Vintage Madness

Former baseball star turned restaurateur Rusty Staub said it best in a letter to the *Wine Spectator* in response to the magazine's criticism of the 1992 vintage for red wine in Burgundy. Rusty, who had tasted two hundred wines in Burgundy, stated: "I must disagree with the picture you have painted about this vintage. The 1992 vintage will not go down in history as a blockbuster or be put in cellars for 15 or 20 years. But it will be a vintage from which the public can enjoy and derive a great deal of pleasure. I sometimes wonder if, in the rush to analyze each new vintage, we judge too soon and too definitively." He calls the '92s wines that the "public can enjoy immensely while waiting for the 1988, 1989, 1990, and 1991 vintages to come around." He goes on to say: "Your panning of the 1992 red Burgundy wines will stop a lot of Americans from ever trying these very approachable, fruity, and affordable wines. We in America must consider the value of vintages that are not of the blockbuster type. We drink too many great wines too young, and we shy away from any wine that doesn't get 90 or above. Good, well-made wines at a fair price: isn't that what we look for the most?"

I take my hat off to Rusty, because he knows that wine is something to be enjoyed rather than fetishized. After all, unless you buy wine as an investment commodity, I believe its flavor and how well it goes with your meal are the most important factors. I know there are many people who are only interested in wines that score 90 or more points by professional wine rating organizations, though they have no real interest in wine. To them it's just another point-scoring snobbism.

Let's say the vintage chart gives 94 points to 1989 Bordeaux and I have only 1992 Bordeaux on the wine list at Montrachet, a vintage that could muster only a lowly 82 points. Although I've been accused of having wines from "off" vintages, I would contend that many 1989 Bordeaux are undrinkable now (and perhaps always will be!) because they tend to be highly tannic, highly alcoholic, and, as a result, hard and astringent on the palate. These wines need time—lots of time (ten to fifteen years)—in which to process their tannin and soften up. They are also very expensive, and value is not about spending a lot of money on wine you cannot drink.

The 1992, on the other hand, is a softer, less alcoholic, and more accessible vintage. It's also a good deal cheaper than the '89. The problem with alcohol and tannin is their tendency to overwhelm the taste of food. With salty food, the wine can taste particularly coarse, but it does better with high-protein dishes of red meat or cheese (tannin, after all, breaks down protein). Generally speaking, wines made in cooler years or cooler climates tend to be lower in alcohol, but they also escape the plaudits of critics, who tend to reserve their highest scores for the most powerful, tannic, and alcoholic vintages. Because these wines do not garner critical raves, they are almost always a better value.

Remember, a serious winemaker will be as meticulous about making wine in an "off" year as in a "great" one. There's the same equipment, year in, year out, and the very important fact of a certain pride in craft that must be satisfied. The winemaker doesn't simply leave the winery to an enological student if the sun isn't shining. That's why it's so important to buy the wine of reputable producers who have been, and are still, in the business for the long haul rather than the quick buck.

Vintage charts can be useful to point out the ripest, most ageworthy vintages, and this can be helpful because some grape varieties do not do well in lighter years (Sangiovese, for example, is a sun-loving grape that shows its irascible side in cold years); but they are hopeless on the irregularities of a vintage within a particular area. For example, in 1980 Burgundy was not rated very highly. But the truth is that if you take the main components of the Côte d'Or—the Côte de Nuits and the Côte de Beaune—the Côte de Nuits would rate 7/8 on a 10-point scale and the Côte de Beaune 5/6. The same was true in Bordeaux in 1987. There were some very good wines from Saint-Émilion and Pomerol, because the earlier-ripening Merlot that dominates these areas could be harvested before the later-ripening Cabernet of the Médoc, which was badly affected by late rains.

What I object to most about vintage charts is the indiscriminate way in which they are used as a substitute for personal experience. Wine isn't a numbers game with strict formulas. Experiment!

APPENDIX IV

Wine and Food

It seems that almost every article or book I read on the subject of matching food to wine begins by saying something like, "It really is not that difficult" or "Don't get intimidated, just drink what you like" or "We are going to lay down just a few simple guidelines." They then go on to weave some grand and convoluted scheme of exactly which kinds of foods go with precisely what kind of wine. By the end of it, you are dizzy and thoroughly intimidated.

The worst service I could offer would be to nail you to a treatise on the art of pairing wine with food. The most important rule is to drink the wine you like and follow your intuition; it will rarely let you down. It's fine to drink white wine with lamb if you like, or Bordeaux with fillet of sole if that tickles your palate, but there are some very general guidelines that may increase your enjoyment. The food recommendations that follow each of my wine selections are meant to serve only as guidelines, not prescriptions. Your tastes are going to be different from mine, but I hope you'll find them useful as an indication of the "weight" and intensity of the dish that will complement the wine.

With food and wine, the sum can be greater than the parts; a merely good wine can rise to greatness with the right dish and vice versa, but rarely will a bad dish be redeemed by a good wine or an indifferent wine rescued by a brilliant plate of food.

The challenge of pairing wine to food is something I encounter every night at the restaurant. What I've discovered is that most people are willing to make compromises as long as the wine is as delicious as the rest of the meal. The restaurant setting is far more challenging than dining at home since at home everyone eats the same dish, while at the restaurant, the game is to match one wine to two, three, four or more different dishes that, combined, have scores of different flavors working together and sometimes against each other. I try to find a wine that works well with all dishes or, if the customer is really looking to turn his dinner into a study in wine matching, I will propose different wines by the glass or half bottles for the different dishes. I look for extreme elements in the dish like high acidity, sweetness, or spice and choose a wine that won't clash. It's best to balance acid with acid and sweetness with sweetness. A highly acidic wine like a dry Riesling will taste less acidic with a dish splashed with lemon juice or vinegar. In contrast, it will taste more tart with a slightly sweet dish like honey-glazed pork. A sweet wine will taste drier with a sweet dish. A very sweet dessert such as tarte tatin will tone down a sweet Sauternes whereas a moderately sweet pastry such as pound cake will increase the perception of sweetness in that same Sauternes. In contradiction to my comments on complementing degrees of sweetness, I find one of the very best matches of all time to be the contrast in pairing sweet wine and salty food as in Roquefort cheese and Sauternes. As for spicy food, it is best to avoid highly alcoholic wine such as a Hermitage or Zinfandel. Drinking these powerful wines would be like throwing oil on the flames. The idea is to cool the heat by adding a little sweetness from a German spätlese or a Vouvray demi-sec, both of which are low in alcohol.

The most important factor as far as I am concerned is the

Port, Madeira, Banyuls	Sparkling Wines	Rosé	Full-Bodied Red	Medium- to Full-Bodied Red	Light- to Med.-Bodied Red	Full-Bodied Sweet White	Full-Bodied Dry White	Medium-Bodied Sweet White	Medium- to Full-Bodied Semi-Dry White	Medium- to Full-Bodied Dry White	Light- to Med.-Bodied Semi-Dry White	Light- to Med.-Bodied Dry White	
	×											×	Oysters, Clams, Mussels
	×	×					×			×	×	×	Shrimp, Crab, Lobster
	×	×					×			×	×	×	White Flaky Fish
	×	×		×	×		×			×			Firm Fish
	×	×		×	×		×		×	×			White-Meat Poultry
	×	×		×	×		×						Dark-Meat Poultry
			×	×	×								Game Birds
	×	×	×	×	×		×		×	×			Pork and Veal
			×	×	×								Lamb and Beef
			×	×									Game
	×	×			×				×		×		Spicy Foods
	×	×			×		×			×			Grilled Fish
		×	×	×	×								Grilled Meats
×		×		×	×		×		×	×	×	×	Mild Cheese
×			×	×		×	×	×	×	×			Strong Cheese
×			×			×		×					Blue-Veined Cheese
	×				×					×		×	Goat Cheese
								×	×		×		Fruit
×						×		×					Sweet Desserts
×													Chocolate

WINE/FOOD CHART 2

	Light- to Med.-Bodied Dry White	Light- to Med.-Bodied Semi-Dry White	Medium- to Full-Bodied Dry White	Medium- to Full-Bodied Semi-Dry White	Medium-Bodied Sweet White	Full-Bodied Dry White	Full-Bodied Sweet White	Light- to Med.-Bodied Red	Medium- to Full-Bodied Red	Full-Bodied Red	Rosé	Sparkling Wines	Port, Madeira, Banyuls
Oysters, Clams, Mussels	x											x	
Shrimp, Crab, Lobster	x	x	x			x					x	x	
White Flaky Fish	x	x	x			x					x	x	
Firm Fish			x			x		x	x		x	x	
White-Meat Poultry			x	x		x		x	x		x	x	
Dark-Meat Poultry						x		x	x		x	x	
Game Birds								x	x	x			
Pork and Veal			x	x		x		x	x	x	x	x	
Lamb and Beef								x	x	x			
Game									x	x			
Spicy Food		x		x				x			x	x	
Grilled Fish			x			x		x			x	x	
Grilled Meats								x	x	x	x		
Mild Cheese	x	x	x	x		x		x	x		x	x	
Strong Cheese			x	x	x	x	x		x	x			x
Blue-Veined Cheese					x		x			x			x
Goat Cheese	x		x					x				x	
Fruit		x		x	x								
Sweet Desserts					x		x						x
Chocolate													x

This chart provides a general guide to pairing different types of wine to food. It should be used with the understanding that you may make a different selection due to a lighter or more strongly seasoned sauce or food preparation.

The wine styles list on the next page will help you identify the wines that belong to a particular category.

intensity of flavor in a dish and how that will shape my choice of wine. There are exceptions to every rule, but generally light foods will be better with light wines; rich foods with full-bodied wines. The sauce of a dish and the way in which the main ingredients have been cooked can have a greater impact on flavor than the basic ingredient itself. Poached sole in a lemon and dill sauce will have a completely different impact on the wine than a simple grilled sole. Poached sole is lighter, less intense than the grilled one.

When orchestrating a meal, it is better to start with the lightest wine and build in richness, just as you would start with the lightest dish and move on to the richer ones. Follow a good wine with a great one; a lighter-bodied with a fuller, because the lighter will always taste insipid if it follows something much more assertive. Build in intensity.

If you are unsure of the wine to serve, choose something that is versatile with many types of meat, fish, or fowl. Light- to medium-bodied wines such as Pinot Noir, Chianti, Rioja, Dolcetto, or Beaujolais-Villages are terrific standbys.

And if you don't want to bother with all of this, just drink what you like!

WINE STYLES CHECKLIST

White

Full-bodied dry

Meursault
Chassagne-Montrachet
Puligny-Montrachet
Corton-Charlemagne and any *grand cru* white Burgundy
Hermitage Blanc
Châteauneuf-du-Pape Blanc
Californian and Australian Chardonnay (oaked)

Medium- to full-bodied dry

Pinot Gris

Sémillon

Graves

Mâcon, Pouilly Fuissé

Bourgogne Blanc

Chablis *premier cru*

Côte de Beaune Blanc

Meursault, Chassagne-Montrachet, Puligny-Montrachet below
    1er Cru

Californian and Australian Chardonnay (unoaked)

Condrieu, Viognier

Côtes du Rhône

Light- to medium-bodied dry

Muscadet

Aligoté

Soave

Entre-Deux-Mers

Chablis

Alsace Riesling

Sylvaner

Pinot Grigio

Orvieto

Verdicchio

Trebbiano

Galestro

Tocai Friulano

Sauvignon Blanc

Sancerre

Pouilly Fumé

Albariño

Pinot Blanc

Light- to medium-bodied semi-dry

German Riesling *(kabinett, spätlese, halbtrocken)*
Grüner Veltliner
Müller-Thurgau
American or Australian Riesling
American Chenin Blanc
Anjoy Blanc
Saumur Blanc
Vouvray *demi-sec*
Montlouis *demi-sec*
Vinho Verde
Muscat
Moscati d'Asti

Medium- to full-bodied semi-dry

Gewürztraminer
Gewürztraminer *vendange tardive*
Alsace Riesling *vendange tardive*
Alsace Pinot Gris *vendange tardive*
German Riesling *(auslese, halbtrocken)*

Medium-bodied sweet

Vouvray Moelleux
Coteaux du Layon
Montlouis Moelleux
Loupiac
Sainte Croix de Mont
German Beerenauslese, Trockenbeerenauslese, and Eiswein
Alsace Riesling *sélection de grains nobles*
Montbazzilac
Vin Santo

Full-bodied sweet

Malvasia
Muscat Canelli

Alsace Gewürztraminer and Pinot Gris *sélection de grains nobles*

Sauternes

Barsac

Tokaji Aszu

Muscat de Beaumes-de-Venise

Port

Banyuls and Madeira

Red

Full-bodied

Châteauneuf-du-Pape

Côte-Rôtie

Hermitage

Australian Shiraz, Cabernet Sauvignon

American Cabernet Sauvignon

Bordeaux classified growths (see page 83)

Zinfandel

Barolo

Barbaresco

Brunello di Montalcino

Medium- to full-bodied

Pinot Noir

Burgundy

Côtes du Rhône

Bordeaux *appellation contrôlée* and *cru bourgeois*

Côtes du Roussillon-Villages

Minervois

Corbières

Faugères

American and Chilean Merlot

Chilean Cabernet Sauvignon

Argentine Malbec and Cabernet Sauvignon
Rosso di Montalcino
Nebbiolo d'Alba
Chianti Reservas
Rioja Reservas
Penedès
Ribera del Duero
Portuguese Dão, Douro, Alentejo, and Ribatejo

Light- to medium-bodied

Gamay
Beaujolais
Bardolino
Valpolicella
Chianti
Dolcetto
Chinon
Bourgueil
Rioja Crianza
Alsace Pinot Noir
Sancerre Rouge
Burgundy
Saumur Champigny

APPENDIX V

Hot Shot Importers to Look For

The chances of finding a good-value wine are in your favor if you look first for the recommended producer, then for the recommended region, then for the recommended importer.

Look for wines selected by the following importers:

Classical Wines from Spain—Spanish wines—
   Tel. 206-547-0255; Fax 206-547-2426

Eric Solomon European Cellars—Tel. 212-924-4949;
   Fax 212-924-0567

Hand Picked Selections (Dan Kravitz)—French wines—
   Tel. 703-347-3471; Fax 703-349-0967

Ideal Wines—French and Italian wines—Tel. 617-395-3300;
   Fax 617-395-3138

ILNA Selections (Rudi Wiest)—German wines—
Tel. 619-753-4244; Fax 619-753-1634

Jack Siler Selections—French wines—Tel. 303-449-8874;
Fax 303-440-1170

Jorge Ordoñez Fine Estates from Spain—Spanish wines—
Tel. 617-327-1613; Fax 617-323-0455

Kermit Lynch Selections—French wines—Tel. 510-524-1524;
Fax 510-528-7026

Kobrand—French and Italian wines—Tel. 212-490-9300;
Fax 212-949-4645

Louis/Dressner—French wines—Tel. 212-319-8768;
Fax 212-754-0198

Martine's Wines—French wines—Tel. 415-485-1800;
Fax 415-485-1215

Neal Empson Selections—Italian wines—Tel. 703-684-0900;
Fax 703-684-2065

Première Wine Merchants—Italian wines—Tel. 212-399-4200;
Fax 212-399-2495

Robert Kacher Selections—French wines—Tel. 202-832-9083;
Fax 202-529-2579

Seagram Chateau and Estate—French wines—
Tel. 212-572-7725

Select Vineyards (Neal Rosenthal)—French, Italian, South
African wines—212-249-6650; Fax 212-744-3354

Terry Theise Selections—German and Austrian wines—
  Tel. 202-895-2469; Fax 202-832-3745

Val d'Orbieu Wines—Languedoc-Roussillon—
  Tel. 800-225-8467; Fax 214-443-9463

Vin Divino—Italian wines—Tel. 312-281-3363;
  Fax 312-281-4054

Vineyard Brands—French wines—Tel. 802-875-2139;
  Fax 802-875-3566

Weygant-Metzler—French wines—Tel. 610-932-2745;
  Fax 610-932-0279

Wines of France (Alain Junguenet)—Rhône wines—
  Tel. 908-654-6173; Fax 908-654-3975

World Shippers and Importers—Portuguese wines—
  Tel. 215-732-2018; Fax 215-732-0122

GENERAL INDEX

INDEX OF WINE NAMES
AND PRODUCERS

INDEX OF WINES
BY PRICES

INDEX OF WINE
AND FOOD